Invisible Governance

Invisible Governance

International Secretariats
in Global Politics

• • • • • • • • • • • • • • • •

JOHN MATHIASON

Kumarian
Press, Inc.

Invisible Governance: International Secretariats in Global Politics

Published in 2007 in the United States of America by Kumarian Press, Inc., 1294 Blue Hills Avenue, Bloomfield, CT 06002 USA

The citations that open the chapters are from *The Complete Yes Minister: Diaries of a Cabinet Minister*, The Right Honourable James Hacker, edited by Jonathan Lynn and Antony Jay (New York: Harper & Row, 1984), and are used by permission from the authors, whose kindness in applying their insights is gratefully acknowledged.

The text of this book is set in 10.5/13 Palatino.

Production and design by Joan Weber Laflamme, jml ediset.
Proofread by Beth Richards.
Indexed by Robert Swanson.

Printed in the United States of America by Thomson-Shore. Text printed with vegetable oil-based ink.

∞ The paper used in this publication meets the minimum requirements of the American National Standard for Information Sciences—Permanence of Paper for printed Library Materials, ANSI Z39.48–1984

Library of Congress Cataloging-in-Publication Data

Mathiason, John, 1942–
    Invisible governance : international secretariats in global politics / by John Mathiason.
        p. cm.
    Includes bibliographical references and index.
    ISBN-13: 978–1–56549–220–2 (pbk. : alk. paper)
    1. International agencies. 2. International officials and employees. 3. Secretariats. 4. International relations. I. Title.
    JZ4850.M368 2007
    341.2—dc22

                          2006032243

16 15 14 13 12 11 10 09 08 07   10 9 8 7 6 5 4 3 2 1   First Printing 2007

Contents

• • • • • • • • • • •

v

Tables and Illustrations

Abbreviations and Acronyms

CEDAW	Convention on the Elimination of All Forms of Discrimination against Women
CFCs	chlorofluorocarbons
CTBT	Comprehensive Nuclear Test Ban Treaty
EPTA	Expanded Program of Technical Assistance
FAO	Food and Agriculture Organization
FBI	Federal Bureau of Investigation (US)
FCCC	UN Framework Convention on Climate Change
GATT	General Agreement on Tariffs and Trade
IAEA	International Atomic Energy Agency
ICAO	International Civil Aviation Organization
ICSAB	International Civil Service Advisory Board
IFAD	International Fund for Agricultural Development
ILO	International Labour Organization
IMF	International Monetary Fund
IPCC	Intergovernmental Panel on Climate Change
NGO	nongovernmental organization
NPT	Nuclear Non-Proliferation Treaty
OCHA	Office for the Coordination of Humanitarian Affairs
OEOA	United Nations Office of Emergency Operations in Africa
OIOS	Office of Internal Oversight Services (United Nations)
ONUC	UN Operation in the Congo (Opération des Nations Unies au Congo)

ONUMOZ	United Nations Operation in Mozambique
UNAIDS	Joint United Nations Programme on HIV/AIDS
UNAVEM	United Nations Angola Verification Mission
UNCTAD	United Nations Conference on Trade and Development
UNDAF	United Nations Development Assistance Framework
UNDP	United Nations Development Programme
UNEF	United Nations Emergency Force
UNEP	United Nations Environment Programme
UNESCO	United Nations Educational, Scientific, and Cultural Organization
UNFPA	United Nations Population Fund
UNHCR	UN High Commissioner for Refugees
UNICEF	United Nations Children's Fund
UNIDO	United Nations Industrial Development Organization
UNIFEM	United Nations Development Fund for Women
UNMOVIC	United Nations Monitoring, Verification and Inspection Commission
UNRRA	United Nations Relief and Rehabilitation Administration
UNRWA	United Nations Relief and Works Agency for Palestine Refugees in the Near East
UNTAG	United Nations Transitional Advisory Group for Namibia
WDR	*World Development Report*
WFP	World Food Programme
WGIG	Working Group on Internet Governance
WHO	World Health Organization
WMO	World Meteorological Organization
WSIS	World Summit on the Information Society
WTO	World Trade Organization

Preface

● ● ● ● ● ● ● ● ●

> *A moment later Sir Humphrey Appleby arrived. He is the
> Permanent Secretary of the DAA [Department of Adminis-
> trative Affairs], the Civil Service Head of Department. He is
> in his early fifties, I should think, but—somehow—ageless.
> He is charming and intelligent, a typical mandarin. He wel-
> comed me to the Department.*
>
> —THE COMPLETE YES MINISTER, 14

International secretariats need their moment in the sun. When I joined the United Nations Secretariat as an entry-level associate social affairs officer in 1971, it was not considered by anyone to be a major player in international relations. When I left the secretariat in 1996 as deputy director of the Division for the Advancement of Women, the world had changed and the United Nations Secretariat had become a major player. For twenty-five years I was one of the new international civil service mandarins, although I would not claim to be either as ageless or necessarily as charming as Sir Humphrey Appleby from the BBC comedy series *Yes, Minister* (Hacker 1984), who could have been our model. However, in many ways we are like the British civil service—whose rules were largely incorporated into the international civil service—represented by Sir Humphrey.

Like the civil servants lampooned in that series, we tried to be invisible, but unlike them, we were not part of a government. The international public service manages organizations that are not sovereign, have no armies or police, collect no taxes, levy no fines, make few formal decisions on their own, and yet deliver a large and growing number of public services. These are services intended to make the world an orderly place and allow nations and their citizens alike to live, in the words of the Preamble to the United Nations Charter, with "better standards of life in larger freedom."

We were invisible because sovereign governments—the member states—are in charge of the organizations, giving them their tasks and their money. Secretariats act through and with those states, almost seamlessly. States are supposed to be seen; their international assistants are not. In fact, the idea that nameless, faceless bureaucrats are running the world would not only be politically incorrect but appalling to most sovereign governments. Invisibility has consequences. First, the international public service cannot defend itself—if it is invisible, what is there to defend? In the wake of the Oil-for-Food scandal (which is discussed in some detail later), the popular press and critics of the United Nations itself use the image of a corrupt, uncontrolled bunch of bureaucrats to discredit the organization. Second, invisibility can reduce accountability. Like government officials, international secretariat managers should have to show that the resources that they have been given have not been wasted. If they are invisible, they can escape this scrutiny.

The idea for the title of this book came from a book published in 1964 by David Wise and Thomas Ross, both White House reporters for major American newspapers. Wise and Ross wrote an exposé of the role played by intelligence agencies like the Central Intelligence Agency in forming national foreign policy. They titled their book *Invisible Government* to reflect the fact that the intelligence agencies maintained a low profile and—the authors claimed—were not accountable to the political process.

The analogy is not completely fair. International organizations are not governments, and they do not govern. Instead, they engage in what has been termed *governance*, a process of steering public policy and services in a non-sovereign world. The secretariats of these organizations make this global governance possible and have been more important than most scholarship would suggest. Their work is a form of invisible governance that needs to be recognized. In recognizing it, their work should be supported but also made more accountable, as the international organizations evolve in the interdependent world of the twenty-first century.

Proper recognition is not easy, since the inner working of the secretariats is not well documented. Few international officials have seen fit to analyze their work, and much of what happened exists in the form of "war stories" told over dinner by current and former international public servants. Only a few of these have reached publication. Other than the marvelous memoirs of Brian Urquhart, the first member of the United Nations Secretariat, or Margaret Joan Anstee's recollections, only a few books have been written by insiders. Most academic analysts have focused on the more visible interplay of states rather than deal with the more shadowy secretariats.

In 1980 I took over from Henri Reymond a course entitled "The United Nations System: Structures and Processes" at New York University. Henri was a retired international civil servant who had started his career with the League of Nations. Henri was, for his time, a *wunderkind*. He joined the international civil service at twenty-one, just after graduating from law school. He started in Refugee Affairs, but in 1931 joined the International Labour Organization (ILO), where he served in the cabinets of successive directors-general. After retiring as the director of the ILO's office at the United Nations and secretary of the International Civil Service Advisory Board, Henri was talked into teaching at the Graduate School of Public Administration at New York University.

Henri expressed the view that, in terms of institutional innovation, the nineteenth century marked the emergence of the nation-state, and historians would mark the twentieth century as the time when international organizations and their secretariats became significant.

In 1971 the only international civil servant who was even noticed in the press was the secretary-general. By 2006 many other international civil servants were considered key public figures. Mohammed ElBaradei of the International Atomic Energy Agency (IAEA) could publicly chide the United States for not protecting nuclear sites in Iraq. United Nations Humanitarian Affairs Coordinator Jan Egeland could embarrass rich countries over their initial response to the December 2004 tsunami, and High Commissioner for Human Rights Louise Arbour could call individual countries to account over human rights issues. The United States president would mention the director of the UN's Electoral Assistance Division, Carina Perelli, by name in several news conferences. Later she was front-page news in the *New York Times* and the *Washington Post* when an evaluation of her office accused her of sexual discrimination. Clearly, something has changed. But has it been recognized, and what does it mean?

International-relations theory is built around states, and since states create international organizations, the focus of attention has been on how states interact. There is ample literature on the Security Council and the General Assembly. An analogy can be made with national politics, and from this perspective, civil society has become a focus as well. Civil society consists of organizations and entities that appear to be similar to domestic political actors. Civil society is considered a non-state actor and, for most of the theory, the only one.

If states and civil society consist of two classes of actors in international politics, a third would be international secretariats. International public service is different in many ways from national public service. The success of international organizations depends on their secretariats, and the success of their secretariats depends on those civil servants who constitute them.

In recognition of these changes an increasing number of international organizations and a few scholars are beginning to document the history of the secretariats. The International Monetary Fund (IMF), the World Bank, and the IAEA have commissioned such histories. The City University of New York has begun the United Nations Intellectual History Project. There have been studies of the international civil service, but almost no one has looked at secretariats as institutions in their own right.

Over a sixty-year period the number of issues with which the organizations of the United Nations system have dealt is truly amazing. I have obviously been selective in drawing a picture of the work of the secretariat, using my own experience, but I also analyze situations where precedents have been set that are still relevant to the issues in international relations today. Bureaucracies can be complex, filled with acronyms, technical jargon, and circumlocutions (we tend to write in the passive voice). My wife, Jan Clausen, has a very low tolerance for bureaucratic writing and has tried to keep the text accessible. My research assistant at the Maxwell School, Loveena Dookhony, assisted me in preparing some of the data used. Jim Lance, the editor at Kumarian Press, helped keep the structure of the book consistent and manageable. My thanks to all of them.

1

• • • • • • •

Why Are Secretariats Invisible?

And their greatest skill of all is the low profile. . . .

So what have I learned after nearly six months in office? Merely, it seems, that I am almost impotent in the face of the mighty faceless bureaucracy. However, it is excellent that I realize this because it means that they have failed to house-train me. If I were house-trained I would now believe a) that I am immensely powerful, and b) that my officials merely do my bidding.

—THE COMPLETE YES MINISTER, 162

The twenty-first century will have a large and vibrant international public sector. A quick perusal of the news shows the breadth, variety, and importance of activities of international organizations, both public and nongovernmental. These range from inspectors determining whether uranium enrichment in Iran is for peaceful purposes; the World Health Organization (WHO) maintaining surveillance on a possible bird flu epidemic; the UN High Commissioner for Refugees (UNHCR) finding ways to protect refugees in Sudan; the World Food Programme (WFP) raising alarms about starvation in Zimbabwe; UN war-crimes tribunals passing judgment on former heads of state and military officers in the Balkans; and in the Balkans, West Africa, and Southeast Asia, a dispute resolution panel of the World Trade Organization (WTO) deciding whether billions of dollars in aircraft sales violate trade agreements.

In monetary terms the international public sector is also growing. The UN's biennial assessed budget for 2006–7 is US$3.6 billion,[1] to which another US$3.6 billion can be added for the specialized agencies of the UN system, not including the Bretton Woods institutions (the World Bank, IMF, and the WTO).[2] This is larger than the national budgets of most countries in the world and can be expected to grow as new tasks are given to international organizations.

International relations scholars have kept an eye on the international public sector over the past sixty years, although their attention has waxed and waned according to changes in world politics. As the international public sector's importance has grown since the end of the Cold War, scholars have focused on how governments interact in multilateral negotiations, peacekeeping, human rights, and development assistance. They have analyzed the growing role of civil society in international politics.

Despite the renewed interest in international organizations, few scholars have looked at international organizations as public administrations, created and maintained to deliver global services. An exception is Barnett and Finnemore who, in *Rules for the World*, examine some of the workings of secretariats like the IMF, the UNHCR, and the Department of Peacekeeping Operations (Barnett and Finnemore 2004). But their focus is still mostly on the governments involved in international organizations rather than on the international public servants who work in the buildings and who are still, in a real sense, invisible.

The question can fairly be asked, if the governance provided by international secretariats is invisible, how can we be sure that it exists? In one sense there is no difficulty in proving that the secretariats exist. They can be seen in office towers all over the world, from New York, Geneva, Vienna, Nairobi, Bangkok, Addis Ababa, Beirut, and Santiago de Chile for the United Nations; and Paris, London, Madrid, Rome, and Montreal for the specialized agencies. Almost every country on the planet has an office of the United Nations Development Programme (UNDP). The secretariats are reflected on the vehicles supplied by the United Nations Children's Fund (UNICEF) everywhere in the developing world or on sacks of grain marked WFP. They are probably more ubiquitous than any public sector in history.

The secretary-general of the United Nations appears in the news almost every day. Refugees, HIV/AIDS, disaster relief, and peacekeeping are normal stories. Nuclear power, the environment, human rights, and trade are all areas where the international public sector is visible.

The breadth and depth of that growth are not so visible nor are their implications for ordinary people. Calculating the extent of the expansion is not easy. For many reasons, including the fact that organizational structures are complicated and reporting on them is uneven, there is no clear indicator of the size of the international public sector or its growth. In the past, when it was politically useful to show how small the United Nations was, supporters would point out that the core budget of the United Nations was smaller than that of the Tokyo fire department and "together with supporting (general service) staff, the core UN Secretariat has a smaller civil service for all these worldwide responsibilities than the City of Winnipeg (9,917 staff) in Canada, or than the staff of the international advertising firm, Saatchi & Saatchi" (Urquhart and Childers 1994, 26).

In reality the international public sector, in budgetary and staff terms, is the size of the public sector of a medium-sized country, and this represents a significant growth over time. Unfortunately, no one has tried to maintain a comparable record of the expenditure of the United Nations system.

However, by looking at expenditure and human resources reports, it is possible to estimate both the present size of the international public sector and its growth over time. This can be seen in three ways: (1) the amount of funds spent, in terms of (2) the tasks the international public sector undertakes, and, linked to this, (3) the number of persons who work for international organizations.

FINANCES

The expenditures of the universal international organizations that belong to the United Nations system have increased dramatically in real terms, even in the context of "zero growth" budgets. In 2003, the latest year for which these figures have been compiled, the combined expenditures of the organizations of the United Nations system amounted to US$12,254,830,400, of which US$3,334,446 were contributions assessed of the member states and US$8,920,383,900 were voluntary contributions.[3] These figures do not include the amounts spent in the World Bank, the IMF, and the International Fund for Agricultural Development (IFAD). It is difficult to chart the growth in the international public sector, because combined expenditure reports have been uneven, have not been expressed in constant (adjusted for inflation) amounts and often are not comparable. The budget of each organization is independently decided by its member states, voluntary contributions have become more significant as a means of funding expanded activities, and the organizations of the United Nations system have resisted combining their expenditure reports.

TASKS

From 1966 to 1984 the United Nations system presented figures showing the subject areas in which expenditures were taking place. This practice has been discontinued, but an earlier study (Mathiason and Smith 1987) showed how the tasks changed over time. The figures in Table 1–1, drawn from official reports, document the growth of humanitarian assistance, for example.

STAFFING

In practice, the international public sector is its staff members, who provide its services and whose salaries and other costs make up most of the combined expenditures of organizations, at least in terms of core budgets. Secretariat staffs have undergone an evolution, both in composition and in approach.

The League of Nations, the first international secretariat, had a staff of 630 at its height in 1929; of these 155 were professionals subject to "geographical distribution." At the same time the ILO had a staff of 371, of which 122 were professionals (Royal Institute of International Affairs 1944, 21n.). By 1986 the United Nations

Table 1-1. Growth in Expenditures by Sector in the UN System, 1966 to 1984

Sector	Percentage of 1966	Percentage of 1984
Political	1.4	4.6
Development issues	7.4	7.4
Natural resources	7.2	5.1
Agriculture	15.1	13.0
Industry	3.0	4.4
Transport	5.4	4.8
Trade	1.5	2.9
Population	0.8	4.1
Human settlements	1.4	16.2
Education	6.0	3.4
Employment	5.0	2.1
Humanitarian aid	13.1	23.9
Social questions	3.7	2.6
Culture	1.0	1.1
Science	5.4	3.1
Total	100.0	100.0

Source: ACC (Administrative Committee on Coordination) Reports on Expenditures by Programme, 1966 to 1984–1985.

Secretariat and its funds and programs had a combined professional staff of 6,135 persons, forty times larger than the League. By 2005 the number had more than doubled, to 13,159. Table 1–2 shows the growth, most of which took place in posts funded from extra-budgetary resources.

But what do these public servants actually do besides occupy offices and do good deeds? And what effect do they have on world politics? The standard role of dominant international-relations theory is not relevant to the role of secretariats. Thus we have to begin with a theoretical framework that will help us to see that role.

Whatever theory one presupposes to be true is the one overlaid on the facts. It often determines what information is considered important, how relationships can be seen and described, and how different pieces of the mosaic of international relations fit together. Theory can also produce a kind of blindness toward events.

WHAT INTERNATIONAL-RELATIONS THEORY TELLS US ABOUT SECRETARIATS

Much of the dominant international-relations theory lacks a place for international secretariats, and observers who are conditioned by that theory will not find them important. While over the past seventy years or so the names of theories used in international relations have undergone change, there are essentially two competing theoretical trends that constitute alternative views of the nature of international organizations and their role. One is *realism*, whose basis is the nation-state as the primary actor in international relations. The other is *functionalism*, whose basis is a vision of what the international system does. A variant is regime theory, which can be seen as a synthesis of both.

The Realist Paradigm: Any Secretariats There?

Realists see states as the building blocks of the international system. Realism was the dominant theory of international relations for most of the twentieth century. Scholars trace its intellectual origins back to the Greek philosophers, to Machiavelli, and to

Hobbes. Current realist theory emerged from the maelstrom of World War II, when scholars like Hans Morgenthau, Arnold Wolfers, and Kenneth Waltz sought to explain the reasons behind conflict among countries. These scholars opposed what they called idealism, a theory that said that international law would lead to a new international order.

Expressed simply, the realist theory states:

- The governments of states act on behalf of their citizens, who are united by various ties of ethnicity, sometimes religion, but more often common experience.
- States provide services to their members and control their borders.
- States have goals and objectives that are grouped under "national interest" (expressed as policies and positions, such as free trade, protectionism, territorial integrity, economic growth, national pride).
- States express these interests in their dealings with other states.
- International relations among states are based on power politics. Stronger states dominate weaker ones. States make bilateral agreements with one another.
- The main currency of power is the ability to use coercive force (military or financial) to induce other states to accept situations or agreements.

Realism assumes that the normal state of nature in the international system is anarchy, so states use various arrangements to force the creation of order. When the state system functions, order is maintained. When it breaks down, order must be reestablished, usually through armed conflict.

In the realist model international organizations provide a space where national interests can be worked out in a multilateral context. When the national interests of most coincide, agreements can be reached and can be honored, as long as states consider that they protect their interests. But at the heart of it all is state sovereignty; the nation-state is the only real building block. Conflict is a characteristic of the system, and political change comes from it.

In this model there is no real place for international secretariats. To the extent that they exist, their purpose is to convey messages from one state to another or write down notes of agreements.

Table 1-2. Professional Staff in the UN Secretariat and UN Funds and Programs, by Source of Funding, 1986–2005

Year	1986			1991			1995		
Source of Funds	Regular Budget	Extra-budgetary Resources	TOTAL	Regular Budget	Extra-budgetary Resources	TOTAL	Regular Budget	Extra-budgetary Resources	TOTAL
UN Secretariat	3,553	322	3,875	3,338	472	3,810	3,555	839	4,394
UN Funds									
UNDP	–	603	603	–	703	703	–	618	618
UNFPA			0			0			0
UNHCR	113	336	449	91	421	512	89	417	506
UNICEF	–	950	950	–	1,165	1,165	–	2,430	2,430
UNITAR	–	15	15	–	10	10	–	12	12
UNOPS		0	0			0			0
UNRWA	14	69	83	120	–	120	82	82	164
ITC	59	18	77	53	21	74	–	71	71
ICSC	23	–	23	18	–	18	21	–	21
UNJSPF			0			0			0
ICJ	15	–	15	19	–	19	24	–	24
UNU	–	45	45	–	23	23	–	20	20
Total	3,777	2,358	6,135	3,639	2,815	6,454	3,771	4,489	8,260

Year	2000			2005		
Source of Funds	Regular Budget	Extra-budgetary Resources	TOTAL	Regular Budget	Extra-budgetary Resources	TOTAL
UN Secretariat	2,925	1,465	4,390	3,133	2,621	5,754
UN Funds			0			
UNDP	—	875	875		1,581	1,581
UNFPA	—	250	250		193	193
UNHCR	77	1,212	1,289	89	1,877	1,966
UNICEF	—	1,103	1,103		2,657	2,657
UNITAR	—	12	12		6	6
UNOPS	—	150	150		665	665
UNRWA	73	13	86	91	36	127
ITC	—	61	61		75	75
ICSC	—	12	12		18	18
UNJSPF	—	42	42		49	49
ICJ	9		9	33	12	45
UNU	—	17	17		23	23
Total	3,084	5,212	8,296	3,346	9,813	13,159

Source: Annual Reports of the Secretary-General to the General Assembly on the Composition of the Secretariat, 1986–2005.

The international system based on unitary states interacting has also been characterized as a billiard game in which the various parties bounce off each other (Krasner 1982, 497). In this image the secretariats are not there at all, unless they are part of the felt on the table, or perhaps the chalk used to prepare the cue.

A better analogy in the realist model would be that secretariats are similar to persons who run the valet parking at a restaurant. The customers arrive, leave their cars with the valets, go inside and complete their business, and then the valets bring the cars from the parking lot and the customers depart.

Anne-Marie Slaughter suggests that the alternative to realism is what she terms liberalism. By this she means that

> Liberals focus primarily on State-society relations. The first Liberal assumption is that the primary actors in the international system are individuals and groups acting in domestic and transnational civil society. Thus where Realists look for concentrations of State power, Liberals focus on the ways in which interdependence encourages and allows individuals and groups to exert different pressures on national governments. Second, Liberals assume that the 'State' interacts with these actors in a complex process of both representation and regulation. Governments are assumed to represent some subset of individual and group actors. (Slaughter 1995, 6)

The international system under this theory is more complex than the realist would have expressed. While states are paramount, other actors are also players. These can include what is now called civil society and can also be government officials who interact with other government officials. They interact through networks, largely informal in nature. Slaughter has made a strong case that the international system is increasingly a network of networks, a new world order (Slaughter 2004).

Liberal theory helps explain a growing role for international nongovernmental organizations (NGOs) in some fields, as well as some informal arrangements among government officials. However, it does not find a place for international secretariats. Secretariats are not, by definition, anchored in national societies. In this theory some international officials can be part of networks, persons who can be contacted or who can provide information, but their formal role is limited and not really very important.

In sum, state-based theories simply do not recognize the existence of non-state actors that are independent of states. Since international secretariats have those characteristics, in terms of these theories international secretariats are invisible.

Realist and other state-centric models have come under considerable criticism for their inability to explain key aspects of international relations. Mark Zacher, a Canadian political scientist, in an essay entitled "The Decaying Pillars of the Westphalian Temple,"[4] pointed out that each of the conceptual pillars of realism was decaying. These include:

- The cost/benefit ratio of wars has reached a point where no state can afford to go to war on its own.
- The ability of the state to provide physical protection to its citizens has decayed, with problems of trans-boundary environmental pollution, epidemics, and the like undermining state competence.
- International economic interdependence has undermined the capacity of the state to control its national economy by public policy.
- Information flows, as a result of technology, have become such that national action cannot control them. (A state cannot stop people from learning about events by stopping newspapers at the border or jamming radio signals.)
- Spread of democracy has meant that the state cannot suppress popular will, and there has been evidence of a global norm.
- Cultural and social heterogeneity has increased, undermining bases for the state based on single cultural models and making identities much more complex.

The Functionalist Paradigm: Predicting an Amoeba-like Growth of Secretariats

The factors enumerated by Zacher are those that the old functionalists assumed would happen. The growth of international secretariats in this context would not be dramatic but would rather be like the growth of amoebas, gradually extending to cover the entire pond of international relations.

Functionalism is a theory that was current early in the modern era of international organizations, but which then fell from favor. Functionalism actually comes from anthropology. Social scientists studying societies (like Bronislaw Malinowski in anthropology and Talcott Parsons in sociology) found that societies held together because certain functions were performed. If these functions were analyzed, we would understand how the society worked. If the functions were not performed correctly or were in conflict, if they were dysfunctional, the societies could break down.

Functionalism came to be applied to international relations as part of an analysis of why the League of Nations, founded on the realist model, dissolved. Scholars found that those aspects of the League that worked best were in the economic and social areas, where the League performed functions such as drug control, refugee placement and assistance, or technical regulations.

David Mitrany saw the number and complexity of these functions growing. He noted that the causes of both conflict and community were rooted in economic and social factors (poverty, perceptions). These functions could not be performed by individual states, so they would have to be performed by multilateral institutions (Mitrany 1946).

After World War II some scholars like Ernst Haas began to see the prospect of the nation-state eroding because transnational functions would need to be performed (Haas 1958). Haas applied the theory to the European community, and it appeared to explain what was happening, but when he applied it to the ILO (Haas 1964) the theory did not seem to work, and he moved on to other interests. As Ruggie et al. point out, Haas was very affected by Charles DeGaulle's use of *realpolitik* in the European community and believed that the functional links that he expected to see would not occur. Haas declared his neo-functionalist paradigm obsolescent (Ruggie et al. 2005, 279), and few other scholars continued the line of thought. Functionalism as an explanation for international relations essentially came to an end. This was probably premature, as will be shown.

Functionalist theory gave a key role to international secretariats. Mitrany argued that an expanding system of functionally specialized international organizations run by experts could become a transformative force in world politics:

> The functional approach . . . seeks, by linking authority to a specific activity, to break away from the traditional link between authority and a definite territory. . . . This approach resolves the dilemma of creating either too loose or too narrow an international organization by building up authorities which would be both comprehensive and solid, in selected fields of common life. (Mitrany 1946, 6)

Haas saw the same in the European community, as did Philippe Schmitter in Latin America. These experts were to be found in the secretariats rather than in the governments, as I found when I examined the relationship between meeting participation and agreement in the UN Economic Commission for Latin America (Mathiason 1972). A few other scholars tried to use functionalist theory, including Ness and Brechin (1988), who looked at international organizations from the perspective of organizational sociology.

In the final analysis by Haas and his successors, the role of global international secretariats did not seem to be very important, and, as a result, secretariats returned to their prior invisibility.

Regime Theory as Fusion: Creating a Role for Secretariats

The weakness of classical realism in explaining why nation-states cooperate with one another offsets its strength in explaining why they conflict. Realism implies that most state interactions are not cooperative or, if they are, will be based on bilateral alliances. Unfortunately, the world is not quite that simple. Much of international order, the kind usually cited to justify the United Nations, is based on multilateral agreements that are respected.

Regime theory explains how these agreements are reached and maintained. It received its greatest impulse with a special issue of *International Organization* in 1982, reporting on the results of a seminar. Regime theory sought to find a synthesis between realism and functionalism, in which "under certain restrictive conditions involving the failure of individual action to secure Pareto-optimal outcomes, international regimes may have a significant impact even in an anarchic world" (Krasner 1982, 186). In other words, regime theorists hold that sometimes power politics do not work and more constructive solutions have to be found.

Regime theory postulated a series of steps that leads to agreement among states to create longer-lasting cooperation agreements. The initial impetus for the kind of thinking that led to regime theory was to explain why states would agree on trading systems, like the General Agreement on Tariffs and Trade (GATT) or on economic integration.

Regimes were defined as "sets of implicit or explicit principles, norms, rules, and decision-making procedures around which actors' expectations converge in a given area of international relations" (Krasner 1982, 186). "Sets" implied that there were boundaries to the agreements. During the 1980s a few scholars sought to analyze regimes, but one difficulty was determining what those boundaries were. Inevitably, when examined, the regimes appeared to be much less solid than originally thought and were found to be difficult to analyze; as a result, few scholars analyzed them. Haggard and Simmons (1987), like Slaughter, argued that to revive the theory, it was necessary to find a link with domestic politics.

Regime theory largely went out of fashion in the academic study of international relations, although a few scholars continued to find it useful. Hasenclever, Mayer, and Rittberger point out that most of those using regime theory see it from the perspective of states (1997, Table 1). They note three competing schools of thought. Realism sees the central variable as power, with weak institutionalism. Neoliberalism sees the central variable as interests, with medium institutionalism. And cognitivism sees the central variable as knowledge, with strong institutionalism. For practitioners, however, regime theory provides a very useful schema for looking at how international negotiations take place, as we will see in Chapter 4, and the role of the secretariat therein.

States enter into agreements because benefits from the situation the agreements produce outweigh specific costs associated with them. They are almost always agreements by consensus, since that is the way in which the value of the larger agreement can be expressed. Consensus is a form of decision-making that is not formally defined. Some argue that if it were defined, it would not work. In practice, a consensus decision is accepted because all parties concerned find that the total positive value of the agreement outweighs any negative aspects. It is, in game-theory terms, a non-zero-sum solution, or a win-win scenario. While the degree of commitment to the consensus can be variable, the decision is legitimate.

Since many of the underlying assumptions in regime theory derive from realism, it is not surprising that most of the analysis that uses the theory does not find a role for secretariats. At best, the secretariats, while being more than parking valets, might be like a hotel concierge, who provides advice on where to go and what to do and works to make the guests—the member states—comfortable while they develop and maintain their regimes.

The assumption is that regimes are created and maintained by states. As we will see, that is not a correct assumption; much of the regime-creation process is facilitated in a very substantive and important way by secretariats who, rather than acting like a concierge, are more like the managers of the hotel, still concerned with the comfort of guests but also with turning a profit.

Still, anyone looking into the regime-theory literature would be hard put to find the international secretariats, and we will have to conclude that international secretariats are still invisible. The next question is, do they provide governance?

To answer that question, we have to look at what governance at the international level implies. That, in turn, requires an excursion into the theory of power.

POWER AND AUTHORITY
AT THE MULTILATERAL LEVEL:
MAX WEBER RETURNS

The coin of the realm for realists is power, but what constitutes power in international relations needs to be elaborated. No one doubts that one type of power is *coercive*. One party can induce another party to do something by the threat (or use) of force. This is what Nye (2004) calls "hard power." While its main currency is military force, it also includes an ability to use economic means to coerce. Coercive power is the most expensive kind of power, both in terms of its physical cost and its longer-term consequences.[5]

A second type of power is what Nye terms "soft power" or "the ability to get what you want through attraction rather than coercion." One party can induce another to do something by providing economic or similar incentives: trading concessions, tax breaks, cultural exchanges, loans or even bribes. This can also be called utilitarian power to emphasize the idea that it is based on some calculation of utility (rather than fear). This type of power can also be relatively costly, particularly if the economic exchanges involved are unequal. A world in which the only forms of power were coercion or utilitarian influence would be indeed anarchic. In fact, any national society in which power was only of these two types would not be a pleasant place to live.

The third type of power was first described by Max Weber, the late-nineteenth-century sociologist, and is termed "legitimate power." Derived from Weber's social-order theory, legitimate power means that a person does something because he or she believes that it is right to do so. Hurd calls it "the normative belief by an actor that a rule or institution ought to be obeyed" (1999, 381). This could be termed very soft power, but it is more than that.

The idea is that the utility of an action is derived from its place in a smooth social order. Goldhammer and Shils, drawing on Weber, saw three sources of legitimate power: law, tradition, and charismatic authority. Of these, the source of legitimate power for international secretariats is not charismatic, since the leaders of international secretariats are anything but charismatic. Tradition is also not a source for legitimate power for international secretariats, at least now, since there is no traditional sanctity for the orders that a secretariat could give. The source of legitimate power is essentially legal. Goldhammer and Shils state that

> legitimate power is regarded as *legal* when the recognition of legitimacy rests on a belief by the subordinated individuals in the legality of the laws, decrees, and directives promulgated by the power-holder. (Goldhammer and Shils 1939, 172)

While this definition involves a tautology, it is clear that legitimacy is in the eye of the beholder. It is something that is believed, and the belief derives from a sense that the orders have been arrived at lawfully.

The international system is above sovereignty, in the sense that it has only that authority which has been granted it by sovereign states. Article 97 of the United Nations Charter, which sets out the responsibilities of the secretary-general as chief administrative officer, reads:

> The Secretary-General shall act in that capacity [as chief administrative officer] in all meetings of the General Assembly, of the Security Council, of the Economic and Social Council, and of the Trusteeship Council, and shall perform such other functions as are entrusted to him by these organs.

In granting authority in the form of principles, norms, rules, and procedures, as regime theory would posit, states have given international secretariats the task of observing compliance with these agreements through the use of information and the exercise of the agreed-upon procedures. In Weberian terms, this could be called bureaucratic authority, based on technical competence, clearly fixed rules, and their neutral application.[6] Secretariats are credible both because of the lawful agreement on which international regimes are based and the secretariats' own characteristics. Barnett and Finnemore (2004) emphasize this point as well, and use a Weberian approach to explain how international organizations function.

Neither Weber nor his successors saw these concepts in terms of transnational organizations. Goldhammer and Shils saw that power relations were either unilateral or bilateral. However, power relations can also be multilateral, where failure of one party to comply with agreements is sanctioned by the other parties, thus giving force to the agreement and a clear role to the secretariats, whose job includes determining whether states are in compliance. The test for international secretariats is how well they use this type of power and with what effect.

APPLYING A FUNCTIONALIST APPROACH: THE FIVE FUNCTIONS

The use of legitimate power provides order at the international level, and within this context international secretariats provide goods and services that allow for the exercise of that power. They perform functions, much as David Mitrany posited, and a return to the functionalist approach is probably the best way to explain what secretariats do. Their primary purpose is to ensure that the global community holds together, and how well they succeed depends on how they perform a series of functions that have been delegated to them by states.

There are five functions: regime creation, information mobilization, norm enforcement, direct services, and internal management. This approach permits a clearer exploration of what the secretariats do, since each involves a slightly different management approach. While they will form a constant method of organization throughout this study, a quick overview of each function sets the stage for the detailed examinations in the different chapters.

Regime Creation

Regime creation is the oldest secretariat function. One of the ways in which international order is maintained is through the negotiation of regimes to govern transnational conduct. This involves first agreeing on the areas in which the actions of nations need to be harmonized, international cooperation achieved, and international machinery employed. The next step is to define the norms that set standards of behavior—defined in terms of rights and obligations—that will govern that cooperation. The result of the process is usually a text, ranging from a treaty to a resolution, that is accepted by governments. This text forms the basis for legitimate behavior by states—and their citizens—as reflected in public policies and programs. Secretariats play a major role in facilitating the agreements that create regimes, as we will see in Chapter 4.

Mobilization of Information

It would not be an exaggeration to state that the world floats in a sea of information. One of the functions of the international public sector is to provide comparative information collected and analyzed according to accepted standards and criteria and made universally accessible. The information thus collected and analyzed provides a common base for policy discourse and allows many decisions to be taken by reference to rules. For example, the designation of countries as least developed, with the corresponding relaxation of international financial obligations and increase in access to concessional resources, is made on the basis of data collected under the UN System of National Accounts.

Mobilization of information has at least two links with regime creation. The first has to do with monitoring the extent to which legitimacy is maintained in the regime through the performance by states of their obligations. In a system where only the exercise of legitimate power is possible, provision of information about illegitimate acts is the only means of compelling compliance. This information must be credibly provided by politically neutral sources. The second is the maintenance of consistency in the interpretation of the obligations under the regime. It is the task of the international organization to be the "institutional memory" that safeguards the consistency of procedures to implement the regime and ensures that the modification of procedures, if required, will be orderly. Mobilization of information can also involve placing facts and interpretation on the international agenda that could help governments or civil society undertake their own actions, even if these are not intended to lead to agreements among states. It can also involve mobilizing information about the United Nations itself. Some of the evolution of information mobilization is described in Chapter 5.

Norm Enforcement

The basic, least costly form of power is founded on legitimacy, where decisions are accepted because they are considered right and rightly made. Enforcement in this context occurs by showing where there has been deviation from the agreed norms and where, by so indicating, the parties concerned are induced to adjust their actions to conform. The function of norm enforcement follows on the adoption by governments of agreements that they hold to be binding.

The types of activities under this function range from the UN Charter–based judicial functions performed by the International Court of Justice, through the monitoring of human rights instruments and, more recently, through the monitoring and administration of international conventions in such diverse areas as law of the sea, elimination of weapons of mass destruction, international drug control, and management of international war-crimes tribunals.

Chapter 6 discusses this function.

Direct Service Provision

Over the past sixty years the United Nations has undertaken a series of functions in which it provides services directly. Cox and Jacobson (1973) consider a number of UN organizations to be service organizations rather than forum organizations. Many of the services are like those that would be provided by a government, if there were one to provide them. The broad function of direct implementation includes three areas: humanitarian assistance, peace and security services, and international economic management. Each has as a common denominator in that the United Nations acts in the same way that a state might. Each has its own distinguishing characteristics and has to be examined separately.

Like the actions of an executive branch of government in performance of this function, those of the international public sector are circumscribed by the enabling legislation that sets limits and by the budgetary allocations that are made available. However, the agencies have considerable latitude in how they seek to provide their services. This is particularly true of humanitarian assistance and international economic management, although for different reasons. It is less true of peace and security assistance because the ability of the United Nations to take action also depends on the countries that contribute troops.

In all three areas the international public sector is an intermediary, sometimes of last resort. In two, peace and security and international economic management, the function is to channel services from donors to recipients, with full recognition of all parties' sovereignty. In practice, all three are funded voluntarily, thus making them to an extent donor driven. Although in the case of peacekeeping missions mandated by the Security Council funding is expected to come from assessments, in practice states can determine whether to contribute troops or not, and some states have purposely refused to accept the assessments.

The actual services this function requires vary according to the specific mandate of each mission but will usually include some administrative tasks such as contracting for service delivery and financial management, policy analysis, provision of direct advisory services, and information dissemination.

Humanitarian Assistance
The United Nations now has the responsibility for providing basic services to persons such as refugees and those displaced by armed conflict and natural calamity who, in the absence of a responsible national authority, have become the responsibility of the international community. National governments once provided many of the services provided by the United Nations, and the growth of United Nations responsibility reflects the inability of many governments in the developing countries to undertake these services.

Chapter 8 considers this service function.

Peace and Security Services
In large measure this function represents the enlargement of the secretary-general's responsibilities, under Article 6 of the UN Charter, to include a wide range of situations in which the United Nations is expected to be an actor when national action is deemed either inappropriate or unlikely. The services range from exercise of good offices in the resolution of conflict through supervising elections, monitoring, training, and organizing policy to the deployment of armed forces and civilian staff to help provide the infrastructure necessary to maintain peace and security.

Perhaps because of its connection with the realist discourse, the peacekeeping function has been subject to considerable analysis, including analysis of its management.

Chapter 7 considers this service function.

International Economic and Social Management Services
International economic and social management is a function that has grown out of the economic and social articles of the Charter, in which the international community provides advisory services, training, and public investment as an alternative to bilateral aid. It is direct implementation in that the service is given directly to

governments by public officials who are employed by the United Nations and involves provision of personnel, financing, and technical support services.

International economic and social management has tended to be seen in policy rather than functional terms, revolving around the North-South debate about transfer of resources and technology, but it should also be seen as a service that the international public sector provides to ensure a stable system of international transactions and movements.

Chapter 9 considers this service function.

Internal Management

A function of all bureaucracies is internal administration and control, actions taken to keep the organization running in a way acceptable to its legislature. Within the United Nations this includes such routine activities as personnel and financial administration, as well as the kinds of activities necessary to provide the organization with a reviewable and accountable structure. These activities include program planning, budgeting, monitoring and evaluation, building maintenance, and security provisions for personnel.

Chapter 10 discusses this function.

An element of management is accountability, the process of showing to stakeholders whether what the organization promised would happen as a result of its work did happen. The issue is particularly important in the international public sector, where so much that is expected to happen is indirect and where, by their invisibility, the secretariats could avoid being held accountable. The solution to the problem has been to install systems of results-based programming and budgeting. How well they have worked is the subject of Chapter 11.

NOTES

[1] A/60/6, "Introduction" (April 4, 2006), 9.

[2] A/59/315, "Budgetary and Financial Situation of Organizations of the United Nations System" (September 1, 2004), Table 1.

[3] Ibid. At different intervals the Chief Executives Board and its predecessors would present expenditure figures, but these were always in current dollars and did not always use the same methodology. Comparison over time is therefore a complicated task that no one has yet undertaken.

[4] Because the system of nation-states is considered to have begun through the Treaty of Westphalia, which ended the Thirty Years War in Europe in 1648, it is often referred to as the Westphalian system.

[5] Military force is most effective when it is not used, as in the theory of deterrence. When it is used, it is easy to use up.

[6] David L. Westby discusses this in detail (1966). While Weber did not deal with international organizations, his analysis of the vital role of the German bureaucracy in fostering state functionality marks a clear analogy with the growth of international organizations.

2

· · · · · · ·

Evolution of the International Public Service (1919–2006)

"Minister," he said firmly, "the evidence that you are pro-posing to submit is not only untrue, it is—which is much more serious—unwise." One of Humphrey's most telling remarks so far, I think. "I have been through this before: the expanding Civil Service is the result of parliamentary legis-lation, not bureaucratic empire building."

I began to think that Sir Humphrey really believes this.

"So," I said, "when this comes up at Question Time you want me to tell parliament it's their fault that the Civil Service is so big?"

"It's the truth, Minister," he insisted.

—THE COMPLETE YES MINISTER, 111

International secretariats and the international public sector in general appeared in the twentieth century. Before that time they simply did not exist. They followed the development of national civil services during the nineteenth century, but in the international environment they underwent their own peculiar transformation.

Unlike many national governments, international organizations run heavily on precedent. International agreements move slowly, but once something has been agreed to it is usually hard to change, since other elements of the agreement are built on it and trying to change earlier agreements often causes more problems. In the international public service, agreements are protected. We start, therefore, with a review of the evolution of those agreements and practices that give the international civil service its form, constrain its actions, and give it flexibility to do its job. It is a history almost a century long.

SOME HISTORICAL ANTECEDENTS TO INTERNATIONAL PUBLIC SERVICE

The first true international organizations, the International Committee of the Red Cross, the International Telegraph Union, and the Universal Postal Union, did not have international secretariats because their staffs were exclusively Swiss. It was only when the League of Nations was founded (and the International Labour Office) that the idea of an international secretariat firmly took hold.

There are many historical precedents for modern national civil services but few for international civil service. The mandarins in imperial China, the bureaucrats of the Ottoman Empire, or the clerks in Medieval Europe were essentially national. Even the central bureaucrats of the Roman Empire were essentially national, even when Rome ruled through indirect means. After the Treaty of Westphalia, when services were needed to support negotiations between different states, the host government provided them, as when the Austrian Empire provided support to the Congress of Vienna. Many negotiations started simply by trying to determine which country would be the host of the conference.

One historical exception was the middle-level bishops of the early Christian church, who formed a multinational secretariat to organize and run the church councils. Convened to reach agreement on established doctrine and fight against heresy, Bishop Eusebius of Caesarea, the secretary of the Council of Nicaea, helped delegates reach a pre-consensus before the council itself began by seeking to find a middle ground for consensus among disputing parties. This kind of function eventually has become institutionalized in the Roman Curia, which is today an international secretariat.

The first two international secretariats, defined as having staff seconded from various national administrations and some immunities, were the European Commission on the Danube, recognized as an international organization in 1878, and the International Institute of Agriculture, founded in Rome in 1905 (Beigbeder 1988, 16–17). Because personnel were loaned to the organizations and were not really independent, the staffs were not really international civil servants.

THE LEAGUE OF NATIONS AND THE IDEA OF INTERNATIONAL CIVIL SERVICE

A permanent secretariat was a significant innovation in the League of Nations Covenant. Its Article 6 specified that the permanent secretariat would be established at the seat of the League. The article stated that the secretariat would comprise a secretary-general and such secretaries and staff as might be required. It provided for the appointment of a secretary-general by the council of the League,[1] with ratification by the entire membership. The covenant required that all staff needed the formal approval of the council, implying that the secretariat was not, in fact, independent. Other than these formal requirements, the Articles did not specify how the secretariat was to be organized or, in fact, what it would do.

The first secretary-general of the League, Sir Eric Drummond, was named in the covenant itself. Drummond was a British diplomat who had been involved in the negotiations. His appointment set the precedent of appointing a civil servant (or diplomat) as the executive head of an international secretariat.[2] His appointment also guaranteed that the national model of a secretariat that would be applied in the League would be that of the British civil service (Langrod 1963, 110). A group of former senior League officials led by Drummond himself in 1944 described the decision in the following terms:

> The first Secretary-General, when framing the scheme for the organization of the League Secretariat, decided that strict international loyalty should be demanded of the staff, thus

discarding the principle of national loyalty which underlay the existing secretariat of the Peace Conference and the Inter-Allied organizations. (Royal Institute of International Affairs 1944, 19)

The detailed evolution of the League's personnel policies designed to ensure independence was analyzed by Henri Reymond and Sidney Mailick (1985); Reymond wrote from his own experience in the League and the ILO. The group of former high-level officials of the League brought together by Drummond on the eve of the United Nations was able to conclude:

> The experiment worked well until the League became the direct object of subtle, then open, sabotage. Whatever their final judgment of the League, observers agree that the concept of international loyalty is practicable, and we can affirm on empirical evidence that an administration based on international loyalty—to the organization in general and its secretariat in particular—can be highly efficient. (Royal Institute of International Affairs 1944, 19)

The League had been vulnerable to national meddling—or even sabotage—because of its requirement that secretariat staff be approved by governments. The principle of geographical distribution of posts often led to the appointment of staff that did not have "international loyalty." Staff members took orders from their national authorities (especially Germany and Italy) and provided confidential information to them as well.

The League secretariat's experience was analyzed, more after the fact than during its twenty years of existence. During World War II, when it was clear that there would be a successor organization, former League staff members came together to reflect on their experience. This included the group of former senior staff put together by Drummond, but also middle-level staff like Egon Ranshofen-Wertheimer (1945), who wrote up his experiences and observations for the Carnegie Endowment for International Peace. Political scientists like David Mitrany (1946) contributed their own analyses.

Two conclusions flowed from this analysis. First, the secretariat had developed a set of unique core values that allowed it to function as an independent actor. Second, the greatest successes of the secretariat had been in areas where a transnational approach was the only realistic means of addressing problems.

A core value that the League (and the ILO) had developed was a sense of international loyalty among the staff. The Drummond group put it this way:

> What is "international loyalty"? It is not the denationalized loyalty of a man without a country. On the contrary, it is the conviction that the highest interests of one's own country are served best by the promotion of security and welfare everywhere, and the steadfast manifestation of that conviction without regard to changing circumstances. (Royal Institute of International Affairs 1945, 18)

This concept was written into the formal staff regulations adopted in 1933, which stated: "The officials of the Secretariat of the League of Nations are exclusively international officials and their duties are not national, but international."[3] Henri Reymond (1994) noted how this had helped secretariat staff cope with the difficulties of their organizations and maintain their own identities and motivation. As learned in the League, it was a significant modification of what realists might expect: staff did not lose their nationality—nationality was something built into recruitment, distribution of posts, and individual identity—but rather they would suspend it in the interest of the international organization.

Ranshofen-Wertheimer expressed this well in his memoir on the League:

> I remember walking to the new *Palais des Nations* early one afternoon with a friend of mine who had preceded me as an official in the Secretariat and who is still working in the League's semi-deserted headquarters at Geneva. It must have been in 1938 or 1939. The day was dreary, the sky was overhung with a bleak veil and the work to which we were returning had assumed, in consequence of the deterioration of the international situation, an air of unreality. The road was uphill and we walked slowly. As we approached the Park Ariana, the *Palais des Nations* stood before us, monumental and as if erected for eternity. A solitary ray of sunlight was

reflected on the marble walls of the Assembly building. I felt decreased, unwilling to work, possessed by a feeling of the futility of my personal contribution in a world that was disintegrating. It seemed senseless to go on with that particular work in which one was engaged. My friend stopped. Suddenly he laid his hand on my shoulder and said: "Cheer up. Do not forget how lucky we are. The only task that is worthwhile in the world of today is ours." (Ranshofen-Wertheimer 1945, x-xi)

When the League experience was reviewed, most experts found that while its political mission was a failure, it exhibited increasing success in dealing with the social and economic problems that transcended nation-states. Article 24 of the covenant provided that international bureaux and commissions that had been established by separate treaties would fall under the jurisdiction of the League.[4] This had the effect of providing a number of them with a common secretariat rather than the ad hoc arrangement that had existed before.

In addition to the International Labour Office, the League aegis included the Slavery Commission, the Disarmament Commission, the Health Organization (which dealt with communicable diseases), the Refugee Commission, and the Permanent Central Opium Board. The last two are particularly illustrative, because they reflected then, as today, functions that cannot be performed by states alone.

THE IDEA OF SECRETARIATS
IN THE UNITED NATIONS

The concept of an international secretariat developed further during World War II, as preparations accelerated toward the creation of a United Nations organization to replace the League. Much of the thinking took place in England, where many former League senior staff had gone and where international relations was a firmly established academic discipline, as well as in the United States, where the ILO secretariat had moved (Philadelphia) and where the Bretton Woods Conferences on the future international financial institutions had taken place.

For the United States, the form and structure of the secretariat was not a major concern. In fact, in the documents from the Washington Conversations on International Peace and Security Organization, October 7, 1944 (better known as the Dumbarton Oaks Conference), the section on the secretariat referred only to the secretary-general.

As the Charter was negotiated, the experience of the League clearly came into play. Table 2–1 shows that while the basis for chapter XV on the secretariat was the Dumbarton Oaks language, the negotiators added several key elements.

First, the secretary-general would be appointed by the General Assembly rather than elected. This meant that he was not an official of the member states, but, while accountable to them, was an independent figure. Once he was appointed, he could not be fired—at least easily—and could serve until the end of his term.

Second, the various intergovernmental bodies did not define the secretary-general's powers and responsibilities until later. Other than the authority given in Article 98 to "bring to the attention of the Security Council any matter which in his opinion may threaten the maintenance of international peace and security" and to act as chief administrative officer, what the secretary-general—and his staff—were expected to do was left completely open.

Third, the Charter specified clearly that the secretariat was to live by "international loyalty" and not seek or receive instructions from governments. This provision was drawn directly from the League's staff rules. However, in addition, states, as a condition of membership, were to "respect the exclusively international character of the responsibilities of the Secretary-General and the staff and not to seek to influence them in the discharge of their responsibilities." This made the independence of the secretariat a responsibility of both the staff and the member states.

Fourth, unlike the provisions in the covenant of the League, the Charter specified that staff would be appointed by the secretary-general and not be subject to review by the intergovernmental organs. Governments would control the staff through their approval of the staff regulations.

Finally, the Charter specified the qualifications that secretariat staff members were to meet. One set of qualifications had to do with personal attributes ("highest standards of efficiency, competence, and integrity"). The other had to do with the necessity of

Table 2-1. Comparison of Text on the Secretariat in the Dumbarton Oaks Conference and the UN Charter

PROPOSALS FOR THE ESTABLISHMENT OF A GENERAL INTERNATIONAL ORGANIZATION (Dumbarton Oaks), October 7, 1944	UNITED NATIONS CHARTER, June 16, 1945
1. There should be a Secretariat comprising a Secretary-General and such staff as may be required. The Secretary-General should be the chief administrative officer of the Organization. He should be *elected* by the General Assembly, on recommendation of the Security Council, for such term and under conditions as are specified in the Charter.	Article 97. The Secretariat shall comprise a Secretary-General and such staff as the Organization may require. The Secretary-General shall be *appointed* by the General Assembly upon the recommendation of the Security Council. He shall be the chief administrative officer of the Organization.
2. The Secretary-General should act in that capacity in all meetings of the General Assembly, of the Security Council, and of the Economic and Social Council and should make an annual report to the General Assembly on the work of the Organization.	Article 98. The Secretary-General shall act in that capacity in all meetings of the General Assembly, of the Security Council, of the Economic and Social Council, *and of the Trusteeship Council,* and *shall perform such other functions as are entrusted to him by these organs.* The Secretary-General shall make an annual report to the General Assembly on the work of the Organization.
3. The Secretary-General should have the right to bring to the attention of the Security Council any matter which in his opinion may threaten international peace and security.	Article 99. The Secretary-General may bring to the attention of the Security Council any matter which in his opinion may threaten the maintenance of international peace and security.

PROPOSALS FOR THE ESTABLISHMENT OF A GENERAL INTERNATIONAL ORGANIZATION (Dumbarton Oaks), October 7, 1944	UNITED NATIONS CHARTER, June 16, 1945
	Article 100. *In the performance of their duties the Secretary-General and the staff shall not seek or receive instructions from any government or from any other authority external to the Organization. They shall refrain from any action which might reflect on their position as international officials responsible only to the Organization.*
	Each Member of the United Nations undertakes to respect the exclusively international character of the responsibilities of the Secretary-General and the staff and not to seek to influence them in the discharge of their responsibilities.
	Article 101. *The staff shall be appointed by the Secretary-General under regulations established by the General Assembly.*
	Appropriate staffs shall be permanently assigned to the Economic and Social Council, the Trusteeship Council, and, as required, to other organs of the United Nations. These staffs shall form a part of the Secretariat.
	The paramount consideration in the employment of the staff and in the determination of the conditions of service shall be the necessity of securing the highest standards of efficiency, competence, and integrity. Due regard shall be paid to the importance of recruiting the staff on as wide a geographical basis as possible.

ensuring the multinational character of the secretariat as a whole ("Due regard shall be paid to the importance of recruiting the staff on as wide a geographical basis as possible").

While nowhere stated, underlying these additional provisions was an understanding that the legitimacy of the organization would be heavily determined by the credibility of its staff. This credibility depended on assured independence, perceived competence, and integrity—and clearly on multinational character.

The details of how the secretariat was to be organized were first embodied in Resolution 13, adopted by the First General Assembly in 1946. This resolution established the departments that would compose the secretariat and authorized the secretary-general to engage staff. It did not, however, make decisions about the secretariat structure or regulations. These proved more complicated; the salary structure was not set until 1951, and the staff regulations not until 1952.

The secretariat was originally established with eight departments:

1. Department of Security Council Affairs
2. Department of Economic Affairs
3. Department of Social Affairs
4. Department for Trusteeship and Information from Non-Self-Governing Territories
5. Department of Public Information
6. Legal Department
7. Conference and General Services
8. Administrative and Financial Services

In various forms these departments have continued for the past sixty years, together with the specialized agencies that were set up subsequently. Thousands of international public servants have worked in them under conditions that have evolved over succeeding generations of officials. A generation can be defined as the stage in the life cycle of an organism or even as a group of generally contemporaneous individuals regarded as having common cultural or social characteristics and attitudes. There have been four generations of international civil servants, reflecting their times.

THE FIRST GENERATION
OF UNITED NATIONS CIVIL SERVANTS:
THE MOHICANS (1945–1959)

The United Nations Secretariat formally came into being with the entry into force of the Charter on October 24, 1945.[5] Of course, the ILO Secretariat had already been in existence since 1919,[6] but its constitution was amended to add the prohibition against national influence when it became the first specialized agency of the United Nations system.[7]

The first generation of UN officials, all of whom have been retired for many years, call themselves Mohicans, from James Fenimore Cooper's novel *The Last of the Mohicans*. They still have an annual dinner in New York and define themselves as UN staff members who served the organization before and during its residence at Lake Success (1946–51).

The first career secretariat member was Brian Urquhart. He was a young military veteran from Britain, born in 1919, who had become the personal assistant to Sir Gladwyn Jebb, the acting secretary-general for the Preparatory Commission for the United Nations.[8] The second secretariat staff member was Margaret Bruce, also a Briton and a veteran. Both moved to New York when the organization was established there. Urquhart became the personal assistant to the first secretary-general, Trygve Lie, and began a career that ended in 1986 with his retirement as an under-secretary-general. Bruce became the head of the women's rights program at the deputy director level and was later president of the Association of Former International Civil Servants.

Some of the Mohicans were veterans of the League of Nations who were recruited to continue with the new organization. Some came from the military of the Allied Powers. Others came from government departments. Many were ideologically peace activists. A surprisingly large number of the professional staff (a quarter) and most of the general service were women. Half of the professional staff at the entry level were women (Mathiason 2001, 27). As Table 2–2 shows, this was a proportion that would not be exceeded for over thirty years.

Table 2–2. Percentage of Women Professionals in the UN Secretariat, by Level, 1949–1993

Year	D-2 and above	D-1 and P-5	P-4 and P-3	P-2 and P-1	All Pro-fessionals
1949	2.00	3.36	19.43	42.88	23.42
1955	0.00	2.15	13.26	30.19	16.76
1960	1.82	3.04	17.93	31.71	18.73
1965	0.00	4.26	20.10	24.65	17.84
1970	5.10	5.90	18.79	36.12	20.18
1975	2.88	7.28	19.38	33.83	19.40
1980	4.72	8.49	24.47	39.08	22.40
1985	4.73	10.60	28.60	40.33	25.36
1990	8.13	15.64	33.79	43.78	29.98
1993	12.75	18.69	33.87	47.46	31.19

Source: Division for the Advancement of Women, compiled from reports of the secretary-general (E/CN.6/1995/1).

The United Nations was in its early stages, but the details of an international service began to take shape. The belief that a new world order had been established after the war was clearly present, and the optimists and internationalists seemed to be in command. The UN Charter was both a realist and a functionalist document, but in setting up an independent international public service, the functionalists were clearly more influential. While this would not last, once precedents are set, they are hard to change.

Two factors shaped each generation of secretariat staff: the secretary-general and the politics of the external environment. The first secretary-general was Norwegian Trygve Lie, who had little experience with international organizations, although, as a legal adviser to the Norwegian Trade Union Federation from 1922 to 1935, he presumably participated in ILO activities. He had become foreign minister of the Norwegian government-in-exile and participated in the San Francisco Conference, where he chaired the committee that drafted the Security Council sections of the Charter. As had been the case with the League, the first executives of international organizations were drawn from diplomats who negotiated the original decisions establishing the organization.

Lie was ousted from the secretary-generalship in the wake of the Korean Conflict and was replaced by Dag Hammarskjöld of Sweden. Hammarskjöld's career had been primarily in Swedish economic policy and as head of the financial civil service, including the Swedish central bank. As such, he had been involved in the creation of postwar international financial institutions. Unlike Lie, he was a career civil servant rather than a politician or diplomat, though at the time of his appointment in 1953 he was a member of the Swedish delegation to the General Assembly.

The secretariat had to deal with the beginning of the Cold War—the rivalry between the Western powers and the Soviet Union and its allies. The superpowers alternatively ignored the organization or sought to coopt it. Relatively few developing countries were members.

For the first years of the secretariat a staff member's life was a continuous process of building. In terms of substance, new issues were added by intergovernmental decision, new specialized agencies were created, functions performed by the League were absorbed into the UN work, a headquarters building was built, and the rules and regulations that would govern the work were agreed upon.

The UN staff started out in borrowed quarters at the Sperry Gyroscope Plant in Lake Success, New York, and later moved into the new, very modern headquarters building on Turtle Bay on Manhattan's East Side. The ILO moved back to Geneva, to the William Rappard Building, while the Palais des Nations was refurbished for the UN's European office.

Establishing the terms and conditions under which the secretariats would work was a major effort during the early years. This included determining the answers to several key management questions: how were staff to be recruited, what would be the standards of conduct, and how would funds be raised to pay the staff. The agreements reached during this early period have carried over into the present.

Precedent 1: Independence of the International Civil Service—Act I

Setting up the secretariat required finding a middle ground among different civil service traditions. The League had been set up on British and French models, but the new United Nations would be heavily influenced by the United States, which had a slightly different model for civil service. Veterans of the League had learned that international civil service was qualitatively different from that of national service. As Ranshofen-Wertheimer expressed it in memoir:

> In its concrete application this implies that there is in the work of the international official an element of uncertainty and indefiniteness absent in the work of the national official and that he cannot therefore, like his national prototype, protect himself behind the law of the country whose servant and executor he is.
>
> Practically everything that has been said regarding the similarity and difference between national public administration and international public administration applies also to the human element. . . . A poor national official is in all likelihood also a poor international administrator. But a good national official will not necessarily make a good international civil servant. The latter must possess nearly all the skills needed for the discharge of important public work in a national administration: the same combination of initiative and meticulousness, the same devotion to duty and accuracy of mind, the same synthesis of personal conviction and the faculty of putting individual views aside in order to execute orders. These qualities must be possessed to a greater degree than the national official, for his initiative, steadiness, devotion to duty, and personal convictions will be tested more severely than in a similar capacity under a national administration. While the national official of comparative rank must have the rare quality of being able to think, and often to act, contrary to all his political and social instincts, the international administrator must frequently think and act contrary to his national instincts—the most severe test to which a

civilized person of the twentieth-century world can be sub-
jected. (Ranshofen-Wertheimer 1945, 10)

While the Charter had solved some of the broad issues of independence of the international civil service, it had left the details to
the staff regulations that would be adopted by the General Assembly.

To set up the secretariat, the First General Assembly (in Resolution 13) authorized the secretary-general to carry over appointments from the preparatory staff and adopted provisional staff
regulations. While intended to be temporary, they contain a number of provisions that have continued over the life of the organization.

Regulation 1[9] defined the nature of international civil service
and set the formal grounds for invisibility:

The Secretary-General and all members of the staff of the
Organization are international civil servants, and their responsibilities are not national but exclusively international.
By accepting appointment, they pledge themselves to discharge their functions and to regulate their conduct with the
interests of the United Nations only in view. In the performance of their duties they shall not seek nor receive instructions from any government or from any other authority
external to the Organization. All members of the staff are
subject to the authority of the Secretary-General, and are responsible to him in the exercise of their functions.

Subsequent regulations outlined the rather stringent nature of
international discretion. International officials do not have the same
privileges and immunities as diplomats. Regulation 4 states, "These
privileges and immunities furnish no excuse to the staff members
who enjoy them for non-performance of their private obligations
or failure to observe laws and police regulations." Regulation 5
specifies that staff are not allowed to communicate with the press:
"They shall not communicate to any person any unpublished information known to them by reason of their official position except in the course of their duties or by authorization of the
Secretary-General."

Not only should secretariat staff not formally communicate with the press (or governments), but their personal behavior must also be above reproach, especially regarding expression of personal beliefs. Regulation 6 states: "Members of the staff shall avoid any action, and in particular any kind of public pronouncement or activity which may adversely reflect on their position as international civil servants. They are not expected to give up their national sentiments or their political and religious convictions; but they shall at all times bear in mind the reserve and tact incumbent upon them by reason of their international status." This includes any political activity or any other outside activity. Staff are not expected to hold any office (presumably in NGOs or the private sector) that is incompatible with functions being performed. If a staff member decides to run for public office, the staff member must resign.

Finally, according to Regulation 1, "No member of the staff shall accept any honour, decoration, favour, gift or fee from any Government or from any other source external to the Organization during the period of his appointment, except for war services.[10]

The regulations embodied a number of key concepts regarding recruitment. The first was that "men and women are equally eligible for all posts in the Secretariat." While this was consistent with the Charter, it was a formulation that was, typically for the era, open to interpretation. Women were eligible to apply for posts on an equal basis, but they did not have to be considered or hired on an equal basis. As history would show, this was a major loophole. Still, the notion of equality in hiring was implicit.

The regulations then specified that appointments should be, as far as possible, competitive. While the method of providing for competition was not specified, the principle was established. Furthermore, while the regulations did not address directly the matter of how to achieve geographic representation, they did address it indirectly. Most of the personnel hired for the preparatory work were from the Allies, especially the British. This would clearly distort the geographic balance, an issue that would recur throughout the organization's history. To address it, the provisional regulations stated:

> With due regard to the maintenance of the staff on as wide a geographical basis as possible and without prejudice to the

inflow of fresh talent at the various levels, vacancies shall be filled by promotion of persons already in the service of the United Nations in preference to appointments from outside. This consideration shall also be applied, on a reciprocal basis, to the specialized agencies brought into relationship with the Organization.

This was consistent with the practice of many civil services to develop career services. The original staff regulations also foresaw the existence of permanent appointment but specified that there be a probationary period. The issue of what a permanent international civil service would mean was not explored. It was assumed that the practice of the United Kingdom would be best, and this was not questioned for over forty years.

The regulations also established the principle that the staff should be involved in decisions about appointment and promotion, implying that the integrity of the international civil service would at least in part be guaranteed by the civil service itself.

In terms of conditions of service, the provisional regulations made temporary arrangements for salary and pension, but included several concepts that have carried on. One of them was that "the whole time of members of the staff shall be at the disposal of the Secretary-General" (Regulation 17), what in 2006 would be called 24/7.

Moving from provisional to final staff regulations took the remainder of Trygve Lie's tenure, but when they were finally adopted at the Sixth General Assembly in February 1952, there were only minor changes, most having to do with staff-management relations, the pension fund, detailed procedures on salary scales, and appeal procedures.

What caused the delay? Behind the discussions were political factors, since both the Soviet Union and the United States took actions that compromised the independence of the international civil service at the beginning of its modern development.

The Soviet Union had come into conflict with its former allies, and this carried over to the United Nations administration. One of the issues dealt with recruitment of staff. The original design of the secretariat had open recruitment, with the secretary-general making appointments, based on competition. In practice, many countries wanted to control hiring. Many of the original staff of the United Nations were from countries that became part of the Soviet Bloc and were now in opposition to their governments. To prevent these people from being hired, and to prevent defection of staff who had already been hired, the Soviet Bloc governments negotiated an agreement that their nationals would be sent to the United Nations "on secondment," which meant that the staff members were actually government officials who had been loaned to the organization. They would be given fixed-term contracts and, when these lapsed, would return to their governments. In practice, these staff members mostly lived in government-supplied quarters, had to return part of their salary to their home government, and were often considered by other UN staff members to be intelligence personnel, or spies, which many were.

Early in 1948, after a communist government took power in Czechoslovakia, the new government requested that Trygve Lie dismiss all thirty-five Czechs on the UN staff. Lie refused, saying, "Only if you give me facts providing unsuitability of any of these will I consider taking action" (McDiarmid 2003, 10).

While the imposition of secondment was detrimental to the integrity of the international civil service, the actions taken by the United States had much longer-lasting negative consequences and deserve to described in detail.

The United States had never been happy with an independent international civil service. It was one of the few countries that did not ratify the Convention on the Privileges and Immunities of the United Nations. Instead, the necessary agreements to give both delegates and staff some kind of legal protection in the United States had been made by executive orders and exchanges of letter, rather than a legally binding treaty, which the United States Senate had been reluctant to ratify.[11]

In the United States there had been opposition to the United Nations among conservatives and anti-communists generated by the East-West conflict. A number of Congressional members, including Senator Joseph McCarthy, alleged that some United States nationals hired by the United Nations were Communists or Communist sympathizers. The Lie administration, based on allegations in the United States Congress, was asked to fire these employees. The provisional staff regulations did not permit the secretary-general to dismiss staff on grounds that their country questioned their national loyalty. The only grounds specified were the person's post being abolished or "if the services of the individual concerned prove unsatisfactory." Trygve Lie was asked to apply a test of national loyalty.

By 1952, 400 of the 1,344 professional posts in the secretariat were occupied by United States nationals. The senior United States national in the secretariat, appointed at the outset in 1946, was Byron Price, assistant secretary-general for administrative and financial affairs, which included personnel matters. A journalist by profession, Price had been the director of censorship in the US federal government during World War II. The intensification of the Cold War had led the UN administration, according to one critic, to reach a secret agreement in 1949 "whereby the Department of State has identified for him [Trygve Lie] United States citizens employed or being considered for employment who would appear to be Communists, with a view to their elimination" (Schultz 1952, 577–78). Agents of the Federal Bureau of Investigation (FBI) were allowed to work in the United Nations, and at least one of Price's senior aides provided information directly to the FBI.[12]

A congressional committee headed by conservative Nevada Senator McCarren subpoenaed a number of the American UN staff members to testify. Most of these invoked the Fifth Amendment of the United States Constitution's protection against self-incrimination. This was considered grounds for terminating their employment. Many of these people had been, in their younger years, members of the then-legal Communist Party or knew people who had been members. They stated that they had "taken the Fifth" because they were afraid that if they did not, and were then asked to name other people, they would be prosecuted for contempt (Schultz 1952). The US government, through the FBI, began to investigate many of the American staff members and to provide information to the United Nations through Assistant Secretary-General Price, who then worked to have them dismissed from service.

Lie was under pressure from the United States, and from the Soviet Union for quite different reasons, and the other countries in the United Nations were uncomfortable with this influence. The Canadian permanent representative, David M. Johnson, wrote to his capital on June 12, 1952, regarding dismissals made that year and pointed out that the dismissals were based on information known to very few persons in the secretariat "because the matter had been dealt with in the Secretariat by a very few people—Mr. Lie and Mr. Byron Price being the principal ones concerned" (Johnson 1952). There were real problems of precedent because staff members' behavior was being judged according to a different standard than that set out in the staff regulations, which stated that members of the secretariat should have "the interests of the United Nations only in view" and should not "seek or accept instructions . . . from any government or other authority." Applying the national loyalty test would invalidate the principle.

The actions of the secretary-general were particularly devastating for the staff members who believed that these were not correct grounds for dismissal. In order to try to obtain some legitimacy, Lie requested a panel of three jurists to determine whether he had the authority to dismiss staff. The three, selected by Lie, included a former Republican attorney general from the United States, a former Conservative official of the wartime British government, and a Belgian lawyer from a Catholic university. The panel was faced with the dilemma that if it advised too broadly, any secretariat employees who fell afoul of their government could be dismissed. It therefore proposed that, because the United States was the host country for UN headquarters, it had a "special relationship" with the UN and could request dismissals of its nationals. Lie accepted the recommendation and began large-scale dismissals, without, among other things, indicating to the staff members the grounds for dismissal.

The staff union had protested the panel's recommendations. As Schultz reported:

> When on December 3 representatives of the Staff Association issued a report—in which they expressed their concern over the recommendations of the jurists, the officers of the association were called to account by Mr. Price, who, it is stated, demanded that the association support the administration policy on the score that the American public would not understand their failure. (Schultz 1952, 578)

The staff was aghast. A. M. Rosenthal, a reporter for the *New York Times* (who later became that newspaper's managing editor), wrote on December 7, 1952:

To most United Nations staff workers this means that for better or worse the concept of an international civil service totally free from the influence of any government has been dropped, if not formally, at least in practice.

Uneasiness is spreading among foreign employees at the United Nations. They, too, are afraid of the lack of definition of subversiveness. Some of them fought in the resistance movements during World War II, were allied with the Communists and wonder if that will be held against them.

But what bothers non-Americans at the United Nations most is the feeling that they are not wanted in the United States. (Rosenthal 1952, E6)

John McDiarmid, who was at the time a senior officer in personnel, commented:

While he [Lie] was widely applauded in the U.S. for his "forthright action," many of his staff felt he had bowed to the kind of government pressure he had inveighed against and had done an injustice to colleagues against whom no improper activity or conduct had been charged, much less proven. (McDiarmid 2003, 11)

In order to protect staff, however, the General Assembly in 1949 had established an administrative tribunal. This was an independent body, elected by the General Assembly, "to hear and pass judgment upon applications alleging non-observance of contracts of employment of staff members of the Secretariat of the United Nations or the terms of appointments of such staff members" (Resolution 351 (I), Article 2, para. 1). The concept of an administrative tribunal was an integral part of British-based systems and was designed to protect staff rights against arbitrary actions of senior management. As established, the decisions of the tribunal were final.

The staff members who had been dismissed appealed to the administrative tribunal, which was made up of three judges: Lord Cook (from New Zealand), Vladimir Outrata (from Czechoslovakia, who had been the Czech ambassador to the United States), and Hamed Sultan (from Egypt). The tribunal ruled that the dismissals were unjustified, and, if the organization was unwilling to reinstate the staff, the United Nations was required to pay compensation.

In January 1953 a committee of the US Senate issued a list of twenty-five UN staff members who had been dismissed, fourteen men and eleven women. The committee listed another eleven serving staff members who were considered to be subversives. During the last month of Lie's tenure, US president Harry Truman issued an executive order requiring a full investigation of all American staff members and all US applicants for positions at the United Nations.

When appointed to succeed Lie, Dag Hammarskjöld moved quickly to reestablish morale. King and Hobbins, drawing on the papers of John Humphrey, the director of the Human Rights Division, note, "During the first weeks of his tenure he reportedly visited, with his Executive Assistant Andrew Cordier, singly or in groups, all of the 3,500 members of the staff" (2003, 344). He accepted the decisions of the administrative tribunal. He also responded to the executive order by ordering John McDiarmid, who was now the head of personnel, to review all information from the FBI. McDiarmid described the process:

> When a few of the FBI reports presented facts that were proved or evident, indicating unsuitability for UN employment, for example, evidence of lack of integrity, the Secretary General ordered dismissal. Many charges were ridiculous—of "undesirable associations," an accusation of disloyalty with only the flimsiest of circumstantial evidence. Even these were sent to the Secretary General, but quickly dismissed. More difficult were the very few cases where Communist associations or party membership were charged against U.S. staff. Here Hammarskjöld informed the U.S. of three decisions. The taking of the Fifth Amendment before the McCarthy Committee would be disregarded if the Secretary General was satisfied with the staff member's explanation. Previous Communist party membership, e.g. as a student, also would be disregarded for staff members with a clean record of service and no record of political activity. Thirdly, any proof of Communist political activity while a staff member would be cause for dismissal. I can't remember a case

in Hammarskjöld's day when this was charged and proved. (McDiarmid 2003, 12)

An additional factor working in Hammarskjöld's favor was the victory of Dwight Eisenhower in the 1952 US presidential election. Eisenhower was committed to multilateral approaches and had the prestige necessary to control the extreme conservatives who had been behind the "witch hunts" in the secretariat. As often happens, a change of administration in the United States led to a change in the US national holding the highest position in the United Nations Secretariat. By May 1953 Byron Price had resigned, leaving Ralph Bunche as the senior American.

Hammarskjöld also approached the issue of the status of the secretariat in a larger context: a general reform of the administration. The reform involved a reduction in the size of the staff (proposed at 10 percent), with a consequent reduction in assessments on member states. In exchange, the member states would, among other things, accept revisions to the staff regulations that would make the kinds of dismissals undertaken by Lie impossible in the future.

One means of clarifying the role of the international civil service was to request the International Civil Service Advisory Board (ICSAB) to define standards of conduct for the international civil service. The ICSAB had been authorized by the General Assembly but set up by the Administrative Committee on Coordination (the committee of heads of UN system secretariats) and consisted of nine members, appointed in their personal capacity.

The nine experts (see Table 2–3) were a "who's who" of eminences from national public administrations. Most had been senior civil servants or members of oversight bodies. Several had been part of the original negotiations for the United Nations. They produced a report entitled "Standards of Conduct for the International Civil Service" in 1954. The secretary of the board, who would have been responsible for much of the initial drafting, was John McDiarmid, who had a Ph.D. in political science from the University of Chicago, had taught at Princeton and the University of Southern California, and had worked with the US States Civil Service Commission during World War II. After the war he had taught at Northwestern University. On leave from teaching, he had participated in the negotiations over the Charter at San Francisco and, after the secretariat was established, had joined the staff in the personnel office. Having been part of the staff that had to deal with real issues of independence when the United States sought to have many of its nationals dismissed, McDiarmid was able to see quite clearly why the statement on standards of conduct was important.

Table 2–3. Members of the International Civil Service Advisory Board, 1954

Member	Country	Background
Thanassis Aghnides	Greece	Diplomat; Greek ambassador to the UK during World War II; rapporteur of the Fifth Committee of the General Assembly's first session
Leon Baranski	Poland	Director-general of the Bank of Poland at the time of Bretton Woods; executive director of the World Bank
Charles H. Bland	Canada	Civil servant; chair of the Public Service Commission of Canada
Ebbe Groes	Denmark	Government official; Groes's wife was minister of trade, industry, and shipping
Luiz Simoes Lopes	Brazil	Economist; founder of the Fundação Getulio Vargas
Roger Gregoire	France	Director of the Civil Service
Sir A. Ramaswami Mudaliar	India	Politician, Dewan of Madras; former president of the UN Economic and Social Council
Dame Mary Smieton	United Kingdom	Senior civil servant; first woman to be named a cabinet secretary in the British Civil Service
Arthur S. Flemming	United States	Former member of the United States Civil Service Commission; member of several Hoover commissions, later secretary of health, education, and welfare in the Eisenhower administration

The report was a comprehensive statement on the need for an independent civil service whose integrity would be based at least partially on the fact that the civil servants behaved in a rational, neutral way, above reproach. Its footnotes show that it drew on British civil service tradition but also on the experience of the League, since it cited as one of its inspirations the report of the Drummond group (Royal Institute of International Affairs 1944).

Because the report was prepared by an internal body and was not approved by an intergovernmental body, it was not a legal text. However, it was used throughout the UN system for forty-five years, was given to incoming staff, and was a factor in decisions by both the United Nations and the ILO administrative tribunals. It was not updated until 2001, and then without substantive changes.

In a series of revisions to the staff regulations, Hammarskjöld built more procedural safeguards for staff into the regulations, and the issue of independence appeared to be largely solved.

Precedent 2: Organization of the Secretariat

Lie essentially left the secretariat as it had been given him by the General Assembly in 1946. Hammarskjöld was a civil servant himself and considered that his mandated task was to "fine tune" the international administration. He stated this clearly in a prepared statement to the press that was issued on his arrival at Idlewild Airport in New York on April 9, 1953:

> Irrespective of the political responsibilities of the secretary-general to which I have just referred, he has an important, indeed an overwhelming job as chief administrator of the UN Secretariat. To me it seems a challenging task to try and develop the UN administrative organization into the most efficient instrument possible. My experience from other administrations tells me that even in the best one there is always much to improve. On the other hand, I feel that an administration inspired by sound self-criticism, never blunted by conceit or false loyalties, and self-improving in that spirit, has a just claim to the respect and confidence of the governments and the public. (Hammarskjöld 1953a)

As the head of the part of the Swedish civil service dealing with financial matters, Hammarskjöld was accustomed to dealing with a relatively compact organization. Like other administrators who were brought into the management of international organizations, he tended to apply his personal experience to the new organization rather than seeing it as qualitatively different.

There were two elements to Hammarskjöld's organizational reforms. On the substantive side he was conscious of the political issues that had affected Lie's tenure. He believed that the organization should be structured to blunt some of the political issues. In 1954 he set up an internal survey group to look at restructuring. This group consisted of director-level managers rather than the more political assistant secretaries-general. The group consisted of Ralph Bunche (the top-ranking director in the Department of Trusteeship and Information from Non-Self-Governing Territories), Julia Henderson (director of the Division of Social Welfare), and Alfred Katzin (director of the Bureau of Personnel) (King and Hobbins 2003, 343). It also seems probable that Martin Hill (deputy executive assistant to the secretary-general) and Bruce Turner (executive officer in office of the secretary-general and later, in 1955, controller), as well as Cordier participated in the group discussions. Most of these were American or British staff members. They proposed to reduce secretariat staff by 284 posts, from 2,865, over the course of a two- to three-year period. Hammarskjöld was emphatic that there should be no terminations on grounds of economy. He therefore instituted a system in which posts were eliminated after retirement or resignation, and personnel were shifted internally as new vacancies arose—staff reductions by attrition. This method would be used frequently in subsequent reforms. The difficulty, not expressed, was that attrition usually did not occur where the posts needed to be eliminated.

Behind that, however, was an effort to depoliticize some of the functions. The reorganization proposals did a number of things, but the most important were to merge the Economic Department and the Social Department. At the same time the Human Rights Division, which had been part of the Social Department, was to be moved to a new Department of Special Political Affairs.[13] The various intergovernmental commissions involved with human rights sought to blunt the effects of the post reductions in that division, probably encouraged by the division's management. This pattern, which was to recur whenever cuts were proposed, made it difficult to target post reductions other than by mechanical across-the-board methods.

The Department of Administrative and Financial Affairs was to be broken up, to reduce its power, with General Services (day-to-day running of headquarters) being made independent. According to King and Hobbins (2003), part of the reason was that Hammarskjöld believed that as chief administrative officer he should have much closer control over the management of the secretariat. He therefore instituted a much greater degree of centralization than had been the case under his predecessor.

Precedent 3: Uncertain Financial Administration

When Hammarskjöld was appointed, the organization was already beginning to face its first financial crises. The Soviet Union was refusing to pay any assessments related to the Korean Conflict, because it considered that they had been illegally imposed. The United States for a time sought to withhold payment of its share of the indemnity payments to dismissed staff that had been ordered by the administrative tribunal. The United States Congress had adopted a non-binding "resolution opposing the awards and warning that appropriations would be refused to cover the United States pro-rata special assessment of $60,000 to meet them" (Gruson 1954).

Perhaps the oldest item on the agenda of the Fifth Committee of the General Assembly (which deals with administrative and financial issues) is "the financial crisis of the organization." The United States's problem was solved by agreeing that the funds would be taken from the staff assessment. The Soviet problem took a long time to resolve, and a point was reached, in the 1960s, when the Soviet Union formally lost its right to vote in the General Assembly as a result of its arrears. At that time another face-saving compromise was reached to write off the withholdings.

The staff assessment was a fund established precisely because the United States had not signed or ratified the Convention on the Privileges and Immunities of the United Nations. That convention had specified that UN employees would be exempt from national taxes on their salaries and emoluments. If the United States was allowed to tax its employees' salaries, but other countries did not, there would be an automatic inequality: US nationals would be paid less than other nationalities.

The resolution of the problem was to set up a two-tiered salary system; each staff member would be given a gross salary and a net salary. The staff member would only receive the net salary, but the member states would be assessed the cost of the gross salary. For US nationals the difference between gross and net was approximately what would have been withheld in taxes. At tax time the US nationals would file as though they were ordinary national employees, and the United Nations would provide their tax payments from the staff assessment fund. For nationals of other countries the difference between gross and net would be deducted from the amounts that their country would have to pay in assessment. Thus, all international civil servants would have to pay taxes, but only US nationals would appear to be doing so.[14]

Because the staff assessment was always in surplus, it could be tapped for other purposes, like paying the indemnities, if the member states agreed, although this implied that non-US member states would be subsidizing the other expenditures. The system has continued to the present.

The second major change completed under Hammarskjöld was to set up a system of multiple accounts to pay for different types of operations. The main account was that established by the assessments for the regular budget of the organization. After the first UN peacekeeping operation (see Chapter 6), there was a separate account for peacekeeping operations although the first military observer missions in Palestine and Kashmir were maintained in the regular budget. Separate accounts were established for technical assistance (see Chapter 8), as well as for other activities that were to be funded on a voluntary basis. Each fund would have its own oversight mechanism. The General Assembly would oversee the regular budget. In practice, the Security Council would oversee peacekeeping. The Technical Assistance Board—and later the UNDP Governing Council—would oversee technical assistance funds. Various other voluntary funds would be overseen by substantive intergovernmental bodies, and a few might be managed only by the secretary-general. This approach carried over to the specialized agencies as well.

Oversight mechanisms were also established. From the beginning of the United Nations an external audit function was put in place. Three national audit agencies, elected by the General Assembly, would oversee the expenditures of the organization. At the budget preparatory stage, an expert body consisting of individuals elected by the General Assembly, called the Advisory Committee on Administrative and Budgetary Questions, reviewed the details of all proposals. This committee had its own secretariat, and its members usually reflected the major contributors.

The End of the Mohican Period

The start up of the United Nations had, for the secretariats of the system, gone from initial optimism to demoralization as the Cold War began to shape the nature of the work and the independence of the international civil service had been tested. When Hammarskjöld was appointed to a second term in September 1957, he told the General Assembly:

> Nobody, I think, can accept the position of Secretary-General, knowing what it means, except from a sense of duty. Nobody, however, can serve in that capacity without a sense of gratitude for a task as deeply rewarding as it is exacting. . . .
>
> Let me mention also the gratitude a Secretary-General owes to his collaborators in the Secretariat from the third basement to the thirty-eighth floor. He is fortunate to profit in his work from a team spirit which renders him unfailing support. He can count on dedication, often to thankless jobs, necessary for the success of the joint effort. He can trust that a challenge will be met with a deep sense of responsibility, broad knowledge, and a truly international spirit.
>
> The significance of what this Organization stands for, as a venture in progress towards an international community living in peace under the laws of justice, transforms work for its aims from a duty into a privilege.

The secretariats of the UN system were becoming accustomed to their role but were still essentially based on the countries that had been involved in World War II. Mostly they were American or European staffed, and most of the issues with which they were dealing were issues appropriate to that group of countries.

All of this was about to change, and a new generation of UN officials was about to enter the secretariats.

THE SECOND GENERATION: GROWTH GENERATION (1960–1975)

During the period from 1960 to 1975 the secretariat expanded in size and in its national composition. The number of members grew from 82 in 1959 to 144 in 1975, as decolonization continued. As new countries joined the organization, efforts were made to recruit their nationals for international service. The new countries had a different perspective on the UN system than did the original members.

The developing countries that were members of the organization took little time in organizing themselves to act in a concerted manner on development issues. They called the caucus the Group of 77 (G-77). The group was established on June 15, 1964, by seventy-seven developing-country signatories of the "Joint Declaration of the Seventy-Seven Countries" issued at the end of the first session of the United Nations Conference on Trade and Development (UNCTAD) in Geneva. It organized its first ministerial meeting in Algiers in 1967, at which time it adopted the Charter of Algiers, a detailed position on trade issues. Over time the group became a vehicle for organizing coherent negotiating positions in all UN forums dealing with development issues.

The total assessed budget of the United Nations Secretariat was US$65,734,900 in 1960 (in 1960 dollars) but reached US$303,016,000 in 1975 (in 1975 dollars).[15] There was a consequent increase in the size of the secretariat staff.

The United Nations Secretariat was headed by Dag Hammarskjöld until his death on September 17, 1961, then by U Thant until December 1971, followed by Kurt Waldheim. The United Nations developed a pattern of a maximum of two five-year terms for each secretary-general. This was less a matter of conscious choice than circumstance. Lie had been in his second term (although only for three years) when he resigned; Hammarskjöld died in the third year of his second five-year term; and U Thant's health did not permit him to consider a third term, even if he could have obtained it.

The leadership of the specialized agencies was more consistent. During this period most of the specialized agencies had executive heads who served for relatively long periods. The median was ten years for those in office between 1960 and 1975.

Precedent 4: Independence of the International Civil Service—Act II

When the Soviet Union questioned the role of the secretary-general at the General Assembly in 1960, it also raised questions about the independence of the international civil service. The secretariat response was prepared by Dag Hammarskjöld in a lecture that he delivered at Oxford University on May 30, 1961, entitled "The International Civil Servant in Law and in Fact." Hammarskjöld worked closely with Oscar Schachter, an American who was the director of the general legal division. The issue at the heart of the matter was whether an international secretariat could be neutral. Hammarskjöld's position was clear:

> The international civil servant must keep himself under the strictest observation. He is not requested to be a neuter in the sense that he has to have no sympathies or antipathies, that there are to be no interests which are close to him in his personal capacity or that he is to have no ideas or ideals that matter for him. However, he is requested to be fully aware of those human reactions and meticulously check himself so that they are not permitted to influence his actions. This is nothing unique. Is not every judge professionally under the same obligation?
>
> If the international civil servant knows himself to be free from such personal influences in his actions and guided solely by the common aims and rules laid down for, and by the Organization he serves and by recognized legal principles, then he has done his duty, and then he can face the criticism which, even so, will be unavoidable. As I said, at the final last, this is a question of integrity, and if integrity in the sense

of respect for law and respect for truth were to drive him
into positions of conflict with this or that interest, then that
conflict is a sign of his neutrality and not of his failure to
observe neutrality—then it is in line, not in conflict, with his
duties as an international civil servant. (Hammarskjöld 1961)

The concepts found in the Hammarskjöld lecture have largely
been accepted. Hammarskjöld's lecture made a strong case for an
international civil service based on permanent contracts, as opposed to seconded national personnel, which was the policy, then,
of the Soviet Union:

A national official, seconded by his government for a year or
two with an international organization, is evidently in a different position psychologically—and one might say, politically—from the permanent international civil servant who
does not contemplate a subsequent career with his national
government.

The issue of the independence of the international civil service
was largely resolved, and subsequent discussions had to do with
details of maintaining it, rather than the principle itself, at least
until recently.

Precedent 5: Politically Realistic Financing

The Congo operation (described in Chapter 7) set another precedent. Countries like the Soviet Union and France that had opposed
the UN operation in the Congo refused to pay their assessments
for the operation. As the amounts of arrears grew, the Soviet Union,
in 1964, would have lost its vote in the General Assembly in accordance with Article 19 of the Charter. France would have lost its
vote in 1965. The crisis was solved when the United States brokered
a deal with the Soviet Union that no votes would be taken at the
General Assembly that year, and the issue of Article 19 would not
come up. Eventually, a compromise was reached:

After a full year without formal voting, it was agreed that
Article 19 would not apply to arrears related to the two

peacekeeping missions, that highly developed countries should make voluntary contributions to help the world body overcome its financial problems, and that the Assembly would return to normal operations. Sensing that the norm had finally been breached, the new US Permanent Representative, Arthur Goldberg, in turn announced that "if any Member can insist on making an exception to the principle of collective financial responsibility with respect to certain activities of the Organization, the United States reserves the same option to make exceptions if, in our view, strong and compelling reasons exist for doing so." (Luck 2003, 33)

The stage was set for subsequent problems, this time affecting the United States. In 1999 the United States was on the verge of losing its vote in the General Assembly because its cumulative withholdings—mandated by the US Congress—had reached a level where it was almost two years in arrears. Its withholdings reflected Congressional unhappiness with some of the decisions made by the General Assembly on issues like Israel and an attempt to force US-favored administrative reforms by choking the organization financially. While the George W. Bush administration agreed in 2001 to repay the withholdings, the US Congress in 2005 again threatened to withhold unless US-favored reforms were instituted.

THE CONSOLIDATION GENERATION (1976–1990)

The period between 1976 and 1990 was characterized by disputes about a new international economic order, the end of the Cold War, and a dramatic consolidation of the role of the UN system. The secretariat role became clearer and more identifiable, if often more controversial. During this period the number of members of the United Nations grew from 147 to 159, a slowing of growth that would change with the breakup of the Soviet Union.

In New York, the US Congress had refused to construct a new building to house an expanding staff, so the City of New York established the United Nations Development Corporation, which erected three buildings across the street from the main headquarters. Still, some organizations had to rent office space. In Geneva, new office buildings were constructed for specialized agencies, as well as a new tower in the Palais des Nations to house UNCTAD and provide new conference facilities. In Vienna, a new United Nations city was constructed to house the IAEA, the UN Industrial Development Organization (UNIDO), and UN Secretariat units. In Nairobi, a new headquarters was built for the UN Environment Programme (UNEP) and the UN Centre for Human Settlements. New buildings were also constructed in the headquarters of the regional commissions (except the UN Economic and Social Commission for Western Asia).

The United Nations was led by Kurt Waldheim until 1982, and then by Javier Perez de Cuellar. The leadership of the specialized agencies continued to be more consistent, with less turnover than in the preceding generation, although the average tenure remained ten years.

By 1975 the management of the United Nations and the specialized agencies was coming under increasing scrutiny as a result of two factors: First, the growing role of the United Nations in development—and the increase in the number of developing countries in the membership—led to a change in priorities that was reflected in efforts to reform or restructure the organization to meet development concerns. Second, the cost of the United Nations to the major contributors was increasing.

The first factor led in 1974 to what was called the restructuring exercise. The second led, in 1986, to what was called the Group of 18. Each had effects that have lasted to the present. In addition, the way staff members for the United Nations Secretariat are recruited changed as a result of growth in the organization and the work of a new oversight body.

Precedent 6: Growth through Reorganization (the Restructuring Exercise)

For the first twenty years of the United Nations there was a fairly stable structure within the secretariats. There was an executive head, under whom there would be a series of deputies who would run equal departments. From time to time a new program would be spun off with its own head, like UNCTAD. The UN system became more complex, as new specialized agencies like UNIDO were created. By 1975 the complexity of the United Nations proper, to which had to be added the funds and programs like UNDP and UNICEF, had grown to the extent that it was considered by many to be unmanageable. For developing countries the secretariat, headed by Kurt Waldheim, with most of the other departments, programs, and funds dealing with development in the hands of Western European or American executive heads, was not responsive.

In 1974 the General Assembly passed Resolution 3343 (XXIX) asking the secretary-general to appoint a group of experts to prepare "a study containing proposals on structural changes within the United Nations system so as to make it fully capable of dealing with problems of international economic co-operation in a comprehensive manner." The expert group's report—the Gardner report—was known for its rapporteur, Professor Richard Gardner of Columbia University.

Expert groups like this one were chosen by the secretariat with careful attention to geographical balance and the political acceptability of the members to their own governments. The group of experts was a typical case and involved a combination of eminent persons and ambassadors, supported by secretariat staff working particularly with the chairman and the rapporteur.

The group worked for four months and reached consensus on its report, which made far-reaching recommendations (United Nations 1975). Some of the recommendations had to do with intergovernmental structure, especially in terms of improving the effectiveness of the Department of Economic and Social Affairs. This recommendation became a standard for reform proposals. However, the experts did not see prospects of significant changes in intergovernmental structure as very likely. Instead, they concentrated on recommendations for a radical reshaping of the economic and social secretariat.

As summarized by Luck there was

> a raft of recommendations on personnel policies, interagency mechanisms, joint research, and intersectoral analysis. The proposed innovation that attracted the most attention, however, was for the creation of the post of Director-General for Development and International Economic Co-operation, to

be placed above agency heads and Under-Secretaries-General, as the second highest official in the world body. The Director-General would be supported by two Deputy Directors-General, one for Research and Policy and the other to head a new United Nations Development Authority. While the Director-General could not exercise authority over the relatively autonomous specialized agencies, he or she would be in charge of interagency coordination and operational activities and would chair a new interagency Advisory Committee on Economic Cooperation and Development. It was suggested that the post be occupied by "a national of a developing country at least during those years when the post of secretary-general is occupied by a developed country." (Luck 2003, 24)

The report also advocated the consolidation of all of the funds for technical assistance and pre-investment activities—except for those of UNICEF—into a new UN Development Authority. The Economic and Social Council would be responsible for reviewing operational activities of the UN system as a whole, and the governing boards of a number of programs would be consolidated or replaced by a new operations board. On the regional level the experts called for structural modifications of the regional commissions and steps to promote cooperation among developing countries. In a politically charged recommendation on a matter of high priority to the capitals of both developed and developing countries, the group urged that the weighted voting systems in the IMF and World Bank be revised "to reflect the new balance of economic power and the legitimate interest of developing countries in a greater voice in the operation" of those institutions.

Many of the group's recommendations were politically unfeasible, such as those having to do with the voting structure of the Bretton Woods institutions. Others were opposed by the executive heads of the specialized agencies. Kurt Waldheim made it clear that he did not favor the idea of a director-general who would dilute his authority.[16] Moreover, the UNDP financial crisis had called into question that organization's capacity to run a centralized fund.

The Gardner report was an input into the Seventh Special Session of the General Assembly, devoted to development and international cooperation. While most of the text adopted at the session had to do with policies, its last section established an ad hoc committee on restructuring of the economic and social sectors of the UN system. The committee was chaired by Kenneth K. S. Dadzie, the permanent representative of Ghana. Dadzie was a former secretariat official. He had joined the United Nations in 1963 and had risen to the level of principal officer in the Office of Interagency Affairs, which provided secretariat services to the interagency coordination machinery. The committee was supported by staff from the Office of Interagency Affairs, with Uner Kirdar from Turkey as secretary. Kirdar had been a staff member of UNDP (and would be again, as secretary of the UNDP governing council for many years). The active delegations working on the committee included such veterans as Miles Stoby, from Guyana, who had been a staff member of the Office of Interagency Affairs from 1971 to 1973.

The committee negotiations carried over into 1977. The main focus was on secretariat reforms, in terms of both structure and procedures for budgeting. The structural reforms, in one sense, were political, to dramatize the commitment of the organization to development. This included new (if only in nomenclature) coordination arrangements. They were also a means of bypassing a problem caused by the budget itself. Because staffing tables were tightly controlled (and difficult to alter), the main means of reassigning personnel resources was to have a "reform." This allowed staff to be shifted among programs as units were combined or divided and also provided an incentive to create new posts.

In 1977 the government of the United States changed, and Jimmy Carter became President. Carter was more committed to multilateral solutions and the United Nations than his predecessors and, additionally, as governor of the state of Georgia, had been a pioneer in program and zero-based budgeting.

By the end of the General Assembly in December 1977 the committee had reached consensus, although it was on much less than had been proposed in the Gardner report. As Luck describes it:

> Though the post of Director-General survived the negotiating process, it was stripped of the authority and support

structures that would have allowed it to be a powerful new locus for policy coordination and advocacy within the system. The two new Deputy Director-General posts were not established, none of the existing Under-secretary-general posts were eliminated, the funds were not consolidated into a UN Development Authority, and their governing boards were not merged. The resolution called for greater uniformity in financial and administrative procedures and extolled UNDP's country-based programming process, but essentially the Director-General was superimposed on the existing highly decentralized structure, without the authority to reshape or redirect it. (Luck 2003, 25–26)

As expected, the reform included a number of organizational changes that increased the number of posts in the secretariat. The director-general for development and international economic coordination post was created, and Kenneth Dadzie was appointed to occupy it. This was not the first nor the last time that a person from the governments that had negotiated an agreement was appointed to occupy the post that the negotiations created.[17] The director-general was given an office on the thirty-seventh floor of the secretariat building, just below that of the secretary-general, and a small staff, all of whom were given relatively high ranks. One of those appointed to the staff was Miles Stoby. The chief of office was James Baker, a career United States foreign service officer who had been part of the US delegation in the negotiations.

The Department of Economic and Social Affairs was divided in two, with one part to deal with policy and the other with technical assistance. The first was headed by a French official, and the second by an ex-diplomat from Niger.

One consequence of restructuring was to increase the size of the secretariat, both in general and in terms of high-level posts. The program-budget approach produced thick budgets but did not seem to be able to contain expenditure increases. By the middle of the 1980s the major contributors had become concerned that the budget process was out of control. The United States Congress, which had to approve the United States payment of its assessed contribution, acted in the form of an amendment sponsored by Senator Nancy Kassebaum:

Finding that the United Nations and its specialized agencies "have not paid sufficient attention in the development of their budgets to the views of the member governments who are major financial contributors," in August 1985 Congress passed the Kassebaum-Solomon Amendment as part of the Foreign Relations Authorization Act for FY1986 and FY1987. It precluded for FY1987 and beyond payment of assessed contributions of over 20 percent to the United Nations or any of its specialized agencies—which meant the withholding of 20 percent of the US contribution—until they adopted weighted voting on budgetary matters "proportionate to the contribution of each such member state." (Luck 2003, 34)

Precedent 7: How to Reduce the Size (the Group of 18)

Faced with a financial crisis brought on by the United States withholding its assessment, the General Assembly decided in December 1985 (Resolution 40/237) to establish a group of eighteen experts to

(a) conduct a thorough review of the administrative and financial matters of the United Nations, with a view to identifying measures for further improving the efficiency of its administrative and financial functioning, which would contribute to strengthening its effectiveness in dealing with political, economic and social issues.

The Group of 18 did have eighteen members, but most of them were not experts. Its chair was Ambassador Tom Vralsen of Norway. It did have one expert, Maurice Bertrand of France, who had done most of the early studies on program budgeting. It did not, however, have a substantive secretariat. As a result, it did not have a staff that could provide it with factual information other than that which might be provided by the Department of Management in response to specific questions.

The Group of 18 quickly identified part of the problem: the structure was "both too top-heavy and too complex," with twenty-eight under-secretary-general level posts and twenty-nine assistant secretary-general level posts under the regular budget, plus an additional seven and twenty-three, respectively, financed through extra-budgetary sources (United Nations 1986). Finding a solution, however, was more complex. The solution was to request the secretary-general to achieve an across-the-board 15 percent reduction in staff by the next biennium (1988–89). How this figure was determined illustrates some of the problems faced by the Group. In the absence of any method to determine where to reduce staff based on program priorities, the only option was an across-the-board cut. The size of the cut had to be determined. One option, it was said, was to use something said by secretary-general Perez de Cuellar as a basis. Once asked by a reporter, "How many people work at the United Nations?" he had replied, "About half." Thus, a 50 percent cut would be acceptable. The 15 percent figure was of the same quality. The group asked the secretariat for an indication of the normal attrition in staff (retirements, ends of contracts, resignations) and was told that it was about 15 percent per biennium. Thus a 15 percent reduction would be painless.

In anticipation of the report of the group, Perez de Cuellar acted to reduce the number of senior posts. He did so by consolidating some of the functions so that he could eliminate ten high-level posts. In Vienna, for example, he transferred the responsibility for the Centre for Social Development and Humanitarian Affairs to the director-general of the UN office at Vienna along with responsibility for the UN drug-control program. This allowed him to eliminate the assistant secretary-general in charge of the Centre as well as an assistant secretary-general in the UN drug-control program.

THE FOURTH GENERATION (1991–2005)

The secretary-general at the start of this period was Javier Perez de Cuellar, in the last year of his second term, but much of the change occurred during the five-year term of Boutros Boutros-Ghali (1992–96). The year 2005 was the penultimate year of the ten years under Kofi Annan. Each had a different leadership style, with Annan's a new type of international management.

In the specialized agencies, major contributors tried to apply a two-term rule for the executive heads. However, the tradition of these organizations was for executive heads to remain as long as they were willing, so long as no insurmountable political problems ensued. By the end of the period the two-term rule did not seem to be holding; for example, Mohammed ElBaradei was elected to a third term in 2005, and subsequently, Jacques Diof was reelected in the UN Food and Agriculture Organization for a third term.

In New York, the old headquarters building, now over fifty years old, needed major rehabilitation. The Secretariat proposed to build a new office tower to serve while the headquarters building was refurbished; later the tower could be rented out. The New York state legislature declined to approve the arrangement, and the secretariat had to build a temporary tower on its north lawn during the renewal of its headquarters. In Geneva, the Canton government developed a plan to increase dramatically the office space available to international organizations. In Bonn, Germany, and the Hague, new United Nations offices were created.

Although most organizations had been required for almost fifteen years to work under zero-growth assessed budgets, they began to increase in size as more responsibilities were given to them, largely funded from voluntary sources. The number of international civil servants in the United Nations Secretariat and its funds and programs grew from 6,454 in 1991 to 13,159 in 2005. The total assessed budgets of the secretariats grew from US$3.2 billion in 1996 to US$3.7 billion in 2005, with further growth expected. In 2003 there was, in addition, some US$8.9 billion in voluntary contributions to the organization (not including the Bretton Woods institutions).[18]

We are now ready to look at the secretariats and their work in detail.

NOTES

[1] The council included the Principal Allied and Associated Powers (the United States of America, the British Empire, France, Italy, and Japan). While these were not given a veto, their membership ensured that a secretary-general would have to have their support. Of course, the United States never participated in the League.

[2] Drummond's appointment also established a precedent, often followed over the next eighty years of appointing as the first executive head

of a new program someone who had overseen its final negotiation. Albert Thomas, the first director-general of the ILO, was a different model. He was a socialist politician who had risen from municipal leadership to a ministerial position in the French government. He was not present at the First Session of the International Labour Conference that elected him.

[3] A more complete text of Article I of the staff regulations reads: "The officials of the Secretariat of the League of Nations are exclusively international officials and their duties are not national, but international. By accepting appointment, they pledge themselves to discharge their functions and regulate their conduct with the interests of the League alone in view. They are subject to the authority of the Secretary General, and are responsible to him in the exercise of their functions. . . . They may not seek or receive instructions from any Government or other authority external to the Secretariat of the League of Nations."

[4] Article 24 reads: "There shall be placed under the direction of the League all international bureaux already established by general treaties if the parties to such treaties consent. All such international bureaux and all commissions for the regulation of matters of international interest hereafter constituted shall be placed under the direction of the League. In all matters of international interest which are regulated by general convention but which are not placed under the control of international bureaux or commissions, the Secretariat of the League shall, subject to the consent of the Council and if desired by the parties, collect and distribute all relevant information and shall render any other assistance which may be necessary or desirable. The Council may include as part of the expenses of the Secretariat the expenses of any bureau or commission which is placed under the direction of the League."

[5] When a multilateral treaty is negotiated, its terms specify when it is to become operational (enter into force). A specific number of states have to have ratified the treaty. The United Nations Charter was opened for signatures in San Francisco, but entry into force had to wait until the deposit of ratifications by the Republic of China, France, the Union of Soviet Socialist Republics, the United Kingdom of Great Britain and Northern Ireland, and the United States of America, and by a majority of the other signatory states. This occurred on October 24, 1945.

[6] Reflecting the view that the secretariat was a distinct entity, the ILO Secretariat is called the International Labour Office.

[7] The original ILO constitution was Part XIII of the Treaty of Versailles. The text on the International Labour Office as adopted then does not contain the provision against seeking, receiving, or giving instructions.

[8] Urquhart himself gave the designation of first career secretariat member to David Owen, who was on Jebb's staff when Urquhart arrived and who became the assistant secretary-general for Economic Affairs

under Trygve Lie and had subsequent appointments in technical assistance (Urquhart 1987, 92). However, Owen was a political appointee, and Urquhart can fairly be called the first career UN official.

[9] When the definitive regulations were adopted in 1952, Regulation 1 was broken into three parts and took up four pages of text, mostly through explanations of what this otherwise clear paragraph meant. Over the years there have been changes and additions, mostly to deal with new issues that have emerged.

[10] This was particularly applicable to United Kingdom nationals. Brian Urquhart and Joan Anstee were only given knighthoods after their retirement. It was possible to request an exception from the secretary-general, but this was unusual. However, as time passed and the number of cases became more complex, this rather straightforward regulation was modified to read: "If refusal of an unanticipated honour, decoration, favour or gift from a Government would cause embarrassment to the Organization , the staff member may receive it on behalf of the Organization and then report and entrust it to the Secretary-General, who will either retain it for the Organization or arrange for its disposal for the benefit of the Organization or for a charitable purpose." In other words, no profit from honor. The rule was also modified to allow some discretion on awards from nongovernmental sources (e.g., honorary degrees) and reads, "No staff member shall accept any honour, decoration, favour gift or remuneration from any non-governmental source without first obtaining the approval of the Secretary-General."

[11] The United States did not ratify the convention until 1970 and then only with significant reservations that essentially said that its provisions would not really apply to United States citizens working for the organization.

[12] The FBI file on Byron Price, released under the United States Freedom of Information Act, is posted on the FBI website. In it there is the copy of an internal memo referring to a telephone conversation between a [redacted] senior official of the UN Department of Administration and an FBI agent, providing internal information.

[13] This was strongly opposed by John Humphrey, who considered it an abandonment of the United Nations commitment to human rights (King and Hobbins 2003).

[14] When the United States finally acceded to the convention in 1970, it entered a reservation that immunity from taxation and immunity from national service obligations shall not apply with respect to United States nationals and aliens admitted for permanent residence.

[15] Figures from "The United Nations Budget: Procedure for Determining the Regular Budget," on the nationsencyclopedia.com website. Because the figures are not adjusted for inflation, the growth is actually less

than would appear, because there was significant inflation during the period.

[16] In 2006, when Kofi Annan proposed to delegate many of his management functions to the post of deputy secretary-general, the G-77 opposed this as being contrary to the Charter.

[17] Other examples include Ambassador Bustani (Brazil), who negotiated the Organisation for the Prohibition of Chemical Weapons and became its first executive head; and Jose Ayala-Lasso (Ecuador), who led the negotiations to create the post of high commissioner for human rights and was the first to be named to the post.

[18] Statistics on expenditures have been reported episodically by the UN system as a whole. The most recent figures are from A/59/315, "Budgetary and Financial Situation of Organizations of the United Nations System" (September 1, 2004), Tables 4 and 7.

3

•　•　•　•　•　•　•

What Do Secretariats Do?
Does Leadership Matter?

> I spelled it out to him. "Humphrey, you are my Permanent
> Secretary. Are you going to support me?
>   "We shall always support you as your standard-bearer,
> Minister—but not as your pall-bearer."
>
> —THE COMPLETE YES MINISTER, III

Managing and working in an international secretariat is not
like working in a national government or a private business. The
multinational culture, complex environment, and difficult tasks
make international work a particular challenge. International organization managers cannot be judged by the same criteria used
to appraise a CEO or a prime minister because the secretariats are
not the same as other public organizations.

We need to first explore these differences and look at the most
visible leaders, the secretaries-general of the United Nations (and
the executive heads of the specialized agencies) and see how well
they do. And we can look at what these differences mean for the
way in which, in general, secretariats go about their work.

HOW INTERNATIONAL MANAGEMENT DIFFERS

First, international organizations are not sovereign entities; only national governments are sovereign. Sovereignty is a key concept in international law under the Westphalian system. It means "supreme authority within a territory" (Phillpot 2003). Someone within a territory, usually a head of state, is invested with the authority to make final decisions that bind everyone else within the territory. In terms of Harry Truman's famous desk sign, it means that "the buck stops here." Absent this kind of authority, it is not clear who can make decisions.

International organizations clearly lack sovereignty, since they do not have territory. Even the headquarters of organizations are, in effect, rented from the countries in which they are located, with the rental terms set out in agreements. International territory only exists as long as a state accepts its existence. For example, New York City police (and federal police authorities) could enter the United Nations premises whenever they want. The same is true of the police in Geneva, Vienna, Bangkok, Santiago, and Nairobi.

More important, the supreme authority for each international organization is vested in its member states, who can request the secretariat to undertake activities or perform functions, if all of the states agree. A state that does not vote for a resolution, for example, is not legally bound by that decision. States can cede authority to transnational organizations by treaty, as has happened in the European Union for some functions where the European Commission has been given supreme authority over some public activities. Over time, more functions may be ceded to international organizations, but until that is done, the organizations remain non-sovereign.

Urquhart describes the dilemma in his usual dry style:

> In the optimism surrounding its birth, there was a popular impression that the United Nations would act on the international level as a government acts on the national level. For better or for worse, the UN is nothing like a government. It has no sovereignty or power of sovereign decisionmaking. It is an association of independent, sovereign states which depends for its effectiveness on the capacity of its members to

agree and to cooperate, and on the ingenuity and dedication with which the secretariat interprets and carries out their wishes. The capacity of governments to agree and cooperate has proved to be quite limited. (Urquhart 1987, 108)

For administration, this means that the executive head of an organization (and anyone within the organization to whom the head delegates authority) is severely constrained in terms of decision-making. Reform proposals at the United Nations are routinely divided between those that can be made under the authority of the secretary-general and those that require action by the member states. Most are of the second type.

Leadership in international organizations is not based on the ability to give orders but rather on the ability to convince member states to endorse proposals and to motivate staff to implement requests. The ability to dismiss recalcitrant staff members is extremely constrained (limited to clear cases of fiscal or criminal misbehavior). The ability to shift resources among budget sections has also been highly limited. The main source of direct authority by executive heads is through the power to appoint staff to positions. Even this is constrained. Many key positions require confirmation by the member states (as in the case of the under-secretary-general for internal oversight services or the head of the UNDP). Most nationals of member states that are to be appointed to senior positions require—in practice, if not in theory— the concurrence of their respective governments. Staff members who have been hired on permanent contracts, of course, cannot easily be removed, although they can be moved from position to position.

As a result, the main means of decision-making within organizations is consensus. Staff members have to be motivated to follow directions. While this is true, to an extent, in all civil services, it is particularly true in international organizations. Decision-making is inherently non-hierarchical, even though the organizations have a clear bureaucratic structure. A rule of thumb for middle managers is that if anything has to be "kicked upstairs" for a decision, the decision-making will become complex and the outcomes difficult to predict. For this reason, most managers solve coordination problems by contacting opposite numbers. This type of coordination is effective in complex organizational settings

(Chisholm 1985), which the United Nations system clearly is. In fact, it has been suggested as a main means by which international relations are organized (Slaughter 2004).

The idea of decisions by consensus rather than by bureaucratic authority makes international management different from national management. At the national level, a senior official can make a decision that subordinates are required to implement. Similarly, within a private corporation an executive can instruct subordinates to carry out orders. At the international level, orders would not necessarily be followed unless the staff members concerned were convinced of their lawfulness and appropriateness. To an extent, setting up the rules that are to be followed solves this, but even these require that the staff members be committed to implementation. Developing a consensus on actions is a way of reducing the possibility of conflict and, as will be seen, international organizations are conflict averse.

Achieving a consensus requires that decision-making procedures be open. This does not mean that all management decisions require the participation of all staff members, but it does require that staff members believe their concerns have been taken into account. More than in a national bureaucracy or in the private sector, information must flow easily. Using information is the main tool of managers, for both their external and their internal environments.

In public administration theory two organizational models are used: closed system and open system. The closed-system model looks at the organization as a thing in itself, self-contained, where the focus is on its internal processes. This model works very well for private corporations, where internal factors dominate the way the organizations function. It works less well for governments, since part of their function is to interact with and provide services to a public, and there is usually some form of legislative oversight. The alternative model, open system, says that an organization's behavior will be determined by its external environment and the interactions between the internal and external structures.

International organizations are almost completely based on the open-system model. Member states are their formal decision-makers, both governments and NGOs are their constituents, and the international organizations work indirectly through these other institutions to achieve results. Even in matters of personnel policy the external environment intrudes in terms of ratifying senior staff and in helping recruit other staff. Management in international organizations means navigating this complex external environment.

One reason that the environment is complex is because, as is often the case with public institutions, results are not reflected in an easily identifiable way. In private corporations results are reflected in profits or losses in specified periods—the bottom line. Even governments can have a kind of bottom line (tax revenues collected, user fees collected, measurable services provided) although many services (like information) are free. In the case of international organizations all services (with very few exceptions) are free, and therefore there is no real monetary bottom line against which to measure performance.

Added to this is the fact that international organizations must work through other organizations, usually governments. Services are typically provided indirectly (the result of a UN study may be that governments adopt its recommendations). The indirect nature of services makes it very difficult to prove that results have been obtained, and if they are observed, to certify that they were caused by the actions of the international organization. This fact makes it more difficult to motivate staff members, who often cannot see a direct result of their work, and to convince a global public about the utility of the organization, especially when it comes under attack.

Managers of international organizations have one advantage over those in national governments and the private sector: they can take a longer-term perspective on issues. Private corporations are judged by their quarterly and annual profit-and-loss statements, while democratic governments are held accountable by regular elections (or other mandate periods). Their perspectives are short term in nature. International organizations are dealing with problems whose solutions are complicated and require sustained efforts over extended periods. Core budgets for most international organizations are relatively stable, and leaders of international secretariats can be reasonably sure that institutional priorities can be sustained. Because they are made up of career civil servants who do not change every time a new executive head comes on board, policies can be consistent over time.

In this sense leadership in international secretariats requires an ability to see both problems and the programs to deal with them in the long term. Strategic planning is a key management factor, more important than in organizations in which political issues or short-term economic factors are more likely to dominate planning.

There will be an increasing need for international managers who can deliver services within a somewhat archaic state-based context. This context creates both challenges and opportunities to the international officials that manage the services.

TOOLS OF THE TRADE

The international secretariats use a number of tools, including acting as a conduit for information, access to bureaucratic rules, the ability to facilitate, and the capability to deliver certain types of services.

Since secretariats are a type of administration that is "above" the national level, but lacking most of the coercive means that are available to a state, information is their main tool. There are two elements to information use. First, secretariats are repositories of information about precedents, agreements, and rules, which are essential to orderly negotiation and the verification of state compliance with agreements. Second, and probably more important, secretariats are in a position to act as conduits of information. Secretariats act as opinion leaders, screening information from diverse sources to determine policy trends. They also can transmit and use information from nongovernmental sources. They collect, process, and make national information comparable through international statistics and are therefore able to structure the factual basis for negotiation and verification of compliance. Finally, secretariats collect information that can be used to constrain and direct state behavior. In this last category falls the information collected by verification organizations like the IAEA in the area of nuclear non-proliferation and the IMF in terms of national financial situations.

Except when the information collected by international secretariats is used publicly (as was the case with the IAEA monitoring of weapons of mass destruction in Iraq that was presented to the Security Council before the invasion of Iraq), information use by secretariats is largely invisible. Collection and analysis are important functions performed by secretariats, but less in the collection and more in the use of the information.

The bureaucratic structure of international organizations themselves is a second tool. There are frequent critiques of UN bureaucracy, but that bureaucratic structure helps give the secretariats their legitimacy and therefore their ability to influence. In a very Weberian sense, as noted in Chapter 1, international secretariats are enabled to act (and then can defend their actions as credible) when they can show that they have followed rules that have been agreed to by member states. The most famous case of administrative failure of the United Nations, the Oil-for-Food scandal, was at least partly caused by ambiguous rules, roles, and responsibilities for administration of the program.

Finally, international secretariats have been able to show that they are able to deliver certain types of public services better than either national governments or the private sector. This is usually because the problems toward which such services have to be directed are transnational in scope and there is no natural alternative to an international administration. Peacekeeping and humanitarian assistance are clear cases of this, especially since the focus has moved from developed to developing countries. Here the main tools for secretariats are their demonstrated competence and their experienced staff resources.

EXECUTIVE LEADERSHIP
IN INTERNATIONAL ORGANIZATIONS

Leadership is the most visible part of management. For most national public organizations the public sees the image of the top managers, whether the president or prime minister or cabinet minister. This is also true of the international public sector, which by design is supposed to be invisible. For most of the UN system organizations' sixty-year history, the executive heads, especially the secretaries-general of the United Nations, have been the most visible representative of the secretariats.

The formal terms of reference for the secretary-general, and by implication, for the executive heads of other UN system organizations are fairly simple: the secretary-general will do whatever the member states request and will act as chief administrative officer of the organization. The art of executive leadership involves helping shape those requests so that they can be implemented and ensuring that administration is open, honest, and effective. The secretary-general, unlike other executive heads, has, under Article 99 of the UN Charter, the power to bring matters to the attention of the Security Council, implying a capacity of individual initiative that is not contingent on member state authorization.

Taken together, these imply two broad criteria for judging secretariat leadership, which applies to executive heads as well as to all other managers in the organizations: an ability to navigate the complex external environment in a way that leads to results, and an ability to manage the administration so that member states are convinced that the resources they provide are being used properly. Put another way, leadership is defined by being able to use the tools noted above with success. Some secretaries-general have been able to do this well, others less well.

Ability to Navigate the External Environment

The external environment for international secretariats includes member states, NGOs, the private sector, the mass media, the academic community, and the general public.

Member states are formally equal in all international organizations, regardless of size or wealth. Thus each state has the right to be dealt with on its own terms. However, some states are "more equal" than others, the permanent members of the Security Council—the P5—for example. Major contributors to the budget carry more weight than minor contributors. Smaller states organize themselves into negotiating groups, like the G-77 for development issues. The designated leaders of these groups require special attention. The task of the secretariat is to get along with all of the states, regardless of importance, while maintaining a sense of political reality.

The role of NGOs, established in the Charter, has also grown over time. Some, like Amnesty International or Human Rights Watch, play a major role in legitimizing state behavior in human rights and act as watchdogs over the United Nations Secretariat. Others, like Greenpeace and WorldWatch, have played significant roles in shaping international environmental policies. In development assistance and humanitarian operations, NGOs like Oxfam, CARE, Medicins Sans Frontieres, and World Vision play an important operational role. The National Rifle Association is an NGO concerned with preventing control of small arms. Like states, each NGO has to be considered as an equal to the others, although NGOs are classified into different categories. Secretariats have to be able to deal with each while ensuring that they do not seem to endorse NGO positions, especially when these are critical of governments, or appear to take sides in disputes among NGOs.

Private-sector organizations were uninterested for some time in the work of the United Nations system, not seeing that it had many implications for their work. There were exceptions: the telecommunications industry was very interested in the work of the International Telecommunications Union, in which 637 large individual companies were given status as sector members and an additional 127 smaller companies as sector associates. The United Nations itself has tried to engage the private sector through the Global Compact, which includes 2,208 private companies that have agreed to subscribe to the Global Compact principles.

The international mass media is a specific constituency for international secretariats. Each organization has a public information program, but these programs have historically been constrained by member state reluctance for secretariats to engage in either public relations or propaganda campaigns. The longest debates during the First General Assembly had to do with the content of the public information program. In the end the consensus was to allow the public information programs to be based on "information products like press releases or information brochures." In addition, the staff regulations limit what international officials can say to the press. Maintaining good contacts with the media without violating either prescription is a major skill.

At the outset of the United Nations there was considerable interest in international organizations in the academic community. As the apparent role of the United Nations began to decline, the academic community lost interest. Only conservative think tanks in the United States, like the Heritage Foundation, undertook research on international organizations, usually from a hostile perspective. However, with the revival of public consciousness of the

role, universities have again begun to focus on international organizations. Leadership includes finding a way to involve these communities in the organization's activities, but this includes dealing
with academics, who often are not interested in what secretariats
do, and do not understand the role of the secretariats.

Promote Agreement among States

As Urquhart's 1987 appraisal suggests, at least for the first forty
years of the organization agreements among states were not easy
to come by. In the last twenty years there may have been more
agreements, but they were no easier to reach. Still, some secretaries-general had a talent for gaining consensus. Probably the most
successful has been Kofi Annan. A career official before he became
secretary-general, he understood the facilitation process from the
inside, including how to maintain neutrality while moving states
toward consensus. Among contemporary executive heads
Mohammed ElBaradei of the IAEA, Jan Egeland of the UN's Office for the Coordination of Humanitarian Assistance, and Juan
Somavia of the ILO stand out. Executive heads that are not able to
facilitate agreements are seldom reelected.

Response to Crisis (Article 99)

While international organizations have typically taken a long-term
view of problems, they have increasingly been called upon to act
in crises. As noted in Chapter 2, the United Nations Charter's Article 99 authorizes the secretary-general to bring to the attention
of the Security Council what the secretary-general determines is a
threat to peace and security. In effect, it says that the secretariats
have an obligation to respond to crises. The difficulty has always
been that, absent a particular fund or mandate, secretariats are
not given the wherewithal to respond, only to alert.

Secretariats have become adept at responding quickly, for example, to the Asian tsunami of 2004. Responding quickly has included finding methods of expeditiously redeploying supplies,
having on-call arrangements with troop and equipment providers, having storage facilities, and being able to dispatch experienced personnel on short notice.

As problems have become defined as global responsibilities,
international secretariats have been mandated to respond within

the terms of their mandates. WHO, for example, has acquired the responsibility of responding to potential epidemics.

This having been said, the organizations are still not set up to deliver services as quickly as they might be. Large-scale increases in funding still require governmental agreement, either through voluntary contributions or changed assessments. Expenditures of existing funds usually still require a mandate based on intergovernmental review. There has been a reluctance of member states to provide contingency funds. Still, the experience of failed operations, as in Rwanda, where the independent inquiry (United Nations 1999d) found flaws in the way the operation was designed and managed, has encouraged managers as well as governments to err on the side of action. Good managers can find ways to adapt the rules and regulations to the needs of the crisis.

Articulation of Vision

The increase in short-term crises with which international organizations have to deal does not change the fact that their greatest strength is their ability to deal credibly with longer-term problems. To see a vision of the future and then plan how to reach it is a key competence in strategic planning. Effective executive heads of secretariats are able to articulate that vision.

Kofi Annan was particularly effective at this. During his first nine years, Annan had to cope with many short-term emergencies, and he handled some better than others, as he himself would admit. However, he clearly managed to articulate the long-term vision on which the legitimacy of the organization is based. He was able to retain a view of the forest as he dealt with the individual trees.

Some predecessors made efforts to express a longer-term vision, notably Boutros-Ghali's Agenda for Peace, but none has been as active as Annan in seeking to articulate an organizational vision for the future built on the experience of the past and the present. The Agenda for Peace codified the functions that over fifty years the secretariat had taken on, and Annan has been able to build on it. Annan's ability to take advantage of the millennium summit to forge an agreement on the millennium development goals stands in contrast to his predecessors. He sought new ways of involving both civil society and the private sector (through the Global Compact) in the organization's processes. The sequence of reform proposals that he has made, starting in 1997 and generated through the use of high-level panels and expert groups, as well as thinking within the secretariat, reflected learning from what went wrong in the short-term emergencies as well as in the evolution of international governance. These proposals have expressed a clear vision for the organization, including changes that would have been impossible for a secretary-general to propose in earlier times, given their scope and implications.

Other executive heads have had similar success. Mohammed ElBaradei was able to articulate a view of how nuclear energy, linked with improved safety and prevention of proliferation, could become again an important part of global energy policy. Juan Somavia has been able to articulate a clear view of improved conditions for labor in the context of globalization.

The United States

Executive heads have to be able to work with all member states (and all NGOs) if they are to be successful, based on the principle of sovereign equality among states, but, as already noted, some are "more equal" than others. The United States, which had a key role in the failure of the League of Nations and in the establishment and much of the success of the United Nations and its system of organizations, is important in its own right. Regardless of how well they do with other states, executive heads must get along with the United States.

The fact that the United Nations political headquarters is located in New York means that the organization's work inevitably becomes interwoven with the domestic politics of the United States. Any secretary-general has to be able to work in that strange context, and most have not succeeded very well. Trygve Lie tried to cope by acceding to the pressure from conservatives in the United States Senate and almost destroyed the international civil service. Kurt Waldheim's past was politically unacceptable in some national circles, and he was sidelined. Although his tenure has not always been marked by success in terms of the vicissitudes of American politics, Annan has certainly done better than any of his predecessors, although when he proposed means to refurbish the crumbling United Nations headquarters building, he faced opposition at all levels of the US government.

Organizations headquartered in Europe have fewer problems with the United States, since their activities are less likely to be visible to a country that is centered mostly on itself. Still, maintaining acceptable relations with the United States is essential. Jose Bustani, the executive head of the Organisation for the Prohibition of Chemical Weapons, defied the United States and became the first elected executive head of a UN system organization to be fired.

Executive heads tend to have senior staff who understand United States politics and who can advise on what to avoid in dealing with that country. The United States has historically been more concerned with defending its positions than with positive advocacy.

Public and Media
In its early years the public image of the United Nations as a concept tended to be favorable, but the image of the organization as a bureaucracy was often negative. Hammarskjöld aside, secretaries-general sought to remain below the public radar. Yet, to be able to influence public policies, the secretary-general or any executive head has to have a positive public image, since this is one of the bases of legitimacy for the office.

Annan, unlike some of his predecessors, has clearly been visible and, in a typically understated way, has articulated positions that previous secretaries-general would not have dared. Moreover, he has provided an example for presenting positions that might contradict those of major powers, which other senior international officials, like Mohammed ElBaradei of the IAEA and Hans Blix, executive chairman of the United Nations Monitoring, Verification, and Inspection Commission (UNMOVIC) in the time immediately preceding the Iraq War, have emulated. Annan's visibility has, in turn, served to strengthen the secretary-general's role, even as it has drawn more attention from critics. The fact that the 2000 Nobel Peace Prize was shared by Annan and his organization, as was the 2005 Nobel Peace Prize by ElBaradei and his organization, shows the identification between executive head and organization.

The difficulty for the organization in presenting a public image, quite apart from the reticence of many executive heads to have one, is that its public information programs are not supposed to produce public relations. Under these constraints the secretariat can do little other than to make its executive heads available to the press for interviews. In periods when the international public sector was not considered important, getting publicity for executive heads was very difficult. Over the last fifteen years, however, the growth in visibility of the United Nations system has meant that there is far more press coverage, and more executive heads, starting with the secretary-general, have become newsworthy, which has served to give them public personas they can use when seeking to exercise leadership.

Ability to Administer

Executive heads are, in constitutional terms, first and foremost the chief administrative officers of their organizations. Yet very often it is this administrative quality that is most absent in executive heads. Because of their complex structures, international organizations are among the hardest bureaucracies to manage. This is not obvious because they are small, relative to most national governments, and deliver few services directly.

Executive heads have to delegate yet remain vigilant about many of the details. As the organizations have become larger, this dilemma has become particularly acute, especially for the United Nations. The independent commission headed by Paul Volcker that investigated the Oil-for-Food scandal concluded:

> A Secretary-General is, de facto, the Organization's chief political and diplomatic officer. In unsettled times, those responsibilities tend to be all consuming. The present Secretary-General, widely respected for precisely those very qualities, has regrettably been undercut by lapses in the administration of the Organization.
>
> The United Nations Charter designates the secretary-general as Chief Administrative Officer. But whatever the founders had in mind, the Secretary-General—any Secretary-General—has not been chosen for managerial or administrative skills, nor has he been provided with the instruments needed for strong executive control, most clearly in the area of personnel, where professional competence must compete

with the political demands of member states. (United Nations 2005, 61)

As will be discussed in Chapter 10, the Oil-for-Food scandal involved the largest United Nations program in its history and, given its flawed structure, made administration particularly difficult. However, it did bring into relief two elements of administration that are critical: the ability to oversee a decentralized administration, and the ability to bring the secretariat along in terms of effectiveness.

Ability to Oversee

The United Nations system is the most complex bureaucratic entity in the world. In addition to the questions of authority, organizations have offices in almost every country, must work in all of the world's currencies, deal with national regulations that differ from place to place, and have a combination of locally and internationally recruited staff that must work in harmony. Overseeing this complex machinery is a major leadership challenge.

Part of oversight is based on rules—program budget instructions and review, accounting procedures, human resources processes. The key element of oversight is when the issues being dealt with, whether crises or complex relations of secretariat officials with their own external environment, require a sense of what the rules mean rather than what they say.

Oversight also means knowing when to investigate and when to leave alone. The Oil-for-Food scandal was a case in which an investigation at an earlier point might have protected the secretariat.

Ability to Bring the Secretariat Along

The secretariat works in a non-sovereign environment in which individual members have their own political connections. Working to rule would be disastrous for delivery of programs, and hierarchy does not function well. According to internal surveys at different times, staff members say that the motivation for their work is the mission of the organization. Effective leadership means bringing the secretariat staff along on the basis of their belief in the correctness of the executive head's ideas and their connection with the organization's purpose. It also includes clear respect for the staff and their rights.

Some secretaries-general of the United Nations have been better able to do this than others. Trygve Lie antagonized the staff in the wake of the United States investigation of staff. Kurt Waldheim, U Thant, and Boutros Boutros-Ghali were considered distant and aloof. Hammarskjöld made a conscious effort to meet the staff, and as a former civil servant himself, was able to convey understanding as well as commitment to the cause. Perez de Cuellar, who had been a staff member, was able to motivate staff, although he also was seen as somewhat distant. Kofi Annan, who was himself a career civil servant, was able to bring the staff along with him, especially in his first term.

Other executive heads, especially those that have come from outside the international civil service, have had more problems, at least until they learned how to deal with the staffs or demonstrated that they would defend the organization and its personnel against outside attacks.

Staff Selection

The final element of leadership is the selection of staff. Although executive heads face some constraints in that most staff are already in place and many have their own political constituencies, they can select their own immediate staff. They also influence who is brought in or up to occupy senior management positions (which are usually distributed geographically), although they are constrained by member states. The problem is how to make a judgment about whether staff appointments will lead to effectiveness.

Executive heads brought in from the outside have more problems with this than insiders, who know other insiders and are more aware of the external constraints. Having worked with other insiders, an executive head has some perception of the assets and liabilities other insiders bring. This can be a disadvantage if rapid change is required, since insiders tend to know why things are done the way they are and as a result are somewhat resistant to change. The external constraints include ensuring that the appointment of staff does not cause problems with the member states. For example, appointing or promoting a staff member who is considered hostile by the state of which the staff member is a citizen would be something to avoid, regardless of the staff member's merit.

For outsiders, the problem is selecting, from among insiders, a cabinet that can respond to the priorities that led to the election of the executive head in the first place. Here the test of the new executive head is to identify those staff who are knowledgeable about the organization, committed to it, and respected by the other staff. When Kurt Waldheim retained Brian Urquhart, even though their personal chemistry, as reported by both Urquhart (1987) and Waldheim (1986) was not very compatible, he made a good judgment. The same has not always been true in other organizations.

The final element in staff selection is to ensure that the Weberian rules of the secretariats are enforced. In many ways these rules are the first line of defense of the secretariats' credibility. If it is clearly apparent that staff members are selected on the basis of merit (even if politics are involved as well), the staff are protected from the charge that they are incompetent. Trygve Lie's failing was that he did not enforce those rules, while Hammarskjöld's success was at least partly based on enforcing and defending them rigorously. Time will tell whether the reforms proposed by Kofi Annan, which include the elimination of permanent contracts as well as the establishment of more transparent processes for appointing senior staff, will have a positive effect.

APPLICATION TO FUNCTIONS

In practice, leadership is practiced out in the specific context of the functions to be performed. Each function has common features, including the need to navigate the external environment and bring along the staff. But they also differ. A manager who can help guide intergovernmental negotiations may not be the best person to direct humanitarian relief. A manager who can help enforce global norms by the use of information may not be the best person to oversee internal management accountability.

These differences will be examined in subsequent chapters that focus on the different functions in today's secretariats.

4

. . . .

Regime Creation

Human Rights, the Internet, the Environment, the Seas, and Drugs and Thugs

> I asked her [his wife, Annie] what she was proposing.
>
> "Make them put more women in top civil servant's jobs. Women are half the population. Why shouldn't they be half the Permanent Secretaries? How many women are there at the top?"
>
> I tried to think. Certainly not many. I'd hardly come across any.
>
> "Equal opportunities," I said. I liked the sound it made. It has a good ring to it, that phrase. "I'll have a go," I said. "Why not? There's a principle at stake."
>
> Annie was delighted. "You mean you're going to do something out of pure principle?"
>
> —THE COMPLETE YES MINISTER, 351

Creating regimes is the oldest function provided by international secretariats, and the most invisible, although part of what secretariats do is visible. If you look at the podium of any

87

international negotiation, you will see an international bureau-
crat, usually behind a placard with an administrative title like secretary or director or assistant secretary-general or chief. The
secretariat officials will mostly be taking notes or handing pieces
of paper to the chairperson—a representative of a member state.
Behind the scenes, and long before the negotiation between states
takes place, the secretariat influences the result. If it does its work
well, it remains unnoticed.

In the twenty-first century international governance is largely
defined in terms of regimes. A regime is a set of agreements by
states to provide order in an area that they have decided needs an
international as opposed to a national or market-based process of
governance. As noted in Chapter 1, regimes were defined in the
international relations literature as "sets of implicit or explicit principles, norms, rules, and decision-making procedures around which
actors' expectations converge in a given area of international relations" (Krasner 1982, 186). Over time, the international system has
evolved into a myriad of interlocking regimes, covering values like
human rights, borderless issues like climate change and the
Internet, and eliminating weapons of mass destruction, rules for
trade and commerce, and protection against international crime.
The rules incorporated into these agreements provide order in relationships among states, for the smooth operation of the market
and for the rights and roles of individual citizens of the planet.

In the nineteenth and early twentieth centuries international
agreements were reached by specialized negotiating conferences
(for example, the disarmament conventions negotiated between
the two world wars). The secretariats of these negotiations were
temporary, or were provided by the state hosting the conference.
Even the United Nations was formed on the basis of negotiations
that were, at least initially, primarily bilateral, although the final
stages were multilateral.

After World War II, it was recognized that the negotiation process on any issue is continuous rather than episodic. The conversion of the United Nations Declaration of Human Rights into
binding international treaties took almost twenty years. It took
almost thirty years (from 1945 to 1974) to agree on a definition of
aggression, a term included in the United Nations Charter. It took
almost fifty years to agree on the WTO as a permanent institution,
and negotiations are still going on regarding elements of its work.

As the United Nations began to evolve, it increasingly became the preferential site for negotiations. In an address to the American Political Science Association in 1953, Dag Hammarskjöld noted the change:

> Traditional diplomatic techniques are in principle, of course, bilateral. That is true even if many nations happen to be represented at the conference table. A truly multilateral approach to diplomacy does not come into being until an instrument is created which represents a denationalized platform for negotiations or a denationalized instrument for a number of governments. In the Annual Report to the Eighth Assembly I have said that I believe we have only begun to explore the full potentialities of the United Nations as an instrument for multilateral diplomacy, especially the most fruitful combinations of public discussion on the one hand and private negotiations and mediation on the other. I added that the opportunities are there to be tested and used. (Hammarskjöld 1953b, 976)

Since then, the number of negotiations around regimes has grown dramatically. As only one indicator, the United Nations Treaty Collection, which catalogues multilateral treaties for which the United Nations is the official depository (and is available online) now includes over five hundred treaties.

ELEMENTS IN THE CREATION OF REGIMES

While there is no formal handbook on how to negotiate a regime, regime theory suggests that the elements and their order have to be agreed upon. The elements are principles, norms, rules, and procedures, each different. As will be seen, they have to be agreed in sequence. In fact, one reason that regime theory has reemerged in international relations is that it describes the negotiation process well. Looking at these elements, the secretariats' role becomes clear.

Defining Principles

Using Krasner's definition, principles are beliefs of fact, causation, and rectitude. For negotiation to succeed there must be a common understanding of the nature of reality in a given subject. The first stage of regime formulation is to agree on the nature of the problem. If there is no consensus on what the problem is, there can be no agreement on what the solutions might be.

In the agreement on principles, Hammarskjöld's notion of a role for the secretariat as a denationalized source of information has clearly been critical. The World Meteorological Organization (WMO), which organized much of the research and consensus building on climate change, used a network of national stations that had been set up and maintained by its staff. These were organized through such programs as World Weather Watch and the Global Atmospheric Research Programme (Paterson 1996). In building consensus that violence against women is a global problem, independent of class, religion, or nationality, the United Nations Division for the Advancement of Women commissioned studies and ran a series of expert groups. They reached the conclusion that violence against women is pervasive, and that women are nine times more likely to be victims of men than men to be victims of women (Mathiason 2001).

The debate over Internet governance, or how to provide public oversight for the most rapidly growing communication technology in history, has had to focus on issues determining what the Internet is. If the Internet is a physical channel, it could be regulated in one way. If it is merely a network of networks linked by commonly agreed protocols, it has to be regulated a different way. If information flow can be controlled at any point, regulation could focus on Internet service providers, while if it cannot be controlled at specific points (other than the sender of messages or the receivers), regulation has to focus on the ends of the communication (Mueller, Mathiason, and McKnight 2004). The Working Group on Internet Governance (WGIG), established by the secretary-general as part of the preparations for the second phase of the World Summit on the Information Society (WSIS), has not yet reached consensus on these principles. The WGIG was supported by a secretariat unit, and the WSIS had its own secretariat, largely provided by the International Telecommunications Union. The next stage of discussion of principles, through an Internet governance forum, will also be supported by a technical secretariat.

Establishing Norms

Norms are standards of behavior defined in terms of rights and obligations. There has to be some agreement by states on the obligations that states agree to take on to deal with a problem. Human rights conventions include acceptance that the State will not discriminate on any of a number of grounds. The UN Framework Convention on Climate Change (FCCC) states that climate change is bad and that states have an obligation to address it with public policies.

The international conventions that deal with the elimination of weapons of mass destruction all include a clear set of norms. For example, in the Nuclear Non-Proliferation Treaty (NPT), states agree that no state that did not already have nuclear weapons when the treaty entered into force should try to acquire them, and that nuclear states should not transfer materials or technologies for weapons to non-nuclear states and should, additionally, take steps to eliminate their own nuclear arsenals. Agreement on the norms was facilitated by secretariats showing that accepting the norms was feasible.

In discussions on Internet governance there was agreement that states should ensure the openness, stability, and security of the Internet. This agreement was facilitated by the secretariat, bringing together scholars, civil society representatives, private-sector representatives, and government officials (the WGIG being only one example, a consultation organized by the United Nations Information and Communication Technology Task Force being another) to explore the norm. One resulting volume issued by the task force was particularly influential in shaping the negotiations because it helped define the existing consensus about norms (McLean 2004).

Elaborating Rules

Rules are specific prescriptions and prohibitions with respect to an actor's behavior. Rules are expressed in "should" and "should not" statements on specific issues. The degree of detail that has to be agreed upon varies from convention to convention. In many, the rules are very detailed and technical.

Rules are particularly characteristic of disarmament conventions. In the Comprehensive Test Ban Treaty, for example, the locations of seismic and other remote sensing sites are set out in the convention itself. This was to guarantee that there would be no way for states to avoid their obligations to permit the construction or use of stations. Ironically, when the secretariat began to set up the stations, it determined that some of these specifications were erroneous.

Similarly, the provisions of the chemical weapons convention are very detailed, both with regard to the chemicals covered and the responsibilities of states to report on them and instructions on how inspections are to take place.

In the NPT the detailed rules are worked out in a set of subsidiary arrangements in the form of safeguards agreements reached between states parties and the IAEA secretariat. The IAEA has developed these agreements through a series of information circulars, which they propose to the agency's board of governors. They are intended to represent a consensus about the information that the agency secretariat needs to be able to verify state compliance with the NPT's broader norms. The rules have been modified in response to experience. By 1988, for example, the Safeguards Department was convinced that the existing rules, which restricted the agency's ability to carry out inspections, would eventually make it impossible to verify state compliance. However, it was not able to make the case successfully. After the 1991 Gulf War, when it became apparent that the inspection procedures used on Iraq's declared nuclear program were not adequate to detect an undeclared program, the agency staff began a process of proposing revisions to the agreements. After considerable negotiation (see Andemicael and Mathiason 2005) the secretariat was able to convince the member states to agree to what were called expanded safeguards that provided for more intrusive inspections as well as unannounced ones.

Negotiations on rules can be particularly complex and time consuming, because they are often extremely detailed. Because of this, a new approach to negotiating agreement is the framework convention, where subsequent agreements on detailed rules are reached. The FCCC was this type. After the treaty entered into force, detailed protocols were worked out at subsequent meetings of the states parties. The Kyoto Protocol, which entered into force in 2005, set out detailed targets for reducing greenhouse-gas emissions.

A similar approach has been advocated for Internet governance and is being considered as part of the negotiations following the WSIS, as well as in the WHO in terms of tobacco use.

A function of secretariats is to provide the factual basis for these agreements, either by mobilizing scientific or engineering evidence from outside experts or by providing it from in-house expertise.

Setting Up Procedures

Procedures are the prevailing practices for making and implementing collective choices. They are the implementation machinery in the form of intergovernmental decision-making bodies and secretariat structures and in the creation of an institutional form for the regime. In these the secretariats are particularly influential, because the procedures have to be built into plans, budgets, personnel management, and organizational structures.

CONSENSUS AND THE ROLE OF SECRETARIATS

Secretariats apply their assets to facilitate consensus among states. These can be summarized as follows:

- The multinational composition of international secretariats reflects many of the national differences that exist. If the international staffs cannot agree on the elements of a regime, it is unlikely that governments can.
- International secretariats are the "institutional memory" of a regime. They know what was agreed and why, and they can help prevent backsliding or deviation.
- International secretariats are brokers between civil society and governments, and among governments.
- International secretariats will have to provide the services that will implement the regime and therefore can judge what is feasible.

- International secretariat staff are encouraged to believe strongly in what they do, and they are motivated to convince others.

THE PROCESS OF CREATING REGIMES

A regime is not created out of thin air. Creating a regime is often a drawn-out process because parameters of the regime have to be modified and refined in the light of experience, national political changes, and other external events.

While any given regime can go through a variety of stages, a careful analysis of the history of many regime creation efforts suggests that six steps have to be taken.

Step One: Raising the Salience of a Problem

A consensus has to be developed that a problem exists and must be addressed. Sometimes this is the result of events. For example, the humanitarian crisis in Darfur drew attention to the need for a doctrine of responsibility to protect and led to the agreement that "the international community, through the United Nations, also has the responsibility to use appropriate diplomatic, humanitarian and other peaceful means, in accordance with Chapters VI and VIII of the Charter, to help protect populations from genocide, war crimes, ethnic cleansing and crimes against humanity" (Declaration of the 2005 World Summit, para. 132). More often, however, governments, civil society organizations, or secretariats, or a combination of these, will take steps to raise the salience of a problem. The impetus can come from any of the three types of parties that are involved in negotiation. A government or group of governments, based on its interest and experience, may call for action. Civil society may call for action in a field where governments have been loath to act (like the environment), often using the mass media. Secretariats can present information suggesting the existence of a problem at an intergovernmental level. There are many examples of each, although the impetus is more likely to come from civil society or secretariats than governments, who are often reluctant to seek multilateral solutions.

During the first phase of WSIS, several governments raised the issue of unilateral control by the United States over the root servers of the Internet. Prior to that point the issue had not been raised at the intergovernmental level. As a result, a discussion of the broader issues of Internet governance has taken place in WSIS and beyond.

While the use of anti-personnel landmines was a feature of warfare for decades, their prevalence in internal armed conflicts made them particularly deadly for civilian populations. NGOs that worked in the reconstruction of areas affected by armed conflicts were the first to call attention to the effects of unexploded ordinance and its effects on noncombatants. They used mass media, based on testimony, to bring the issue of banning these weapons to the public consciousness.

NGOs concerned with the environment have taken the lead in raising awareness of the existence of these types of problems. Similarly, in the human rights area, NGOs like Amnesty International and Human Rights Watch have called attention to the need to address, in a practical way, violations of the Universal Declaration of Human Rights. A more recent case is the effort by organizations of persons with disabilities to obtain agreements from governments to negotiate an international convention on the rights of persons with disabilities. They began their effort at the World Conference against Racism in Durbin in 2001, where a disability caucus succeeded in getting persons with disabilities listed as a group facing discrimination. Subsequently, organizations worked with governments, like Mexico and Ecuador, to have a negotiating committee established.

Because secretariats are formally supposed to respond to governmental requests rather than lead them, secretariats are not often the visible provocateurs of regime creation. However, they can channel and support initiatives from civil society or governments. They can help validate the initiatives by either certifying the connection between the new proposal and existing regimes or by showing factually that the problem exists.

Step Two: Defining the Parameters of the Problem

Once negotiations have been set in motion, the next step is to define parameters for action. Much of the activity in this step is prior to formal negotiations. In intergovernmental bodies, academic discussions, and interagency meetings within the United Nations system the outlines of the facts about the problem can be discussed.

Once there is some agreement about what is at issue, action can be called for. A large part of this step takes place with the active involvement of secretariats. Bringing this step to a successful conclusion is one of the main added values of the international civil service.

Secretariats were critical in setting the basis for the United Nations Convention on the Law of the Sea. Two lines of analysis coalesced: (1) evidence that there were likely to be increasing disputes about regulating traffic on the high seas and over offshore petroleum exploitation and fishing, and (2) technological advances that would make the deep seabed beyond national jurisdictions a resource over which states might have conflicts. Governments sensed the first issue, secretariats the second. However, preceding the negotiations the secretariats played the central role in obtaining a consensus about what had to be agreed.

In the area of advancement of women, the issue of violence against women was originally propelled by NGOs, particularly in the United States and Europe. The focus was primarily on violence in the streets, as reflected in such movements as Take Back the Night in the United States. Over a ten-year period, from 1975 to 1985, the issue's salience was raised from safety on the streets at night and "intra-familial conflict," as the 1975 Conference on Women in Mexico City put it, through "battered spouses" in the second conference at Copenhagen in 1980, to "violence against women" in the Nairobi Programme for Action. From 1986 through the adoption in 1991 of the UN Declaration on the Elimination of Violence against Women, the UN Division for the Advancement of Women provided a focus for expanding the understanding of the factual dimensions of the problem (Mathiason 2001).

Similarly, when the IAEA was tasked with defining the expanded safeguards agreements for nuclear inspections, the secretariat organized expert group meetings, as well as evaluations of its own work, to suggest what had to be addressed in the revised agreements.

Step Three: A Major Event to Establish a Framework

While consciousness and facts are essential steps, for them to be translated into binding agreements an extraordinary event is usually necessary to establish the key negotiation framework. This is because "normal" processes take place at a level of political importance that is too low to ensure success. Since the 1960s, world conferences have provided the incentive for states to reach agreements. Most of the time the agreements are on the first two elements of a regime, principles and norms, but they may agree also on procedures.

Secretariats often encourage the convening of conferences under the hypothesis that a conference or summit meeting can be the excuse for its preparations (Mathiason 2005). The calling of a conference or summit tends to focus attention on an issue, and the need for an outcome document often provides the incentive to define the parameters that need to be negotiated to establish a new regime or modify an existing one.

The 1968 World Conference on Human Rights set the basis for beginning the negotiation of the Convention on the Elimination of All Forms of Discrimination against Women (CEDAW). Similarly, the existence of the United Nations Conference on Environment and Development provided an incentive to complete the negotiation of the FCCC. The summit at the General Assembly in 2005 led to an agreement to reform the UN's human rights machinery by creating the Human Rights Council.

In the disarmament regimes the periodic review conferences provide a focus for adjusting the regimes. Even when these conferences fail, as was the case with the Fifth Meeting of States Party to the Biological and Toxin Weapon Convention or the 2005 review conference of the NPT, the conferences can provide new perspectives on what needs to be agreed.

In structuring preparatory activities for the conferences the secretariats can have considerable influence on the result by organizing expert groups (and helping select their members), preparing their own analyses, and facilitating the negotiations of final documents.

Step Four: Initial Implementation and the Structuring of Institutions

With few exceptions, new international regimes involve the creation of new international institutions. The state commitments involved in the regime usually require some mechanism to verify compliance. Decision-making requires an institution to prepare for intergovernmental meetings. Often the regime requires a neutral office to collect, analyze, and present information. While sometimes these new functions can be grafted onto an existing institution, often an entirely new institution is needed, either because states are reluctant to expand the authority of an existing institution or because no institution exists. As a result there are negotiations to set up the details of the new implementation machinery. These can often be very contentious, since this defines the extent to which states are willing to cede functions or even sovereignty to an international organization. The negotiations also involve cost, since each additional institution implies a new commitment of national resources to an international public entity.

In UN terms this is when discussion turns on a "statement of program budget implications." In order to prevent states that pay little into the budgets of international organizations (in absolute terms) from determining the tasks that these organizations should perform, most have adopted rules that say that before any decision is adopted, the secretariat must indicate whether implementing the decision will require additional financial resources, will change programs of work, or can be absorbed within existing resources. In determining whether a proposal has program budget implications, a secretariat faces a difficult choice. By showing that a proposal has implications, the secretariat can effectively block its adoption, because major contributors may object to the cost. However, if the secretariat favors a proposal, it may try to avoid showing increased cost by stating that it can absorb the new activity "within existing resources."

For example, after the 1985 Conference on Women in Nairobi, states at a special session of the Commission on the Status of Women in 1987 proposed to triple the number of reports that the secretariat should prepare for each session of the Commission on the Status of Women while annualizing the sessions that had previously been biennial. The secretariat felt that, although its workload would increase dramatically, if it requested additional resources the proposal would fail and the organization's program for advancement of women would be damaged. It accordingly said that it could absorb the additional work within its existing staffing (Mathiason 2001).

When the Comprehensive Nuclear Test Ban Treaty (CTBT) was in its final stages of negotiation, the issue of a verification organization was raised. One option was to give the responsibility to the IAEA, which deals with other aspects of nuclear weapons. The agency indicated its willingness to take on the assignment, but stated that it would require additional resources in the area of seismology, a field in which the IAEA had not worked. With this proposal in hand, a number of states argued that there would be a different pattern of states party to the CTBT than were party to the NPT, and as a result, there could be confusion. Others argued that until the treaty entered into force, the secretariat for the CTBT would be temporary and that therefore a new organization would be preferable. Still others argued that the costs of existing international organizations, because of their grade structure, benefits, and pension systems, were too high and that a new organization could be less costly. A separate organization was established.

Step Five: Periodic Review of the Regime and Elaboration of Details

The role of secretariats increases when the regime has been established. There is usually a work program to explore details of the agreement with a view to modifications of the regime within its broad parameters. The work program includes further information mobilization, review of compliance, and proposals for further negotiation.

For many regimes that are embodied in conventions, the process is reflected in periodic review conferences. These allow for revisions and adjustments based on experience. The preparations for the review conferences are supported by secretariats. In the case of the biological weapons convention the periodic review conferences led to efforts, still unsuccessful, to agree on a verification protocol. The last periodic review of the NPT has had the effect of exposing weaknesses in the regime.

The FCCC was adopted with the procedure that implementation details would be worked out at the regular meetings of states parties and, in fact, each successive meeting has further elaborated the agreements, including the Kyoto Protocol. Since states have the option of not joining protocols, the process allows further negotiations in which all states parties can participate, an openness whose importance will be seen as the regime develops.

The role of the executive head of the body supporting the negotiations as spokesperson for the regime has also been growing. For example, the high commissioner for human rights now speaks on behalf of the regime and can publicly affect the direction of negotiations.

Step Six: Implementation through Institutional Work

Assuming that the regime has been set in place, the machinery for implementation is expected to work effectively, with the government role shifting to oversight of the activities and outcomes. At this point the international public sector swings into action.

The extent to which the secretariat will function will depend on the responsibilities assigned. However, these responsibilities have been increasing as the international regimes have become both more complex and more authoritative.

The Dispute Resolution Body of the WTO now has a significant role in managing the global trading system. The WTO secretariat has the responsibility for setting up dispute resolution panels, collecting information on the facts of the disputes, and supporting the discussions of the panels. Similarly, the Law of the Sea Tribunal, set up under the terms of the UN Convention on the Law of the Sea, has begun to adjudicate disputes relating to such aspects of the law as boundaries of economic zones.

The institutions created in older regimes, such as the international monetary regime set up under Bretton Woods, now function as independent bodies. Their annual meetings reach agreements that are influenced by the technical work of their secretariats. This is also the case when a secretariat has been given the responsibility for providing services directly, as the World Intellectual Property Organization does with regard to international registration of trademarks and copyrights. Both the Bretton Woods institutions, and to an extent the World Intellectual Property Organization, are able to finance their secretariat operations from user fees. The IMF and the World Bank finance their secretariats from interest on loans; the World Intellectual Property Organization is allowed to charge for registrations it performs.

The human rights regime functions through a series of monitoring committees that review state reports. With seven monitoring committees and up to 190 parties to a given convention, the machinery has become increasingly complex. Some committees, like the Human Rights Committee and the Committee on the Elimination of Discrimination against Women, now meet three times a year. Faced with an increasing load, the Office of the High Commissioner has been working to find ways to streamline reporting and monitoring.

Finding ways of streamlining implementation machinery is likely to increase, as is the number and coverage of different machineries. The issue of coordination, which has been a concern of states since the beginning of the United Nations, will also become more important.

REGIME CREATION CASES

We can best see the processes by which international regimes have been created and the specific roles played by the concerned secretariats by looking at specific stories. None of the international regimes is yet fully articulated because the normal pattern is to create a central regime and then build on it, expand it, or deepen it by subsequent agreements that respond to experience. That makes the regime creation stories fascinating; they are never over and they are always relevant.

Women's Rights Are Human Rights, If They Are Exercised

When Hillary Rodham Clinton said, at the fourth Conference on Women, that "women's rights are human rights and human rights are women's rights" (Clinton 1995), she was only partially accurate. The United Nations Charter, the Universal Declaration of Human Rights, the UN International Covenant on Civil and Political Rights, and the UN International Covenant on Economic, Social and Cultural Rights all state that men and women have equal rights. However, the women's movement argued that while the rights existed, they were not exercised equally due to lack of appropriate public policies. A regime for women's equal exercise of their human rights was needed, and the United Nations Secretariat became a major player in the process.

The year that the two international covenants were adopted (1966), the Commission on the Status of Women, through the Economic and Social Council, forwarded a draft declaration on the elimination of discrimination against women modeled on the UN racial discrimination declaration. The declaration functioned as a low-level human rights instrument, but it foreshadowed another notion, pushed by the secretariat, that the *exercise* of rights is as important as having them. The declaration stated that women's rights were contained in the covenants, but there was enough discrimination on the basis of sex that the rights could not be enjoyed. This began a parallel process of elaborating the CEDAW, drafts for which were prepared by 1974.

According to Donnelly's analysis of the human rights regime, the negotiation and entry-into-force of the CEDAW helped push the creation of the larger human rights regime further (Donnelly 1986). The process took about as long as negotiating the UN Convention on the Elimination of Racial Discrimination, but the content of the convention was much broader. International Women's Year and the 1975 Conference on Women in Mexico City provided the major event to dramatize the need for the convention. The draft of the convention was completed in 1976 and forwarded, through the Economic and Social Council, to the General Assembly.

Other human rights conventions had been prepared with the support of the Division for Human Rights. The CEDAW, in contrast, was prepared by a secretariat unit that since 1946 had supported the Commission on the Status of Women. Initially part of the Human Rights Division, when that division was transferred from New York to Geneva in the 1960s, the Status of Women Section remained in New York, only loosely part of human rights. In 1972, with the appointment of the first woman to a post at the assistant secretary-general level, a new unit was created that merged the Status of Women Secretariat—renamed the Branch for the Promotion of Equality between Men and Women—with elements of the Social Development Division. Discrimination against women as a human rights issue became the responsibility of a secretariat unit that was independent. More important, by the time it became the Division for the Advancement of Women, its staff had changed from being comprised exclusively of lawyers to a combination of lawyers, economists, sociologists, demographers, and political scientists (see Mathiason 2001). The secretariat saw human rights in a much more dynamic context—more as a matter of public policy. The Commission on the Status of Women welcomed this approach.

The convention, after several years of negotiation by a working group of the Third Committee of the General Assembly, where the main issues had to do with the implementation mechanism rather than substance, was adopted in 1979 and entered into force in 1981. A treaty monitoring body, the Committee on the Elimination of Discrimination against Women, began operation in 1982, joining the Human Rights Committee, the Committee on Economic, Social and Cultural Rights, and the Committee on Racial Discrimination as norm enforcement functions.

The convention was strengthened in 1999 by the adoption of an optional protocol that recognizes the competence of the Committee on the Elimination of Discrimination against Women to receive and consider complaints from individuals or groups within its jurisdiction. The optional protocol had been stimulated by the 1995 Conference on Women in Beijing and was considered an integral part of its follow up. The Division for the Advancement of Women, providing information on precedent and need, made it easier for governments to adopt what was a fairly far-reaching agreement.

Law of the Sea: High, Middle, and Below

Creating a regime for managing the seas and oceans was a major success of the United Nations, but it too took many years and required the active involvement of the secretariat. The Law of the Sea was the first expression of international law, so the process of creating the current regime has deep roots.

Hugo Grotius (1538–1645), widely considered the father of international law, wrote in *Freedom of the Seas*:

Can the vast boundless sea be the appanage of one kingdom alone, and it not the greatest? Can any one nation have the right to prevent other nations which so desire, from selling to another, from bartering with one another, actually from communicating with one another? Can any nation give away what it never owned, or discover what already belonged to some one else? (Grotius 1916)

Grotius perceived that there was space beyond national control that needed regulation for orderly use. The Law of the Sea, as it developed, provided rules for the free navigation of the high seas and limited national sovereignty to countries' immediate seacoast (three miles from the shoreline). This essentially customary law was observed until 1945, when the United States, to protect its offshore oil interests, extended its claim of sovereignty to the continental shelf, a concept as yet undefined in international law. Other countries followed suit, and Ecuador, for example, extended its claim to two hundred miles to protect its fishing grounds.

The matter of defining the continental shelf was sent to the International Law Commission, a subsidiary of the General Assembly. The commission, using secretariat papers as its basis, proposed a definition of the continental shelf, but this had no binding legal authority. In order to deal with the issue, as well as others, the United Nations convened the First United Nations Conference on the Law of the Sea in 1958. The conference resulted in four draft conventions, one each on the territorial sea and contiguous zone; high seas; continental shelf; and fishing and conservation of living marine resources in the high seas. These conventions were considered by many states to be imprecise, and their ratification and entry into force were slow and not universal.

In the meantime, technological changes affected the process. Oil exploration became possible in deeper waters; industrial fishing became more common, allowing "factory ships" to stay in fishing grounds for long periods; and the technology for exploiting mineral resources like manganese nodules in the deep seabed seemed ready for application to mining operations.

The issue of deep seabed mining had been raised in the context of the Advisory Committee on the Application of Science and Technology to Development rather than in committees dealing with international law. The advisory committee was serviced by the Division for Natural Resources and Energy in the Department of Economic and Social Affairs, whose staff included engineers and economists who saw the connection with the legal regime. The advisory committee's 1966 report to the Economic and Social Council led the council to request a survey of "knowledge of the resources of the sea beyond the continental shelf, excluding fish, and of the techniques for exploiting these resources" (Resolution 1112 (XL), "Non-agricultural Resources"). Between the council meeting in March and the General Assembly in September, more work was done. When the matter was taken up in the General Assembly's Second Committee, there was a clear mood to go beyond the narrow survey that had been proposed. The General Assembly requested, in addition to the council-mandated survey, "a comprehensive survey of activities in marine science and technology, including that relating to mineral resources development, undertaken by members of the United Nations family of organizations, various Member States and intergovernmental organizations concerned, and by universities, scientific and technological institutions and other interested organizations."

The mandate permitted the secretariat unit on ocean economics and technology to set the parameters for negotiation. Headed by Yugoslav economist Vladimir Baum, an assistant director of the Division of Natural Resources and Energy, the unit included French economist Jean-Pierre Levy, who was particularly interested in the field. They organized a collaborative effort to determine the economic and scientific dimensions of the issue.

The issue was also placed on the agenda of the next General Assembly, and a report of the secretary-general was prepared to stimulate debate. Material from the secretariat's work also found its way to Malta's permanent representative to the United Nations, Arvid Pardo, who had been part of Hammarskjöld's office.

Trained as an international lawyer, Pardo saw the economics of the seabed as a vehicle for promoting a wider law of the sea regime. As the ambassador of a member state, he requested the inclusion of an agenda item at the 1997 General Assembly entitled "Examination of the question of the reservation exclusively for peaceful purposes of the seabed and the ocean floor, and the subsoil thereof, underlying the high seas beyond the limits of present national jurisdiction, and the use of their resources in the interests of mankind."

The secretariat quickly produced a report on the subject (A/C.1/952), which described activities of the various organizations of the United Nations system regarding seabed resources and concluded that "(a) the legal status of deep sea resources and (b) ways and means of ensuring that the exploitation of these resource benefit the development constitute two major gaps." The report suggested that the General Assembly request a more comprehensive report.

Pardo was the only speaker when the item was taken up on November 1, 1967, and he made the most of it. His speech took three hours to deliver but set the basis for the negotiation process that led, in 1976, to the adoption of the United Nations Convention on the Law of the Sea. His claim that "the high seas are the common heritage of all mankind" was recognized in the General Assembly resolution on the item, which created the ad hoc Committee to Study the Peaceful Uses of the Seabed and the Ocean Floor beyond the Limits of National Jurisdiction. With secretariat services provided by both the Ocean Economics Branch and the Office of the Legal Counsel, this body eventually recommended the convening of the third United Nations Conference on the Law of the Sea to negotiate a comprehensive convention.

The process of preparing for the first meeting of the conference enabled the secretariat to mobilize information, prepare position papers, and help structure the process. The first meeting of the conference took place on December 3, 1973, in New York. The negotiating process continued for eight years.

The complex negotiations were completed by 1982, and the convention was adopted on December 10, 1982. The negotiations involved trading interests of coastal states with those of landlocked states and those of industrialized countries with developing countries. When the time came to adopt the convention, consensus was not possible. The United States, under the Reagan administration, opposed elements of the convention related to seabed mining, especially the arrangement for an international enterprise. As a result, the convention was adopted by a vote of 130–4, with 17 abstentions. The negative votes were the United States, Israel, Turkey, and Venezuela, each for different reasons.[1]

Because the United States has the largest coastline, as well as navy, its refusal to sign the convention meant that the convention was unlikely to work. Sixty states were needed to ratify the convention for it to enter into force, and many of the states involved decided to ratify slowly to prevent the crisis of a universal convention coming into force without a major party.

For the secretariat, which knew by 1982 that there would be a considerable delay before the convention entered into force, the task was to prepare the ground for the regime. To do so, the secretariat developed an ocean-affairs plan, which it included in the medium-term plan for the period from 1984 to 1989. The plan brought together two different offices, the Ocean Economics and Technology Branch, which was concerned with issues like seabed mining and mapping of boundaries, and the Office of Legal Affairs, which was concerned with legislation and treaty interpretation. The two offices worked out a sequence of objectives prior to entry into force, including preparing *travaux* (documents explaining why provisions were included), establishing procedures for arbitrating boundaries on the sea, and establishing preparatory documents for the institutions to be created when the convention entered into force. They also trained national officials in the significance of the treaty and provided public information about its provisions. By undertaking these activities the secretariat could ensure a smooth transition when the convention entered into force.

The convention finally entered into force in November 1994. A main factor was that the United States convinced the states parties to renegotiate Part IX of the convention, which dealt with deep seabed mining beyond limits of national jurisdiction. The changes removed objections that the United States had entered in 1982. After the agreement, other states ratified, and the convention came into force, although the United States has not yet become a party.

One of the first consequences of the entry into force was the creation of two institutions: the International Tribunal for the Law of the Sea, and the International Seabed Authority. The tribunal was set up in Hamburg, Germany, in 1996 to adjudicate cases arising from the convention. Its first registrar (head of secretariat) was Gritakumar Chitty of Sri Lanka, who had been a long-time staff member of the Ocean Economics and Technology Office. He held office until 2001, when he retired. Over the first nine years of operation, the tribunal decided thirteen cases.

The International Seabed Authority was established in November 1994 in Kingston, Jamaica. Its functions relate primarily to deep seabed mining. Since this has not really begun, the initial work has been to establish rules and regulations for implementing the convention. The first secretary-general of the authority, Satya

Nandan, was one of the negotiators of the convention (for Fiji) and was later head of the UN Secretariat unit in New York that dealt with the law of the sea.

Is the Heat On? Climate Change

Like the seas and oceans, the world's physical environment is clearly beyond the control of individual states. The United Nations system was not involved initially in environmental matters, which were seen as scientific research issues rather than matters of policy. The International Geophysical Year, 1958–59, was organized and run by an NGO, the International Council of Scientific Unions. UNESCO also was working on aspects of climate, as was the WMO, which had been set up in 1950 to link national meteorological services. Enough data had been collected and concerns expressed, especially by civil society groups, for governments to become interested at the policy level, pushed by the secretariats.

The most important consequence of the 1972 Stockholm conference on the environment was focus on climate change as a global policy issue. Connected to the preparations for Stockholm was the formulation of a specific program to deal with climate change issues—the Global Atmospheric Research Programme—a joint enterprise of the International Council of Scientific Unions and the WMO. The program was intended to collect scientific evidence of climate change, about which concern was beginning to be expressed in the scientific community but about which there was little interest among policymakers.

Partly as a result of the preparatory activities, the declaration of the Stockholm conference stated that there was a potential problem between pollution and climate:

> We see around us growing evidence of man-made harm in many regions of the earth: dangerous levels of pollution in water, air, earth and living beings; major and undesirable disturbances to the ecological balance of the biosphere; destruction and depletion of irreplaceable resources; and gross deficiencies, harmful to the physical, mental and social health of man, in the man-made environment, particularly in the living and working environment.

Little was said about what to do about climate change, although Recommendation 70 in the Programme of Action requested governments to "carefully evaluate the likelihood and magnitude of climatic effects and disseminate their findings to the maximum extent feasible before embarking on such activities." It would be another fifteen years before this evaluation process led to further regime creation.

Development of a regime to deal with issues of climate was slow but steady, guided and reinforced by the work of technical secretariats who contributed studies, analyses, and syntheses of information cutting across epistemic communities. The process was given relevance because of other events that led to international conferences.

Following the Stockholm conference, a series of other UN conferences—food (1974), water (1976), and desertification (1977)—included the issue of climate change. These conferences were called because of perceived crises in these areas (including the first Sahelian drought in the 1970s, where the main focus was on humanitarian intervention).

In 1979 the WMO together with the International Council of Scientific Unions organized the first World Climate Conference, which, among other things, noted that the amount of carbon dioxide in the atmosphere was increasing and that this might have consequences for humans. One result of that conference was the establishment the World Climate Programme to coordinate full-scale research. The World Climate Programme provided a mandate to WMO and its epistemic community to justify focusing research on the specific issue of human-caused changes to the environment.

The idea that scientific research could lead to international agreements was also being tested in another area: ozone depletion. Satellite imagery had shown that the earth is surrounded by a layer of ozone, and the ozone was beginning to be depleted. This observation caused considerable alarm among scientists:

The ozone layer absorbs a portion of the radiation from the sun, preventing it from reaching the planet's surface. Most importantly, it absorbs the portion of ultraviolet light called UVB. UVB has been linked to many harmful effects, including various types of skin cancer, cataracts, and harm to some crops, certain materials, and some forms of marine life. (US Environmental Protection Agency 2006)

Once the ozone depletion was detected, there was an effort to mobilize research to detect factors that could explain the phenomenon. Researchers quickly identified chlorofluorocarbons (CFCs) as the main culprits. These chemical substances had been used for over fifty years for refrigeration, as solvents, and as a key ingredient in aerosol sprays. They were being used on a worldwide basis, and it was clear to scientists that addressing their use required global action.

The issue of ozone depletion was first discussed by the governing council of the UNEP in 1976. A meeting of experts on the ozone layer was convened in 1977, after which UNEP and the WMO set up the Coordinating Committee of the Ozone Layer to make periodic assessments of ozone depletion. The conclusion drawn was that the only way to mitigate ozone depletion was to eliminate CFCs.

Intergovernmental negotiations for an international agreement to phase out ozone-depleting substances started in 1981. During the early years of the 1980s satellite imagery and an analysis of observations that had begun in 1961 demonstrated that a hole had developed in the ozone layer over Antarctica and that it was growing. This gave greater incentives for action and led to the adoption of the Vienna convention for the Protection of the Ozone Layer in March 1985. The Vienna Convention encourages intergovernmental cooperation on research, systematic observation of the ozone layer, monitoring of CFC production, and exchange of information. Based on further analysis, it was found that the process of ozone depletion required a rapid response and negotiations began on a protocol to the convention to set targets.

The Montreal Protocol on Substances that Deplete the Ozone Layer was adopted in September 1987. It was designed so that the schedules for phasing out CFCs could be revised on the basis of periodic scientific and technological assessments. The protocol has been adjusted to accelerate the phase-out schedules. It has also been amended to introduce other kinds of control measures and to add new controlled substances to the list. A secretariat unit was created within UNEP to service meetings of the parties to the convention and subsidiary bodies, but more important, to receive and analyze data and information from the parties on the production and consumption of ozone-depleting substances. These data form the basis for the periodic assessments of ozone depletion.

Changes in the ozone layer were highly visible, and the cause was clear. That was not true with regard to global warming. Not only was the presumed cause, carbon dioxide accumulations, not easy to establish with credibility, but the data on which change could be measured were much less easy to come by, if only because they had been collected only over a relatively short period of time. The role of the secretariat of the World Climate Programme was to compile the available data and to bring experts together to review that data and to draw conclusions. The ozone-layer issue clearly provided a model.

By 1985 enough information was available that an international conference was organized by the World Climate Programme in Villach, Austria. The theme was "Assessment of the Role of Carbon Dioxide and Other Greenhouse Gases in Climate Variations and Associated Impacts." The conference concluded that there was a relationship, and that global warming was in fact taking place.

The next issue was how to bring this emerging scientific consensus to governmental attention. According to Paterson, the issue of climate change reached the political level in 1988 when, at a legislative hearing, James Hansen, the chief climatologist of the US government, stated that the greenhouse effect was occurring (Paterson 1996). The statement came on the heels of six of the hottest ten years in history and a major drought in the United States.

At the same time, the Canadian, UK, and Soviet delegations at the General Assembly began to mention the importance of the problem. The developing countries, however, did not see this as their problem, since the studies had shown that the main sources of carbon dioxide were the developed countries. Convincing the developing countries that climate change, while not their fault, was their concern took some time. Scientific civil society was not well rooted in those countries. Efforts to reduce greenhouse gases would have an impact on development. In addition, the United States had its own problems with industrial organizations that were concerned that air quality controls would cost money and slow growth of the economy.

One solution to the problem was to create, in 1988, an Intergovernmental Panel on Climate Change (IPCC) to agree on the facts and their implications. While the initiative had come from the secretariats of both WMO and UNEP, the creation of the panel was formally authorized by the WMO assembly. The members of the panel would be drawn on a geographical basis from recognized climate scientists to ensure both its scientific credibility and its political neutrality. The panel set up three working groups, one each on available scientific information on climate change, environmental and socioeconomic impacts of climate change, and formulation of response strategies. Again, to ensure political neutrality as well as to draw on national research resources, the chair of the first working group was from the United Kingdom, the second from the Soviet Union, and the third from the United States.

The IPCC reported to the second World Climate Conference in 1990, where the assembled scientists called on politicians to do something. The General Assembly, in Resolution A/45/212, noted the findings of the IPCC and decided to initiate negotiations for an effective framework convention on climate change, which was to be completed prior to the UN Conference on Environment and Development in June 1992. That conference, called the Earth Summit, had been convened on the occasion of the twentieth anniversary of the Stockholm conference. The resolution requested that the head of the ad hoc secretariat of the negotiations cooperate closely with the IPCC to ensure that the panel could respond to the needs and requests for objective scientific and technical advice during the negotiating process. In the negotiation the work of the IPCC had to be taken into account, in particular the paper on legal measures.

Michael Zammit Cutajar, a long-time career official of the UN from Malta, was appointed to head the secretariat. An economist by training, Zammit Cutajar's career had been mostly associated with UNCTAD but had also involved work with UNEP. His appointment reflected the importance of economics and development in the debates on climate change.

The FCCC was negotiated quickly and was opened for signatures in June 1992 at the Earth Summit in Rio. It entered into force two years later. One reason that the process went quickly was the scientific consensus that human behavior could change the global climate. The main reason, however, was that as a framework convention the FCCC was limited to general principles and norms rather than details, whose negotiation would have been difficult. The convention established the Conference of Parties as its supreme body and tasked it to reach subsequent agreements on how to address global warming.

The FCCC also formally set up a permanent secretariat unit to support the convention, located in Bonn, Germany, and headed by Zammit Cutajar. The secretariat was able to draw on the work of the IPCC, which continued its review of scientific evidence. The secretariat was structured to be able to provide support to an extensive negotiations process. By 2005, in addition to a unit to service the meetings of the conference, the secretariat had specialist units dealing with, respectively, (1) methods, inventories, and science, including methodological work, compiling data on climate, and providing links with the scientific bodies concerned; (2) the integration of climate-change concerns into the sustainable development priorities and programs of the parties; and (3) support for the further development and implementation of the three mechanisms under the Kyoto Protocol—the clean development mechanism, joint implementation, and emissions trading—and for activities implemented jointly under the pilot phase.

By the third conference, which took place in 1997 in Kyoto, Japan, there was broad agreement that climate change should be addressed by limiting the emission of greenhouse gases, primarily in industrialized countries. This would be reflected in a protocol to the FCCC. The negotiations on this were difficult and turned on a combination of political and scientific factors. Developing countries argued that they should be exempted from the targets on the grounds that compliance would retard their development and, in any case, they were not the major polluters. This was the political dimension. The scientific dimension was determining what reduction meant in practical terms. This included determining emission levels in 1990, the target year, and the extent to which natural phenomena called sinks would affect national targets.[2] There were no agreed facts on the extent to which the effort to reduce emissions would affect the economies of the developed countries. Based on fears that the effect would be negative on the US economy, the US Congress passed a resolution stating that it would not ratify the Kyoto Protocol. Because the details of how to implement the protocol were vague, subsequent negotiations were necessary before states were willing to ratify.

The Kyoto Protocol would only come into force when states accounting for 55 percent of the total carbon dioxide emissions for 1990 had ratified. With the United States refusing to ratify, the minimum was reached only in 2005, when the Russian Federation ratified. The period covered by the protocol is 2008 to 2012, at which point it will have to be renegotiated. The conference in Montreal in November 2005 began that process, which continues, supported by the FCCC secretariat.

Verification of Disarmament

Disarmament was one of the original purposes of the United Nations. Constructing a working disarmament regime, however, has not been easy. One area where progress has been made, although not steadily, has been in verification of the elimination of weapons of mass destruction, defined as nuclear, chemical, and biological weapons. The construction of a regime began in 1955, when, under the heading of peaceful uses of atomic energy, the establishment of the IAEA was negotiated. The motivation was the fear that nuclear weapons would proliferate from those states that had already acquired them to other states. The nature of the Cold War, however, meant that the issue had to be placed into a larger context of peaceful uses. This also reflected an understanding, which began to emerge as the number of developing countries grew, that states who had no direct interest in a subject (nuclear weapons or nuclear power) because they did not have the elements, should be given a reason to join the organization.

The IAEA had come into existence in 1957 and had begun its work in different areas (nuclear safety, applications, and nuclear energy). Its safeguards program was designed to help ensure that nuclear materials and technologies were not diverted to non-peaceful means. The Chinese detonation of a nuclear weapon impelled the United States and the Soviet Union to reach an international agreement to prevent proliferation. Starting in 1962 the NPT was negotiated through the Conference on Disarmament. There were a number of problems, but, as Bunn summarizes the process:

In the compromise, the United States gave up on the multilateral force; the Soviets gave up on a prohibition against U.S.

deployment of nuclear weapons in West Germany (and other allied countries), provided the weapons remained under sole control of U.S. personnel. The non-nuclear-weapon states were asked to accept draft language which prohibited them from having nuclear weapons and which called for the IAEA to be permitted to carry out inspections to guarantee that their nuclear programs were limited to peaceful uses. In addition, the United Kingdom, the Soviet Union, and the United States agreed to provide assistance to non-nuclear-weapon NPT members in their pursuit of peaceful uses of nuclear energy and agreed to conduct future negotiations to halt the nuclear arms race and reduce their nuclear weapons with the goal of achieving nuclear disarmament. (Bunn 2003, 4)

The treaty assigned the IAEA the responsibility for carrying out inspections and otherwise verifying that the terms of the convention, which was signed in 1968 and entered into force in 1970, were being met. The treaty established the role of the IAEA Safeguards Department as the public-sector body responsible for assuring that any violations by states of their obligations under the convention were detected.

The 1991 Gulf War provoked a major advance in the international regime for verifying the elimination of weapons of mass destruction. The historical use of chemical and biological weapons by the Saddam Hussein government in Iraq and fears that they could be used again prompted agreement on the Convention on the Prohibition of the Development, Production, Stockpiling and Use of Chemical Weapons and on Their Destruction in 1994, and the consequent establishment of a secretariat verification organization, the Organisation for the Prohibition of Chemical Weapons. The convention is extremely detailed and has made major demands on the new organization. A second consequence of the Gulf War was an increase in efforts to negotiate a verification protocol to the Convention on the Prohibition, Production and Stockpiling of Bacteriological (Biological) and Toxin Weapons and Their Destruction, which lacked a verification organization. A protocol was almost agreed upon, but the incoming Bush administration in 2001 essentially stopped the effort.

The development of a verification regime increased the responsibility and authority of the IAEA. In the course of inspections after the end of the Gulf War, the agency discovered that the Iraq government, which had a declared nuclear program that had regularly been inspected, also had an undeclared program. Starting in 1988 the Safeguards Department within the IAEA became convinced that its procedures were inadequate to detect an undeclared program and were even limited for declared programs, primarily because there were limits on the use of remote sensing and on unannounced inspections.

Faced with criticism that it had not detected the Iraqi undeclared program, the agency proposed to strengthen the safeguards agreements that it was to reach with states parties to the NPT. After several years of debate the IAEA board of governors agreed to establish "enhanced safeguards" and to request that states party to the NPT accept them. As described in depth in Andemicael and Mathiason (2005), the process involved a constructive dialogue between the IAEA secretariat and the governments on what was desirable and possible.

The role of the IAEA and the temporary UNMOVIC in the period before the 2003 United States invasion of Iraq demonstrated the changed role of the organizations undertaking verification. Charged with inspecting Iraq for weapons of mass destruction, both Mohammed ElBaradei of IAEA and Hans Blix of UNMOVIC concluded that there was no evidence of such weapons or weapons programs. On the basis of this, many members of the Security Council decided not to support the United States and its allies in the war with Iraq.

While efforts to establish a verification organization for the biological weapons convention are on hold, there are indications that the process of negotiation will start again soon.

Drug Lords, Thugs, Terrorists, War Criminals, and Other Not Nice People

The growth of international drug trafficking, organized crime, and terrorism, all of which require multinational cooperation to combat, has led to an increase in international agreements to address key elements of these problems, mostly since 1991. To this list must be added war criminals, who, after a gap of almost fifty years from the Nuremberg and Tokyo tribunals in 1946 to the International

Criminal Tribunal for the former Yugoslavia in 1993, are now dealt with by an international regime.

Control of illicit drugs was one of the first functions assigned to modern international organizations. The League of Nations Opium Control Board morphed into the International Narcotics Control Board, and the Division of Narcotic Drugs was established in Geneva to deal with broader aspects of the problem by supporting a United Nations Commission on Narcotic Drugs. During the physical reorganization of the secretariat in 1979, when offices were moved from New York and Geneva to Vienna, the UN drug-control secretariat was moved. At the same time, in order to assist national governments implement an international strategy and policies for drug control, the UN Fund for Drug Control was established in 1981, funded from voluntary sources. The largest contributor to the fund was Italy, and an Italian national was appointed to head the organization, also located in Vienna.

Since the narcotics control board had the treaty-based responsibility for setting the amount of licit narcotic drugs to be produced in a given year,[3] the rudiments of an international regime already existed. However, although the Single Convention on Narcotic Drugs mandated states parties to combat drug trafficking through international cooperation to deter and discourage drug traffickers, it lacked specific measures to be taken.

International drug trafficking grew in scale over the intervening years, and in 1987 an International Conference on Drug Abuse and Illicit Trafficking was organized to dramatize the problem and to reach consensus on actions to be taken. The secretary-general of the conference was Tamar Oppenheimer, a career secretariat official from Canada who had started her career in the Division on Human Rights. She was convinced that crime and drug trafficking needed to be dealt with together. The conference mandated the negotiation of a third international drug convention, which took place very quickly compared to other regimes, a feature that has characterized most of the subsequent crime-and-drug conventions. Unlike previous conventions, the 1988 Convention against the Illicit Traffic in Narcotic Drugs and Psychotropic Substances provides for comprehensive measures against drug trafficking, including provisions against money laundering and the diversion of precursor chemicals. It provides for international cooperation through, for example, extradition of drug traffickers and transfer of proceedings.

The most important breakthrough was in terms of money laundering. However, no formal mechanisms were established to counter this, although groups of countries have worked out informal networking arrangements to deal with the problem (Benning 2001).

The agreements led to an expansion of what has become the UN Office on Drugs and Crime. One of its main functions is to support treaty implementation. Its creation reflected the idea that drugs and crime were related and led to an expansion of the international regime to deal with crime.

The original UN mandate in the area of crime had come from a League of Nations convention on the treatment of prisoners as well as an early UN concern with juvenile delinquency. These had been embodied in a series of international congresses on the prevention of crime and the treatment of offenders that have taken place at five-year intervals since 1955. These conferences, in addition to providing a vehicle for police and justice officials to exchange information, had reached normative agreements (such as the United Nations Standard Rules for the Treatment of Offenders). However, in the present period, the nature of international crime has led the governments to negotiate and adopt a series of conventions on organized crime and terrorism, both of which are classified as falling within the remit of the Office on Drugs and Crime.

By 2000, the UN Convention against Transnational Organized Crime had been adopted; it entered into force in September 2003. The convention deals with activities through which organized crime functions, like money laundering and corruption. It sets the legal basis for formal cooperation. The convention has three supplemental protocols, negotiated separately because of difficulties in getting complete acceptance from all parties to the larger convention. These deal with trafficking in persons, especially women and children; smuggling migrants by land, air, and sea; and illicit manufacturing of and trafficking in firearms, their components, and ammunition.

Terrorism, although still not formally defined, has been addressed in a sequence of twelve international conventions, each adopted after a major event. These include conventions related to aviation and shipping, all of which involve international jurisdiction, attacks against diplomats and international officials, hostage-taking, and similar activities. The support of these conventions, most of which have not involved standing verification machinery, has also been given to the Office on Drugs and Crime. A comprehensive convention on terrorism will define both the concept and the international responsibilities, from which additional tasks will be given to the secretariat.

An international criminal tribunal was established in February 1993 by the United Nations Security Council as a result of "continuing reports of widespread violations of international humanitarian law occurring within the territory of the former Yugoslavia, including reports of mass killings and the continuance of the practice of 'ethnic cleansing'" and the council's determination "to put an end to such crimes and to take effective measures to bring to justice the persons who are responsible for them" (Resolution 808 (1993)). The International Criminal Tribunal for the Former Yugoslavia was established in the Hague and has, on an increasing basis, been prosecuting persons accused of crimes who would not have been prosecuted in national tribunals. The processes and precedents have been worked out by the tribunal's secretariat, which has been headed by eminent jurists like Louise Arbour, who became high commissioner for human rights, and Carla Ponti.

In November 1994, in the wake of the Rwanda genocide, the Security Council decided to establish a second international tribunal with "the sole purpose of prosecuting persons responsible for genocide and other serious violations of international humanitarian law committed in the territory of Rwanda and Rwandan citizens responsible for genocide and other such violations committed in the territory of neighbouring States, between 1 January 1994 and 31 December 1994" (Resolution 955 (1994)). The International Criminal Tribunal for Rwanda was established in Arusha, Tanzania, the following year.

Both of these tribunals were invested with judges and prosecutors as well as facilities, all financed with special assessments. Many governments saw that crimes going beyond national boundaries were likely to increase and that, rather than creating ad hoc tribunals whenever a new situation emerged, it was time to develop an international judicial mechanism. The International Court of Justice, established in 1945, deals exclusively with juridical issues between states; there was no mechanism to deal with individuals other than national courts. The experience of both the former Yugoslavia and Rwanda showed that there would be cases where the prosecution of criminals would exceed the capacity of national courts, either because of problems of jurisdiction or willingness of national courts to try the cases.

In 1998 a negotiating conference in Rome adopted the Statute of the International Criminal Court, to be established in the Hague. Most countries ratified the statute. The major exception was the United States, which, under the George W. Bush administration, even sought to withdraw the country's initial signature to the treaty. Nevertheless, the statute entered into force in July 2002, and the court is now functioning. Three situations (Democratic Congo, Uganda, and the Darfur Region of the Sudan) have been referred to it. The international criminal justice regime is likely to grow as more transnational crimes are referred to it.

NOTES

[1] The abstentions were the United Kingdom, the Federal Republic of Germany, Belgium, the Netherlands, Luxembourg, Italy, Spain, Thailand, and the Soviet Union and its allies, with the exception of Romania.

[2] A sink is a phenomenon like new forest growth that absorbs carbon dioxide naturally.

[3] The board's responsibilities were set out in the Single Convention on Narcotic Drugs, 1961, and the Convention on Psychotropic Substances, 1971. These superseded earlier treaties going back to the beginning of the twentieth century.

5

• • • • • • •

How Information Is Mobilized

> *"Minister," said Humphrey in his most injured tones, "you said you wanted the administration figures reduced, didn't you?"*
>
> *"Yes," I agreed.*
>
> *"So we reduced them."*
>
> *Dimly I began to perceive what he was saying. "But . . . you only reduced the figures, not the actual number of administrators!"*
>
> *Sir Humphrey furrowed his brow. "Of course."*
>
> *"Well," I explained patiently, "that was not what I meant."*
>
> *Sir Humphrey was pained. "Well really, Minister, we are not mind-readers. You said reduce the figures, so we reduced the figures."*
>
> —THE COMPLETE YES MINISTER, 178

The international system is fueled by information. Trade patterns, exchange rates, population projections, migration rates, life expectancy, and employment figures are all data needed by private corporations, governments, universities, and even individuals in order to make policy or personal decisions. Moreover, we need analysis about what this information means, so that we can deal with present problems and anticipate future ones. Information for the international system needs to be comparable, and the conclusions drawn from it need to be credible and neutral. *Neutral* in this sense means that the methods used to collect, analyze, and present the information have to be technically sound and balanced in terms of alternative explanations.

Mobilizing this kind of information has been a major and growing task of international secretariats. This is not exciting work, but it probably contributes more to effective governance than the more newsworthy functions of the international public sector.

One of the significant achievements of the League of Nations was to bring together leading economists to examine international trends and provide policy recommendations. The League became a focus for the collection of economic statistics. Leading economists of the inter-war period, including Gottfried Haberler, Bertil Ohlin, and Jan Tinbergen, were on the League staff and were significant contributors to economic theory and to the development of postwar trade policy (Howson 2004).

One of the first functional commissions of the UN Economic and Social Council was the Statistical Commission, which was set up to harmonize standards for the collection of statistics. During the Mohican generation the economic and social statistical series started under the League and the ILO were moved to the United Nations proper, and the Statistical Division was set up in the secretariat. As the regional economic commissions were established, they too began to recruit economists and statisticians. In the Economic Commission for Latin America, Raúl Prebisch was beginning to explore the nature of trade in the postwar world. Hans Singer was beginning to develop the discipline of development economics. The role of the early United Nations as a center for thinking on development economics was profound. Emmerij, Jolly, and Weiss point out:

> From the point of view of intellectual history, it is important to note that ten Nobel laureates in economics (Jan Tinbergen, Ragnar Frisch, Gunnar Myrdal, Wassily Leontief, James E. Meade, W. Arthur Lewis, Richard Stone, Lawrence Klein, Theodore W. Schultz and Amartya Sen) have spent a substantial part of their professional lives working as UN staff

members and/or consultants contributing to the UN's ideas and activities. (Emmerij, Jolly, and Weiss 2005, 222)

As each of the specialized agencies was established, it undertook the task of collecting and publishing statistics in its areas of operations: education and media statistics (UNESCO), health statistics (WHO). In 1924 the ILO took over a survey that had been undertaken by the British government to collect statistics on wages and food prices in sixteen capitals with the aim of comparing the levels of real wages. When the ILO became a specialized agency, this was revised and continued as a regular activity (Young 2003). The IMF started operations in mid-1947, and by mid-1948 it had produced the first issue of *International Financial Statistics*. The first *Balance of Payments Yearbook* was issued a year later.

Social and economic policy analysis, based on statistics and other data, became a staple to help international secretariats form the basis for intergovernmental decision-making on policy matters. In developed countries this function was performed by national governmental institutions or academic centers, but for developing countries the international secretariats often became the place where ideas were developed and propagated. At the initiative mostly of developing countries in the new organization, a number of regional economic commissions were established—in Asia, the Pacific, and Latin America. The Economic Commission for Latin America (later the Economic Commission for Latin America and the Caribbean) was founded at the initiative of Hernan Santa Cruz, the Chilean permanent representative (and later assistant director-general of the FAO). It became a major focus for policy analysis in that region under the leadership of Raúl Prebisch, an Argentinian economist. The prestige of the institution, the uncertainty of government or academic employment, and United Nations salaries enabled the secretariat to recruit from among the best economists and sociologists (Pollock, Kerner, and Love 2001).

Although policy directions were formally made by intergovernmental negotiations at the secretariat's governing body meetings, an analysis of the decision-making process showed that the main actors in developing agreements were the technicians of the secretariat (Mathiason 1972).

During the period 1960–75 the leadership role of regional economic commissions like the Economic Commission for Latin America and the Caribbean continued and was expanded to new institutions. When UNCTAD was created in 1966, it was specifically tasked to play a leadership role in the area of trade. The appointment of Raúl Prebisch as the first UNCTAD secretary-general reinforced this role.

In 1971 a largely unnoticed event took place that had an effect on the willingness of the United Nations Secretariat to provide provocative policy analysis. The background to this event went back a number of years, during which time one of the publications of the United Nations in the social field had been the "Report on the World Social Situation." This report had been prepared by the Division for Social Development (or its predecessors) since 1951, as part of a concern to provide a holistic view of social aspects of development, in contrast to an economic-only perspective.[1] The report was seen in the Third Committee of the General Assembly (economic reports are examined in the Second Committee).

The secretariat report was a deadly dull description of what was presumed to be happening in the world, mostly based on official reports. It had two parts: the first described regional developments, and the second, sectoral developments. It was long, dense, and bureaucratic in tone, and it is not likely that many people actually read it. However, from 1968 there had been significant political unrest in the United States and Europe. It seemed that major social and political changes were taking place, and the secretariat staff drafting the report tried to reflect these development in sections of the report. However, the secretariat also tried to be politically cautious, and, since many of the Eastern European staff members who saw the draft were on secondment from their governments, they commented on the draft from their perspectives. As a result, the draft was more critical of those countries that were more open to criticism than of those that were not.

The report, cleared and issued in the name of the secretary-general, had been reviewed by the Commission for Social Development and by the Economic and Social Council, although the review of the latter was perfunctory. Normally, the debates in the General Assembly would focus on issues rather than on the document itself. However, in 1971 the United States representative to the Third

Committee was Daniel Patrick Moynihan, a well-known social scientist. Moynihan read the report, was incensed, and protested sharply. As he recounts in *A Dangerous Place:*

> Having spent much of my years as a graduate student read-
> ing the procès verbaux of committees of the League, I had
> settled comfortably into the work of the Third Committee of
> the UN, when the Report on the World Social Situation came
> my way. The Report had begun some years earlier as a sur-
> vey of "social development" in the developing nations, and
> in time was extended to the whole membership. The draft
> now submitted to us for final approval had been three years
> in the making, the subject of a succession of conferences in
> the pleasanter parts of Europe and of endlessly circulated
> drafts, the whole presided over by a Finnish member of the
> secretariat reporting to the Finnish chairman of the Third
> Committee. The result was a totalitarian tract. The nations of
> the world were assessed in terms of social well-being. The
> measure of social well-being was the presence or absence of
> dissent. The presence of dissent indicated the absence of so-
> cial well-being. Czechoslovakia came out as just about top
> country. The situation in the United Stales seemed criminal.
> (Moynihan 1978, 12)

The secretariat staff members who had drafted the report were shocked. The director of the Social Development Division, Kurt Jansson, wrote a letter to the *New York Times* defending the report, mostly on the grounds that it had been extensively reviewed. In-side the secretariat there was some sense that part of Moynihan's critique was accurate. At the management level there was clearly a fear of future criticism of the report, and, in a reorganization that was related to the appointment of the first female assistant secretary-general and the creation of a Centre for Social Develop-ment and Humanitarian Affairs, the section responsible for the report was moved from the Social Development Division to the Centre for Development Planning, Projections, and Policies, which was concerned with the preparation of economic surveys, and was considerably more conservative. The next "Report of the World Social Situation" was much more economic in orientation and made an effort to be purely descriptive. Although prepared in 1974, the report was not reviewed by the General Assembly until 1976, and the review was perfunctory. The experience meant that secretariat policy research on social aspects of development essentially stagnated. In fact, social policy analysis only really resumed with the UNDP *Human Development Report.*

The information publications issued by the secretariats of international organizations have become more important. Drawing on a combination of official statistics, information obtained in the course of development activities (especially for the World Bank and UNDP), and the large number of seminars and expert groups that are organized by most international organizations, these reports have become a major source of development thinking. To a large extent this is because the reports reflect the consensus among the professional communities about the nature of the world and the social and economic changes occurring in it. The first, and still most important, of these is the *World Development Report.*

Part of the approach taken by Robert McNamera to make the World Bank a leader of the development process at the international level led him, with the encouragement of his senior staff, to place the World Bank at the forefront of the development debate. The World Bank had begun to acquire considerable statistics of its own, not all based on official national statistics, through its connections with ministries of finance and central banks. At the same time the policy analysis of the United Nations itself had become less adventuresome and more reflective of agreements made by governments. McNamara authorized the World Bank staff to prepare the *World Development Report* and expressed his vision in the introduction to the first edition in 1978:

> The World Development Report, 1978, along with its statistical annex, is the first of what we expect will be a series of annual reports providing a comprehensive assessment of the global development issues. . . .
> . . . Whatever the uncertainties of the future, governments have to act. They are faced with the necessity of daily decisions. And hence the quality of the information and the range of available choices on which those decisions will have to be made become critically important.
> That is why we have undertaken this analysis. The World Bank, with its broad-based membership, its long experience,

and its daily involvement with the development problems of its members, is in a unique position to analyze the interrelationships between the principal components of the development process. To the extent that these are more clearly understood, the institution itself, and all of its member governments individually, will be able to cooperate more effectively in accelerating economic growth and reducing the intolerable deprivations of massive poverty.

There were two novelties in the WDR, as it came to be called. First, it was issued as a report of the president of the World Bank, not of its intergovernmental management, the board of governors. It was clearly presented as the view of the World Bank staff, who were identified as individuals in the introduction. The first version was drafted by D. C. Rao, later director of the International Economics Department, under the direction of Ernest Stern, the World Bank's senior vice president for policy. Subsequent editions were prepared by teams led by senior World Bank staff. Second, the report drew heavily on and presented statistics that allowed comparison both among countries and over time.

Table 5–1 shows the subjects that the WDRs have covered since 1978.

The WDR has continued to be a forum that lays out issues in terms of the World Bank's goals. The shift in subject matter, from external to internal factors (corruption, good governance), suggests the changes in development thinking. If the first period focused on internal policies and the second and third focused on external policies, the present development period returns to the matter of national policies and institutions.

The success of the WDR, published commercially by Oxford University Press, led other organizations of the United Nations system to create their own reports. UNICEF, for example, began to issue *The State of the World's Children* in 1980.

The United Nations system continued to collect and publish statistics. However, increasingly these were used, following the World Bank model, to provide the factual basis for advocacy. One area where this became an important tool was in advancement of women.

In 1988, UNICEF, the United Nations Population Fund, the United Nations Statistical Division, and the United Nations Division for

Table 5-1. Subjects Covered in the *World Development Report*, 1978–2005

Year	Subject
2005	A Better Investment Climate for Everyone
2004	Making Services Work for Poor People
2003	Sustainable Development in a Dynamic World
2002	Building Institutions for Markets
2000–2001	Attacking Poverty
1999–2000	Entering the Twenty-first Century
1998–1999	Knowledge for Development
1997	The State in a Changing World
1996	From Plan to Market
1995	Workers in an Integrating World
1994	Infrastructure for Development
1993	Investing in Health
1992	Development and the Environment
1991	The Challenge of Development
1990	Poverty
1989	Financial Systems and Development
1988	Public Finance in Development
1987	Industrialization and Foreign Trade
1986	Trade and Pricing Policies in World Agriculture
1985	International Capital and Economic Development
1984	Population Change and Development
1983	Management in Development
1982	Agriculture and Economic Development
1981	National and International Adjustment
1980	Poverty and Human Development

the Advancement of Women agreed to undertake the preparation of a major statistical study of the position of women relative to men over time (see Mathiason 2001, 156–59). Called *The World's Women: Trends and Statistics,* the project had its origins in two different prior developments. First, the UN Statistical Division at the time was headed by William Seltzer, a career UN official who had been in charge of social statistics. He had several professionals on his staff, like Joann Vanek, who were innovators in the field of gender statistics. As part of the follow up to the Nairobi Conference on Women, the Statistical Division had a created a database of gender statistics. The Division for the Advancement of Women had begun to use these in its analysis.

At the same time, *The State of the World's Children* was being supervised by UNICEF's deputy executive director, Richard Jolly. Jolly had come to UNICEF in 1982 from academia. He had been director of Sussex University's Institute for Development Studies. He was interested in finding ways to make social statistics, such as those being used in UN publications, more popular and accessible, based on the model of the annual publication of the United Kingdom Statistical Office *Social Trends,* which had been in existence since 1970. The problem was that in many areas international statistics were not available on a consistent basis.

Whenever progress reports on international conferences or plans of action were requested, the main secretariat tool was to send a questionnaire to governments. As the number of conferences and plans of action had proliferated, governments felt increasingly burdened. One alternative was to base the reviews on UN statistics.

The process for *The World's Women* included assembling and analyzing the series, but also finding editors that could make the result more interesting, both stylistically and graphically. While the publication was not completed until 1991, it became the best-selling United Nations publication in history and was only out-sold by its successive versions in 1995 (for the fourth Conference on Women) and 2000 (for the fifth anniversary of the Beijing Conference on Women).[2]

While *The World's Women* was initially designed to be part of a series on social trends, its success led to its continuation as a sequence of reports used for policy purposes. The existence of credible statistics to show changes (or not) in the situation of women relative to men was used extensively as an advocacy tool.

While both the WDR and *The World's Women* compared countries, they did so only on individual statistics. A qualitative change occurred with the first publication of the *Human Development Report* by UNDP in 1990. The report was an initiative by Mahbub Ul-Haq, who had been a vice president of the World Bank. He believed that a means of encouraging countries to adopt sound development policies was to show where they stood relative to other countries. The key feature of the *Human Development Report* was a composite index constructed from key economic and social indicators. This permitted states to be ranked by human development scores. The report became immediately controversial because countries were not used to being rated without their consent by international secretariats.

The fact that it was not even issued in the name of the administrator of the UNDP demonstrated that it was a secretariat product. Instead, it was issued, as the UNDP website states, as "an independent report . . . commissioned by the United Nations Development Programme (UNDP) and is the product of a selected team of leading scholars, development practitioners and members of the Human Development Report Office of UNDP."

UNDP staff have prepared the *Human Development Report* annually. Under the leadership of Ul-Haq and then Richard Jolly (who moved over from UNICEF), the reports continued their policy of rating national performance by a standard index. These were often accompanied by national or regional seminars to explore the reasons for low ratings, which served as a catalyst for policy changes in many governments. One notable case was the issuance, in 2004, of a *Human Development Report* for the Arab region that was considered to be very critical. In order to maintain governmental support for the *Human Development Report*, UNDP now organizes regular briefings for governments about preparations.

With the creation of the WTO, the role of UNCTAD as a source of information about trade and trade issues increased. By design, the WTO did not envisage a research capacity, so UNCTAD, which was already responsible for collecting and processing global trade statistics, has had its role as a shaper of policy increased. Its annual *Trade and Development Report* and the *World Investment Report* provide a factual basis for many countries seeking to integrate with the global trading and investment system. The first is prepared just in advance of the annual meeting of the Trade and Development Board and is intended to shape policy discussions there.

NOTES

[1] The first issue, "Preliminary Report on the World Social Situation" (UN publication, sales no. 52.IV.11), was fairly influential in shaping the UN social agenda at the time. A policy-oriented supplement followed in 1955, and full reports were issued in 1961 and 1967.

[2] No update of the statistics was prepared for 2005. Instead, a methodological report was issued, "The World's Women 2005: Progress in Statistics," with updated statistics in an annex.

6

· · · · · · ·

Norm Enforcement

Human Rights,
Weapons of Mass Destruction,
War Crimes, and Trade Disputes

"Minister, Government isn't about morality."

"Really? Then what is it about?"

"It is about stability. Keeping things going, preventing anarchy, stopping society from falling to bits. Still being here tomorrow."

"But what for?" I asked.... What is the ultimate purpose of Government, if it isn't for doing good?"

"Government isn't about good and evil, it's only about order and chaos."

—*THE COMPLETE YES MINISTER*, 454

If international governance is to work, the norms that states have agreed to follow need to be enforced. Over sixty years the international public sector has developed means—imperfect as they are—to provide incentives to states to comply with their obligations. In an increasing number of regimes the responsibility

for norm enforcement has been given to international secretariats, a change from earlier practice. In a purely Westphalian system international norms should be self-enforcing. States that are
party to multilateral treaties are expected to act themselves to ensure compliance from fellow states parties. Fear of reprisals from
other states is expected to deter a given state from violating obligations that it has taken on. Enforcement is based on the kind of
global "shaming"; the good opinion of others is an incentive for
compliance.

When the United Nations was established, self-enforcement was
built into its institutions. The only type of coercive power available to international organizations was that which was established
under Chapter 7 of the Charter, by which the Security Council can
authorize states to use military force to deal with a threat to the
peace, breach of the peace, or an act of aggression. This force has
been used with increasing frequency in recent years, including
punishing Iraq for its invasion of Kuwait in 1991; authorizing the
Economic Community of West African States to reverse a coup
d'etat in Sierra Leone; authorizing NATO to use force in Bosnia
and Kosovo; and authorizing Australia to lead an international
force to reestablish order and permit independence in East Timor.
Enforcement of early disarmament treaties, like the Biological and
Toxin Weapons Convention, was based on state challenges that
were referred to the Security Council.

The International Court of Justice, established under the Charter, also follows the model of self-enforcement. The court receives
and rules on disputes between states over the interpretation of
their obligations under existing treaties. However, once a judgment is entered, it is for the states concerned to enforce it.

Over the past fifteen years new institutions have been established or older institutions strengthened in ways that have given
international secretariats an increasing role in norm enforcement.
This includes a role in fact-finding in the context of threats to peace
and security, managing an international criminal court system,
adjudicating trade and other disputes, and verifying the elimination of weapons of mass destruction. Each of these cases illustrates how the secretariat role is evolving, but before examining
each, the conditions that are necessary for that role to be played
need to be examined.

CONDITIONS NECESSARY
FOR EFFECTIVE NORM ENFORCEMENT

Norm enforcement is related to the final stages of regime creation, an agreement about the procedures to be followed in ensuring that rules are followed. Three conditions can be proposed for effective norm enforcement. First, the regime has to be truly agreed in the sense that states parties to the agreement really intend for it to govern their actions. Second, the rules and procedures set out in the treaties have to be practical in the sense that they can be implemented within the existing resources of states. Finally, secretariats must be given the political and resource tools to be able to undertake enforcement.

Condition 1:
The Regime Is Truly Agreed

The underlying basis for the norms obviously has to be solid. Regimes are created by the states parties (with the assistance of relevant non-state actors) who perceive that their individual interests can best be served by an international agreement. States must fully intend to implement the provisions of the agreement and the agreement has to be one to which states will continue to adhere, even if governments change.

For most current regimes this condition has been met. However, the experience of the NPT, which allows for withdrawal of states after a six-week notification, and the bilateral anti-ballistic missile treaty suggests that instability is possible. An additional factor in stability is the number of states that do not become party and therefore, in effect, do not agree with the regime. The fact that the United States is party to less than half of the human rights conventions clearly weakens that regime. The absence of a verification mechanism for the Biological and Toxin Weapons Convention weakens that regime. And the fact that the United States is not party to the Rome Convention establishing the International Criminal Court will, over time, weaken that regime.

The agreement on the GATT that led to the formation of the WTO has so far held steady. Stable trade relations based on increasing trade flows are agreed to be essential for development, and so far the total positive consequences of the regime have outweighed the issues that have led to disagreements and permitted the dispute-resolution system to function.

Similarly, the consequences of unregulated use of the seas and oceans are considered sufficiently bad that the regime's adjudication processes are functioning, even though the United States is not yet a party to the United Nations Convention on the Law of the Sea.

There is agreement that international action is needed to prevent the proliferation of nuclear weapons.

Condition 2:
The Underlying Treaties Are Practical

While it would be difficult to reach agreement on a convention that was not practical, often this aspect is worked out as the treaty comes into force. What appeared workable when the treaty was negotiated, particularly in terms of verification of compliance, may have problems later. For example, there were serious problems with the Chemical Weapons Convention when initial understandings about inspections and how they were to be financed turned out to be inadequate. Similarly, interpretation of provisions of the NPT has not been as clear or consistent as had been hoped.

Most regimes have practical procedures, even if they are not always implemented. The role of the monitoring bodies for human rights is clear, as are the state obligations to report periodically. Many states have had problems meeting the schedule, in part because of delays in consideration of national reports, and in part because it has been difficult for some states to allocate the resources necessary to prepare reports.

In contrast, the dispute-resolution system established under the GATT has worked well because it is practical. Each state has the option of claiming that other states are not complying, and a procedure is in place that allows agreeable adjudication of the dispute. A similar situation exists with regard to the Law of the Sea Tribunal.

Condition 3:
A Credible International Secretariat Is in Place

Increasingly regimes are designed to have an international secretariat perform coordination, verification, and revision functions. This recognizes that international agreements, on the whole, can no longer be effectively self-enforcing. Earlier conventions assumed that states were headed by "gentlemen" who would respect their obligations. In the current world, history has shown that not all states are run by "gentlemen" or that, if they are, other "gentlemen" will not necessarily recognize the fact.

Most international agreements now make provision for an implementing secretariat. These can include an existing organization that is given additional responsibilities, as when the World Intellectual Property Organization undertook to implement the Internet conventions. It can involve a change and expansion in an existing secretariat, as when the GATT secretariat became the WTO. It can also include a completely new secretariat established specifically for the convention, as was the case with the Comprehensive Nuclear Test Ban Treaty Organisation, Organisation for the Prohibition of Chemical Weapons, the UN Framework Convention secretariat, and the prosecutor and registrars offices for the International Criminal Court. For these secretariats to be effective in norm enforcement, they must be credible.

The foundation of legitimate power at the international level is that the secretariat, as the arbitrator of whether states are in compliance with their obligations, is believed by the states parties to be politically neutral, technically competent, and, in general, obeys the rules that set it up. This bureaucratic authority is the basis of secretariat norm enforcement. Moreover, the secretariats become credible advocates for the norms. Barnett and Finnemore state:

> Having established rules and norms, IOs [international organizations] are eager to spread the benefits of their expertise and often act as conveyor belts for the transmission of norms and models of good political behavior. There is nothing accidental or unintended about this role. Officials in IOs often insist that part of their mission is to spread, inculcate, and enforce global values and norms. They are the missionaries of our

time. Armed with a notion of progress, an idea of how to create the better life, and some understanding of the conversion-process, many IO staff have as their stated purpose to shape state action by establishing best practices and by articulating and transmitting norms that define what constitutes acceptable and legitimate state behavior. (Barnett and Finnemore 2004, 33)

For a number of regimes the secretariat has credibility because of its history. For example, the Office of the High Commissioner for Human Rights, first as the Human Rights Division, later as the Centre for Human Rights, has been in business for fifty years. Its staff members are considered competent and neutral. Now that the position of high commissioner has been established, and depending on the actions of the incumbent, the office can have credible leadership, and any of its judgments about compliance will be given credence.

As secretariats acquire experience, their credibility grows. The WTO secretariat's credibility has been increasing as the dispute resolution system evolves and is perceived by all parties to be fair. The secretariat of the International Tribunal for the Law of the Sea is also considered credible. Its initial staff was drawn from officials like Kumar Chitty, its first registrar, who were involved in the negotiations from the beginning.

In the area of verification of obligations regarding weapons of mass destruction, the Safeguards Department of the IAEA has proven its effectiveness over a forty-year period, especially in the inspections of Iraq after the first Gulf War, in the denuclearization of South Africa, in verifying North Korean compliance with the NPT, in inspections preceding the second Gulf War, and in the disputes about the Iranian nuclear program.

TOOLS IN NORM ENFORCEMENT

By joining regimes states have undertaken to comply with the obligations that the treaties to which they are party specify. In the early days of the United Nations these were expected to be self-enforcing. States that had problems with the compliance of other states would act, by diplomatic pressure, trade retaliation, immigration restrictions, and other actions that were within the capacity of the individual state. As international relations have become more interdependent and complex, determining whether states are in compliance or not can no longer be left to the judgment of individual states, whose neutrality and competence are questionable.

The new approach to norm enforcement emphasizes the creation of institutions to verify state compliance and to provide a structure for resolving disputes. The secretariats of these institutions will determine their effectiveness and use a number of tools: fact-finding, constructive dialogue, judicial mechanisms, and dispute-resolution processes.

Fact-finding

The one explicit power of the United Nations secretary-general, to bring to the attention of the Security Council threats to peace and security, has led to the growth of fact-finding in potential conflict situations by secretariat officials. Most often, these are missions by special representatives of the secretary-general. Often they are part of the exercise of the secretary-general's "good offices," which are part of "preventive diplomacy," as the Agenda for Peace calls it.

A recent case is the mission sent by the United Nations to investigate the assassination of the former prime minister of Lebanon, Rafik Hariri. Because of the political situation in the Middle East, a neutral investigation was required, and the secretary-general, under Security Council authorization, appointed Detlev Mehlis of Germany as the commissioner of the UN investigation commission. Mehlis was a prosecutor in the German judicial system. He began the mission, supported by secretariat staff, in May 2005 and was expected to complete his investigation in October 2005. As the *New York Times* reported on September 17, 2005:

> In Beirut, Mr. Mehlis is piecing together the myriad scraps of evidence, hundreds of witness statements and mounds of intelligence to answer a fundamental question still dogging Lebanon: who really killed Mr. Hariri? More manager than hands-on detective, he oversees a team of 100 investigators

who produce evidence that is shared with Lebanese judges and prosecutors, who then take legal action.

The investigative team interviewed over three hundred people as it began to narrow down responsibility. As an immediate consequence of his investigation, four senior Lebanese officials were charged with the assassination. Mehlis was chosen because of his national experience and his nationality, although he was not a career international official. He was supported by career officials. For example, the administrative head of his mission was Keith Walton, a recently retired career staff member from the United Kingdom with extensive experience in humanitarian and political missions as well as in UN management.

The fact-finding power was also used in Iraq. After the first Gulf War, when it was believed that the Iraqi government had been clandestinely developing weapons of mass destruction, the IAEA and the United Nations Special Commission had undertaken to find and destroy those weapons and to make the programs nonfunctional. The monitoring programs had been suspended in 1998, but a new organization, the UNMOVIC, had been established, headed by the former director-general of the IAEA, Hans Blix. When the United States and others questioned whether the Saddam Hussein government was restarting the banned programs, UNMOVIC and the IAEA were tasked with determining, factually, whether the programs had been reconstituted. Although the time was very short, the two organizations undertook rigorous inspections and concluded that there was no evidence that the programs were being reconstituted. While the United States and its allies still invaded Iraq, the inspection results kept enough members of the Security Council from supporting the invasion that no mandate was given.

What were the factors that led to the IAEA's success? There are many, some unique to the nuclear field and others more general. Among the unique factors are that no alternative organization developed to deal with nuclear issues, and as peaceful use of nuclear power became less popular, the institution's secretariat became the center of an epistemic community. A nuclear expert resident in one of the countries where nuclear power was on the decline could find employment at the IAEA.

Among the more general factors is the development of a career corps of safeguards inspectors who provided a professional cadre of civil servants to perform a function that no other organization could undertake. When the IAEA was established, it was assumed that safeguards inspectors would come from the military or intelligence services of the nuclear powers. As the agency matured, however, it became clear that inspectors had to be drawn from non-nuclear countries as well and that the agency would have to train them. The Safeguards Department developed its own training program, which guaranteed both the professionalism and the neutrality of the inspectors. While the agency was established with a strict rotation principle for staff (the normal assignment was to be three years, extendable to five, with an absolute maximum of seven years), staff of the Safeguards Department were frequently exempted from this provision, since most had no alternative employment options in their countries. Over time, this created a career service.

The matter of leadership continuity was also important, as were the styles of the last three (of four) directors-general. The agency also took a longer-term approach to promoting international agreements, including a process of organizational learning that led to the development of and agreement on expanded safeguards that significantly strengthened the agency role.

Concern for elimination of weapons of mass destruction will lead to significant increases in the international role, which is now more public than it has been at any time, and will provide challenges for the current and new international organizations dealing with verification.

The ability to find facts credibly is determined by the qualifications—both professional and in terms of nationality—of the head of mission and by the quality of the staff. The secretary-general's representatives are inevitably from countries considered to be neutral in a given situation. Over time, career officials increasingly have a variety of experiences that permit them to support the fact-finding effort with skill.

Constructive Dialogue and Shaming

Of all the regimes that have been created, the regime dealing with human rights has been the most problematic. While the conventions were expected to be self-enforcing, they each included a provision for monitoring by independent committees. Composed of experts elected by the states parties but serving in their individual capacities, the various committees include the Human Rights Committee (International Covenant on Civil and Political Rights), Economic, Social and Cultural Rights Committee (International Covenant on Economic, Social and Cultural Rights), Committee on the Elimination of Racial Discrimination, Committee against Torture, Committee on the Elimination of Discrimination against Women, the Committee on the Rights of the Child, and the Committee on Migrant Workers.

Each state party to a convention agreed to submit an initial report on the steps it had taken to meet its obligations and then to submit periodic updates. The monitoring committee reviews the report in a public session. When a report is considered, national officials and the committee experts engage in "constructive dialogue" by posing questions to the state making the presentation in order to determine those areas where the state's performance could be improved. On the basis of the dialogue, the committee makes comments and recommendations to the state party to be taken into account in future implementation. The committee can also prepare general comments, based on its review of many state reports, on the meaning of the treaty provisions in practice. This form of judicial interpretation assists states in interpreting their obligations.

In the process of reviewing reports NGOs provide information to the monitoring committees to help shape the questions to be posed, often in the form of alternative reports.

The enforcement mechanism is based on a form of "shaming," in which the weaknesses in state compliance are publicly available to both the citizens of the country and to other states. This spotlight of legitimacy is intended to provide an inducement to states to adjust their policies and practices to conform to the terms of the convention.

The role of the secretariat—the Office of the United Nations High Commissioner for Human Rights for all except the women's convention—in this function is formally passive. It organizes the meetings, receives and translates the reports, helps the committee prepare its comments, and finalizes the formal committee report for publication. The secretariat edits and translates the reports as official documents. It also sends comments and information provided by NGOs to the experts.

The main secretariat role is to ensure the transparency of the process, in part by providing public information. The secretariat staff members who support the expert committees provide the institutional memory that allows the committees to retain their neutrality. They ensure that rules are followed, both by reporting countries and by committee experts. They are repositories of information about precedent. They can help prevent the experts from making conclusions and recommendations not based on the facts presented. They also help facilitate participation by civil society organizations.

Support of the human rights processes requires both background and experience. For example, support to the Committee on the Elimination of Discrimination against Women from 1996 to 2004 was provided by Jane Connors, an Australian expert on human rights law who was chief of the Women's Rights Unit of the Division for the Advancement of Women. Connors was a recognized expert on, among other things, violence against women. She oversaw the expansion of the committee's work, including the arrangements for implementing a complaint procedure. She then went on to perform the same function for other human rights committees under the jurisdiction of the Office of the United Nations High Commissioner for Human Rights.

The secretariat performs other functions as well. The basis of the review system is the periodic report of states parties. Both the Office of the High Commissioner for Human Rights and the Division for the Advancement of Women undertook advisory missions and organized training for national officials in how to prepare periodic reports. The effectiveness of the review system at the national level is based on access by national NGOs to the results of the constructive dialogue. These are formally reported in United Nations documents as well as in press summaries. In earlier times these documents were largely inaccessible, but now the Internet makes almost instant communication possible. The secretariat maintains the websites on which the information is found.

For most of the first fifty years of the United Nations, the secretariat worked to remain invisible, working through the expert committees, the Commission on Human Rights, and the system of special rapporteurs. While this protected the secretariat, it meant that it could not act on violations of human rights. This problem was addressed when the post of high commissioner for human rights was established after the World Conference on Human Rights in 1992. The post had been initially proposed by John Humphrey in 1963 to give a political face to the secretariat work. José Ayala-Lasso, the first incumbent in the post, graded at the under-secretary-general level, was a cautious diplomat who did not press issues of compliance. However, Mary Robinson from Ireland soon replaced him. As the former Irish head of state and a known human rights lawyer, she was able to speak authoritatively about human rights violations, and she did so. She established the precedent that the secretariat, rather than governments, could speak about the extent to which states were in compliance with their obligations. Mary Robinson was critical of United States policies and actions after the Iraq War, especially regarding the use of torture, and this was clearly one of the factors that kept her from being reappointed. Her style has been continued, nonetheless, by Louise Arbour of Canada, who became high commissioner in 2004 after serving as the chief prosecutor in several war-crimes tribunals.

An International Judicial System

As the international legal system built around treaties has evolved, new international judicial mechanisms have been developed to supplement national enforcement of international norms, particularly in the area of humanitarian law. This includes such issues as war crimes and, soon, terrorism, where national means have been found wanting.

Prior to the late 1990s international prosecution of war criminals, who were not easily dealt with by national means, had been very episodic. The Nuremburg and Tokyo trials after World War II had been essentially ad hoc in nature and were only nominally international. They were undertaken by the victorious allies against personnel of defeated countries. Subsequently, persons charged with war crimes and other violations of humanitarian law were tried by national courts.

The United Nations War Crimes Commission, which was established in 1943 to oversee the collection of information and prosecution of war criminals, undertook an examination of the Nuremberg trials and other prosecutions of German and Japanese war criminals with a view to determining the general rules. The staff studies began a process of defining both war crimes and crimes against humanity (Meron 1998, 467 n. 25). However, this was not followed up until many years later.

Events in the former Yugoslavia and Rwanda, and later Sierra Leone, showed that the existing system did not function well when states broke apart or administration of justice failed. The role of courts in achieving closure based on a sense that justice has been done has become part of post-conflict peacebuilding. National courts would be seen as being engaged in acts of vengeance and would not be considered legitimate by all parties, while international courts could make judgments considered to be fair.

The judges, prosecutors, and investigators of the International Criminal Tribunal for the Former Yugoslavia have been able to prosecute war criminals from all of the states of the former Yugoslavia. This provides a form of balance. The power of the tribunal, however, was demonstrated most clearly when the chief prosecutor, Carla Ponti, was given the authority to determine whether Croatia (and eventually Serbia) had complied with the court as a prerequisite for being considered for membership in the European Union.

The first modern war-crimes tribunals were temporary and episodic. They, however, led to the creation of a standing body with a permanent secretariat, many of whose members were drawn from the temporary tribunals. The International Criminal Court, whose headquarters is in the Hague, was established to prosecute any major violator of international humanitarian law that had escaped prosecution by national authorities. The premise is that a neutral juridical institution would make prosecution both fair and inevitable.

The first use of the court has been in the context of the humanitarian crisis in the Darfur region of western Sudan, where the Security Council requested that the court investigate and prosecute leaders of the militias that were causing people to flee from their homes and were attacking refugee camps and international relief officials. Even though the United States had strongly opposed the International Criminal Court, it was compelled to agree to its jurisdiction in this case.

The credibility of the temporary courts, as well as the new permanent court, will depend on the perceived competence and neutrality of its senior officials—the judges, prosecutors, registrars, and investigators.

Dispute-resolution Mechanisms

In the original design of the international system, the International Court of Justice was expected to resolve disputes about obligations taken on by parties to various conventions. Most conventions, whether in the human rights area, disarmament, or the environment, have a dispute-resolution clause, giving that authority to the court. In practice, this provision has been used very infrequently and, increasingly, states have formally opted out of International Court of Justice jurisdiction. The United States, for example, opted out of the court mechanism when it lost a case in which Nicaragua—under the Sandinista government—accused the United States of seeking to overthrow its government by force. The result of the case, Military and Paramilitary Activities in and against Nicaragua *(Nicaragua v. United States of America)*, was that the United States recused itself from all jurisdiction of the court.[1] The largest single source of reservations on human rights treaties is the article on dispute resolution, suggesting that many states do not wish that mechanism to be used against them.

The development of more complex regimes, however, has required states to find alternative dispute-resolution mechanisms. The United Nations Convention on the Law of the Sea established the International Tribunal for the Law of the Sea, headquartered in Hamburg, Germany, with the responsibility for adjudicating disputes about boundaries of exclusive economic zones and territorial seas, as well as disputes about interpretation of different provisions. It has already considered a number of cases, with some success.

The most influential institution, and one that is being used as a precedent, is the dispute resolution mechanism created by the GATT and located in the WTO. When the WTO was established, it had essentially two functions: to negotiate further agreements, and to provide for compliance review of existing agreements. For general compliance review, a subsidiary body of the General Council called the Trade Policy Review Body was established to function somewhat like a monitoring committee of a human rights treaty. More important is the Disputes Settlement Body, designed to mediate disagreements about the application of the treaty provisions by states. There is a three-stage mechanism. First, states, with the facilitation of the WTO or directly, can seek to solve the dispute themselves or with the assistance of a third party. This method is similar to practice that was current before the international structure was present. If that fails, consultations can be arranged. In these consultations, on request, the WTO secretariat can provide good offices, conciliation, and mediation services. Finally, if these do not resolve the dispute, a panel is established consisting of neutral experts proposed by the secretariat from a list of experts that it maintains. The experts must be agreeable to both parties. The panel is presented with evidence, including that provided by both sides in the dispute, and makes a determination. If a party is not satisfied with the result, it can appeal the decision to the Appellate Body. This is a permanent group of seven experts in trade issues and trade law in charge of reviewing the legal aspects of the reports issued by panels.

As of September 2005 there were 333 disputes. By 2003 fifty-one had been resolved and thirty-nine settled outside (for a completion rate of about 38 percent).

The importance of the secretariat in maintaining the system, which has survived and prospered even though some major trading powers, like the United States, have lost cases, is clear. The WTO secretariat:

- guards the norms established under the GATT;
- sets agenda and vets facts;
- services meetings;
- develops new norms through analysis of law and decisions; and
- maintains surveillance of trade trends.

THE SECRETARIAT ROLE IN NORM ENFORCEMENT

The role of norm enforcement among international secretariats is clearly increasing. As more regimes are created and institutions established to manage them, monitoring and verification of state compliance, as well as institutionally based dispute resolution, will clearly become more important. Secretariat roles in implementing the enforcement tools are clear, if not particularly visible. One factor in the successful implementation of international norm enforcement will be the ability of the secretariats to maintain the confidence of both states and civil society in their competence and integrity.

NOTE

[1] For the case summary, see the International Court of Justice website.

7
● ● ● ● ● ● ●

Providing Services
for Peace and Security

*"To put it absolutely bluntly, Minister, confidential investiga-
tions have revealed the existence of certain documents
whose provenance is currently unestablished, but whose
effect if realised would be to create a cabinet vacancy and
precipitate a by-election."*

I didn't know what he meant. I asked him.

"You are on a death list, Minister."

—The Complete Yes Minister, 215

Peace and security operations are the most visible and dramatic of all services provided by international secretariats. They
are men in uniform, weapons, cease-fire negotiations, and, too
often, tragedy, all in situations of armed conflict. This is the most
public face of the United Nations, the space where the non-sovereign secretariats interact most tangibly with the system of sovereign states. The number and type of peace and security operations
have evolved over the past sixty years. Within that evolution, the
role of the secretariats has grown in scale and complexity. While
initially there was only one service provided—peacekeeping—
there are now several, including services to deal with terrorism, a
new challenge for the international public sector.

CHAPTER VII OPERATIONS

The UN Charter assumed that the main method for achieving peace and security was the combined action of states on the basis of decisions of the Security Council. It made no real provision for the types of peacekeeping operations that are now common. Chapter VII of the Charter states: "The Security Council shall determine the existence of any threat to the peace, breach of the peace, or act of aggression and shall make recommendations, or decide what measures shall be taken . . . to maintain or restore international peace and security" (Article 38). It then specifies a sequence of steps, culminating in authorizing states, individually or in combination, to utilize armed force.

The ineffectiveness of this provision was demonstrated when it was first used, in 1950 in Korea, and it has seldom been used since. Chapter VII of the Charter was invoked when the Democratic People's Republic of Korea suddenly invaded the Republic of Korea in June 1950. The Cold War was fully under way, and the Soviet Union, one of the permanent members of the Security Council, had been boycotting its sessions since January to protest that the seat for China had not been given to the government in Beijing. By General Assembly Resolution 116 (II) the United Nations had established the Commission on Korea in October 1947 to provide for reunification; the country had been occupied after the war by the Soviet Union and the United States. The commission, therefore, was in a position to state factually whether an invasion of the South by the North had taken place, and did so. In short order the Security Council, in Resolution 86 (with only Yugoslavia voting against), authorized members of the United Nations to "furnish such assistance to the Republic of Korea as may be necessary to repel the armed attack and to restore international peace and security in the area."

The role of the secretariat in this process was minimal. As Urquhart recalls:

> In any case, after the initial proceedings in the Security Council, in which the United States rushed through a decision for the UN to intervene with force before the USSR woke up to

what was happening, the United States was designated as the Unified Command for the operation and took full control. The UN had little or nothing to do with the military action. (Urquhart 1987, 120)

The Cold War prevented any subsequent Chapter VII operations until 1991, when the post–Cold War Security Council authorized a coalition of states to reverse Iraq's invasion of Kuwait. Another case was Australia's intervention in East Timor in September 1999 to stop violence. However, when the United States and the United Kingdom sought a resolution to place their invasion of Iraq under Chapter VII provision, they failed. A subsequent effort to use Chapter VII in connection with Iran's nuclear program similarly failed.

One consequence of the weakness of Chapter VII was the development of alternative means that depended more on the work of the international public sector than on national initiatives.

PEACEKEEPING

Peacekeeping emerged in the early years of the United Nations as an extension of the traditional means of halting conflict by interposing a force between two combatants to certify that cease fires were being maintained and withdrawals accomplished. The two original operations interposed military observers between combatants in Israel and in Kashmir.

The Charter envisaged two approaches to dealing with peace and security: Chapter VI defined the peaceful-resolution/good-offices function of the work of the Security Council, into which the secretary-general would feed. Chapter VII defined peace enforcement by member states under Security Council authorizations. Both were quickly tried. During this period humanitarian relief was largely connected with these conflicts.

The most visible early use of Chapter VI was in the Arab-Israeli conflicts that accompanied the creation of Israel under United Nations auspices. Mediators appointed by the secretary-general from the secretariat played a key role and won Ralph Bunche the Nobel Peace Prize. Bunche was himself a Mohican. He had been a political scientist who joined the US Department of State during

World War II. After the war, in 1946, he was tapped by Lie to become head of the Trusteeship Department. The temporary resolution of the Arab-Israeli war led to two additional service operations. The truce brokered by Bunche was supervised by the first peacekeeping operation, the United Nations Truce Supervision Organization, set up in 1948 and still in existence.

The UN Truce Supervision Organization was followed in quick succession by the United Nations Military Observer Group in India and Pakistan. The partition of India and Pakistan in 1948 included a dispute about the border between the two countries in Kashmir. As part of the truce that ended hostilities (brokered by a United Nations commission on India and Pakistan), a military observer group was established in July 1949. The group was made up of unarmed observers from neutral countries that would be stationed between the warring parties and would monitor compliance with the terms of the cease fire. This group, like the UN Truce Supervision Organization, is still in existence and both are now funded from the assessed budget of the organization.

The two groups were extensions of practices that could be traced back to the nineteenth century and were in that sense not unusual. They were also somewhat passive; observers were usually unarmed, and if they noted something untoward, they would report it and withdraw.

Subsequent operations, of which there have been approximately forty, have been built at least in part on the assumption that the peacekeeping role is one of providing a buffer between competing forces. The first of these set the pattern for this type of operation.

The British-French-Israeli invasion of Egypt to secure the Suez Canal led to the establishment of the first real peacekeeping operation, called the United Nations Emergency Force. The UN had been involved in the Arab-Israeli issue since 1947. While the origins were complex, the operation itself set precedents for subsequent operations. The Security Council was unable to agree on steps to deal with the situation because two permanent members (the United Kingdom and France) were parties to the conflict, so the authority passed to the General Assembly.

In order to separate the combatants (and then extricate the French and British expeditionary forces), the UN Secretariat proposed to the governments the idea of a large multinational military contingent. The secretariat played the key role in determining how to implement the peacekeeping, through a report by the secretary-general. Several concepts were agreed as set out in the secretary-general's second report, dated November 6, 1956.

First, the commander should be appointed by the United Nations itself and in his functions should be responsible ultimately to the General Assembly and/or the Security Council. His authority should be so defined as to make him fully independent of the policies of any one nation, and his relations to the secretary-general should correspond to those of the chief of staff of UNTSO (A/3302, para. 4). The force commander would recruit the other officers for his staff, rather than having them named by member states.

Second, the force should be recruited from member states who are not permanent members of the Security Council. In this context the secretary-general observed that the question of the composition of the staff and contingents should not be subject to agreement by the parties involved because such a requirement would be difficult to reconcile with the development of the international force along the course already being followed by the General Assembly.

The force should have no rights other than those necessary for the execution of its functions, in cooperation with local authorities. It is more than an observer corps, but in no way a military force temporarily controlling the territory in which it is stationed; nor should the force have functions exceeding those necessary to secure peaceful conditions, on the assumption that the parties to the conflict will take all necessary steps for compliance with the recommendations of the General Assembly.

An important concept that was presented and decided (and was then followed for military contingents in all subsequent peacekeeping operations) was expressed in paragraph 14 of the report:

> General experience seems to indicate that it is desirable that countries participating in the force should provide self-contained units in order to avoid the loss of time and efficiency which is unavoidable when new units are set up through joining together small groups of different nationalities.

This established the precedent of peacekeeping forces being made up of national contingents that, as will be seen, can be independent of United Nations command and control.

How the force should be financed required further study. A basic rule, which could be applied provisionally, would be that a state providing a unit would be responsible for all costs of equipment and salaries, while all other costs should be financed by the United Nations outside its normal budget. It was obviously impossible to make any estimate of the costs without knowledge of the size of the force and the length of its assignment.

Within three weeks the secretary-general prepared another report (A/3383), which contained several principles. First, the funding for each peacekeeping operation would be separate from the general budget and would be placed in a special account. Second, the funding would be for short periods but renewable as required. Third, the financing would be based on the normal assessment of member states. Fourth, in addition to direct costs, the United Nations would finance the foreign exchange costs of national participation.

For most of the next fifty years this approach was used in a multitude of peacekeeping operations involving different states. This fundamental concept was expressed by Urquhart in his meditation on the 1973 Yom Kippur War:

> Much of my career at the United Nations was involved in peacekeeping, especially in the Middle East. Peacekeeping depends on the non-use of force and on political symbolism. It is the projection of the principle of non-violence onto the military plane. It requires discipline, initiative, objectivity, and leadership, as well as ceaseless supervision and political direction. It takes time to develop the full effectiveness of a peacekeeping operation and to secure the confidence and cooperation of the conflicting parties with which it is dealing. (Urquhart 1987, 248)

This presumption was clearly tested in the Congo and was retested in subsequent operations such as Bosnia and Herzegovina, Somalia, Rwanda, Sierra Leone and Liberia, where the combatants were parties in civil war. Inevitably armed conflicts become international responsibilities because states determine that they are, usually through the Security Council. This aspect is still realist politics, but what has changed is that the management of the peacekeeping (and other elements) depends on the skill and re-sources of the secretariats.

ONUC set the precedent for many subsequent peacekeeping operations. It was the first United Nations peacekeeping opera-tion that was linked to the emergence of newly independent de-veloping countries, and one that led to the death of the secretary-general and to the second great United Nations finan-cial crisis. It created a network of secretariat staff members whose bonds had been created in peacekeeping service.

The facts of ONUC are well known.[1] The Republic of the Congo became independent from Belgium on June 30, 1960, and was clearly unprepared for independence. The Belgians had not estab-lished either the necessary military or civil infrastructure, unlike the British or French in Africa, and shortly after the independence celebration violence broke out. The Belgian government sent its troops back to contain the mutiny of the Congolese troops. UN Secretary-General Dag Hammarskjöld decided to invoke Article 99 and bring the matter to the Security Council. Because neither the United States nor the Soviet Union wanted to take the lead on dealing with the problem, which would have set a precedent for future situations, Hammarskjöld was able to persuade the Secu-rity Council that the United Nations was the only alternative.

With very little planning (there was no contingency planning in the secretariat at the time) the Congo operation began. It in-volved bringing in national military contingents, using airlift ca-pacity from the United States (mostly) and the Soviet Union (some), reestablishing services and trying to reestablish political order. It included a major mobilization of UN system agencies. As Brian Urquhart, who was sent to the Congo at the outset, recalls:

We brought in all sorts of people: we brought in air control-lers through ICAO, we brought in doctors from WHO, UNICEF took on the emergency food supply—in fact they overdid it; they acquired about 70 times as much food as the Congolese could possibly eat. It was amazing. One could hardly move in Leopoldville for stocks of emergency food, but that was finally stopped. We had to clear Matadi [the main port], which General Wheeler did. We had to try to get the Belgians out, which was an enormous problem entailing endless negotiations with the Belgian soldiers and the Ambassador. We had to deploy the Force in order to give a pretext for the Belgians to leave, and that was a complication because there wasn't any headquarters. We were just bringing people in. It was a completely virgin country as far as that was concerned; there wasn't anything there at all. (Urquhart 1984a, 9–10)

The Congo operation lasted from 1960 to 1964 and was the first that could be called an operation in a failed state. As such, it should have produced a number of lessons for the future. It is not clear whether lessons were learned, at least formally, since there was no official history written about the operation. In part this was because Hammarskjöld, who had risked the UN's prestige to undertake the operation, was killed in an airplane crash in September 1961. In part it was because the operation involved peacekeeping (in the sense of interposing United Nations forces between warring parties), peace enforcement (putting down the Katanga rebellion), and what would now be called post-conflict rehabilitation, and these were not consolidated. And no one was assigned to write the history.

While the initial mandate of the Security Council was more or less straightforward, the major powers soon entered into conflict, which significantly damaged the secretariat. At the 1960 General Assembly the Soviet Union attacked Hammarskjöld personally and tried to replace the secretary-generalship with a troika (three executive heads, one each from West, East, and South). Other major contributors, at different times, opposed the secretary-general.

Urquhart remembers:

The uproar created a tremendous trauma in the UN generally, because it divided the Organization completely down the middle. It wasn't just the Russians and the West; the African Group was divided, the non-aligned Group was divided, everybody was divided. Everybody was very discontented with the Congo Operation, nobody knew what to do. We were stuck with going on with it, because if we pulled out at that point what was just a horrible situation would have become a blood-bath. There is no question of it. Hammarskjöld was completely stuck with this, and it was a terrible situation. I think it took a great toll on him; he became extremely irascible, extremely emotional, on this subject—I think with good reason—and it really was a very gloomy time. It was pretty awful. (Urquhart 1984a, 25)

In terms of peacekeeping, ONUC demonstrated some of the problems that using national contingents could produce. Many of the contingents were African, and some of the African leaders took sides in the internal conflicts in the country. For example, the Ghanaian battalion, under orders from Kwame Nkrumah, the country's president, sided with the pro-Lumumba faction. Command and control were problems, as they were later in other operations. But perhaps the longest-lasting lesson was that the United Nations had great difficulties using military force in a peacekeeping mission.

For the secretariat it was somewhat exhilarating, at least at first. Urquhart recalls:

What was very interesting about it—to me, at any rate—was that that was the only two months in my whole nearly 40 years here when the secretariat was actually running something entirely without interference, because nobody was anywhere near it, nobody would get in because they were too frightened, and we just had to do what we thought was right and couldn't even get instructions, because nobody told us what to do. (Urquhart 1984a, 12)

There were problems of staffing. The operation quickly depleted existing United Nations staff and new staff had to be recruited for mission service. Some were very good, some not. Urquhart has very strong views that some of the senior appointments made were unfortunate.

The issue of finance was always a problem. The operation was mandated by the Security Council, but as it developed, the Soviet Union and several other major contributors began to have problems with it and began to withhold funding. The scale of the operation meant that the financial implications were, relative to previous United Nations undertakings, high. The United States, as the largest contributor to the budget, was supportive, but others were not.

Eventually, with the level of conflict reduced, U Thant decided to recommend terminating the operation. No similar operation was attempted for some fifteen years, although UNEF-type peacekeeping did continue. For many, the Congo operation was a failure, although the secretariat staff concerned did not share that view. Urquhart concludes: "My view is that it was a remarkable effort which deserved to succeed better than it did and in fact did succeed quite a bit. And I doubt if we shall ever do anything like that again" (Urquhart 1984b, 26). He was, of course, wrong in his prediction.

In the 1992 Agenda for Peace, Boutros-Ghali specified five types of peace and security activities. Of these, all but one, peace enforcement, make demands on the secretariat to provide services. The activities include providing mediators and fact-finders, organizing troop contingents, and coordinating relief and development activities in conflict situations.

One of the success stories of the 1980s was the operation in Namibia. If the Congo provided bad examples to the Secretariat, the Namibia operation provided good ones that have been used in successive complex emergencies.

There were two secretariat elements to the peacekeeping operations of the 1980s. First, the secretariat organized the missions: identifying troop contingents and observers, providing them with minimal equipment (UN identification and communications equipment[2]), and securing their transport to the operation site. Once there, United Nations civilian personnel would provide administrative support and act as liaison with local authorities. Cedric Thornberry, the administrative deputy in the Namibia operation, characterizes this in the following way:

> In the 'Good Old Days', pre-1989, peacekeeping was relatively simple, and was organized and run by a handful of people in the atmosphere of a multi-national gentlemen's club somewhere in the world's northwestern quadrant. (Thornberry 1997, 377)

The Security Council, sometimes at the initiative of the secretary-general, would ask the secretary-general to report on the possibilities and practicalities of the new operation, a report prepared by a small office of the under-secretary-general for special political affairs. The office would bring together the various management units concerned, make an estimate of requirements, and, once approved, roll the requirements through the normal program and budget process.

The second element involved the overall management of the operation. Increasingly, the authority for an operation would be given to a special or personal representative of the secretary-general, who would normally be the person responsible for finding a political solution to the problem that had led to the peacekeeping operation in the first place. While these were sometimes drawn from member states diplomats, increasingly they were drawn from secretariat staff. For example, a Central American operation was under the responsibility of Alvaro de Soto, who, while having started as a Peruvian diplomat, had become a senior UN staff member.

The United Nations Transitional Advisory Group for Namibia (UNTAG) was the most important and successful operation of its time. Some of the political circumstances were unique to Namibia, but the ways in which the organization was managed were applied to subsequent missions.

Namibia (as Southwest Africa) had been a League of Nations mandate that had passed to the United Nations. It had been administered by South Africa since the end of World War I, but as South Africa's apartheid policy had continued, the mandate had been revoked by the General Assembly in 1966 and the United Nations itself took on the responsibility.[3] In 1973 the post of commissioner for Namibia was established, and in 1977 Martti Ahtisaari, who had been Finland's ambassador to Tanzania, was appointed to the post. It was hoped that progress could be made toward transferring authority from South Africa to a new Namibian government. Negotiations took place among members of the Security Council, the government of South Africa, and neighboring governments. A round of proximity talks, held in New York in February 1978, produced the "Proposal for a Settlement of the Namibian Situation," which, on April 10, 1978, was presented to the president of the Security Council.

The proposal, which was adopted by the Security Council in Resolution 435,

contained a negotiated compromise. Described as a "working arrangement" which would "in no way constitute recognition of the legality of the South African presence in and
administration of Namibia", it allowed South Africa,
through an Administrator-General designated by it, to administer elections, but under United Nations supervision
and control exercised through a Special Representative of
the secretary-general, who would be assisted by a "United
Nations Transition Assistance Group" (UNTAG). The Contact Group stated that the Proposal addressed all elements of
resolution 385, but "the key to an internationally acceptable
transition to independence is free elections for the whole of
Namibia as one political entity with an appropriate United
Nations role". All other elements of the Proposal were intended to facilitate this central objective of a democratic exercise in self-determination. (UNTAGFT, n.d.)

Ahtisaari was named special representative and plans were put
in motion for UNTAG, which would involve a complex sequence
of steps that would permit South Africa to withdraw peacefully
and a legitimate government of Namibia to be installed. Unfortunately, South Africa insisted on maintaining part of Namibia as its
territory, and the Namibia issue became intermingled with the
problems of neighboring Angola, which, upon becoming independent, had had a civil war in which the United States and the Soviet Union—through its Cuban ally—had become involved. The
solution to the Namibia question was eventually based on a pack-
age deal, part of which was to establish UNAVEM I, the UN Agnola
Verification Mission, a peacekeeping operation in neighboring
Angola, and part of which was to implement UNTAG.

UNTAG had as complex a mission as had ever been given to a
UN peacekeeping operation. In a country that had no tradition of
democratic government, a system based on racial discrimination,
and both an armed independence movement and a modern military (South Africa), UNTAG was supposed to guarantee a smooth
transition to independence. It did so, and in the process set several key precedents.

UNTAG had both civilian and military elements. The military
aspect was not unlike other peacekeeping operations, in that the

function of observers and contingents was to supervise the disarming or departure of armed elements, both of the independence movement and the South Africans. The civilian element, however, was more innovative.

Some of the civilians would replace South Africans in running the country, while others would work to involve communities in the process. Others from the UNHCR would oversee the repatriation of refugees who had fled the country. For this purpose the country was divided into districts, each of which had a UN office headed by a career civil UN official. In addition, the United Nations would replace the South Africans as the police authority in the country. A civilian police contingent was set up, with UN police recruited from many countries but, unlike the military, serving in mixed units. This set a precedent for using civilian police as part of UN operations.

To supervise the elections, additional UN civilian personnel were brought in. This was the first time that the United Nations provided electoral supervision on this scale.

At its maximum strength, the United Nations deployed 4,493 military, 1,500 civilian police, and fewer than 2,000 international and local staff. The mission was reinforced by approximately 1,000 additional international personnel who came specifically for the elections. In peacekeeping operations before UNTAG, some UN officials were loaned for "mission service" from their regular jobs. UNTAG involved an unprecedented deployment of regular UN staff, drawn from the secretariat, funds and programs, and the specialized agencies. Two lessons were learned: international officials who had been hired for other functions could do very well on political missions such as UNTAG, and the experience of the mission improved their performance in their jobs. The precedent was established to draw on regular staff to provide key personnel for short-term political missions.

Over time, the secretariat has become increasingly adept at the process, although it has had to learn some very difficult lessons. In 2000 the Independent Panel on Peace Operations was convened under the chairmanship of Lakhdar Brahimi to review the lessons (United Nations 2000). The report of the panel has led to significant reform of and improvement in the secretariat's capacity to deliver this critical service. For analytical purposes the process can be broken down into three aspects: planning and design of operations, contracting of troop contingents and other personnel, and day-to-day management of the operations.

Planning and Design

In 1956 a small group of staff together with Dag Hammarskjöld planned the first modern peacekeeping operation. That time is long past. The proposals made by the secretariat to the Security Council now shape the mandate. The proposals can determine the size, composition and cost of the operation, which are significant elements.

More important, these elements determine the rules of engagement and other limitations of the mission. When these are correct and realistic, the mission has a high probability for success, and most of the peace and security operations, particularly those concerning interstate conflict, have been successful. It has taken much longer for the secretariat to cope with planning for intra-state conflicts or failed state conflicts.

The first Somalia operation, which was designed to protect humanitarian relief, did not succeed because it did not take into account the clan-based politics in the country. The most notorious cases, however, were Rwanda and Bosnia-Herzegovina.

The Rwanda genocide is probably the largest failure of peace and security operations in the organization's history, although it is closely followed by Srebrenica. The independent inquiry commission set up to review what went wrong in Rwanda concluded: "The overriding failure in the response of the United Nations before and during the genocide in Rwanda can be summarized as a lack of resources and a lack of will to take on the commitment which would have been necessary to prevent or to stop the genocide" (United Nations 1999b, 30). To a large extent, this was a failure of planning and design. The inquiry (p. 31) found that

the decisions taken with respect to the scope of the initial mandate of UNAMIR were an underlying factor in the failure of the mission to prevent or stop the genocide in Rwanda. The planning process failed to take into account remaining serious tensions which had not been solved in the agreements between the parties. The United Nations mission was predicated on the success of the peace process. There was no fallback, no contingency planning for the eventuality that the peace process did not succeed. (United Nations 1999b, 31)

The dilemma of the secretariat here is clear. In proposing a mission, it had to take into account the external constraints—especially the difficulty in obtaining troop contingents after the previous failure of peacekeeping in Somalia—as well as the internal conditions. A cease fire between warring parties in Rwanda was arranged as a result of a conference in Arusha that had been mediated by the United Nations, where one condition was the establishment of the peacekeeping force. Yet there was little support for a large-scale mission. As a result, the secretariat planners felt that they had to make the most optimistic of assumptions about conditions, which did not turn out to be correct.

International secretariats have increasingly been called upon to plan operations based on optimistic assumptions. Early experience with peacekeeping, when the combatants were states, suggested that the risk of error was not high. But as peacekeeping began to center on failed states, the risks have become increasingly greater. One consequence has been that the secretariat has ·devoted more resources to acquiring accurate information about the situation on the ground.

Another reform, suggested by the Brahimi report, was that peace operations should have clear, consistent, and achievable mandates and that

(a) The Panel recommends that, before the Security Council agrees to implement a ceasefire or peace agreement with a United Nations-led peacekeeping operation, the Council assure itself that the agreement meets threshold conditions, such as consistency with international human rights standards and practicability of specified tasks and timelines;

(b) The Security Council should leave in draft form resolutions authorizing missions with sizeable troop levels until such time as the Secretary-General has firm commitments of troops and other critical mission support elements, including peace-building elements, from member states. (United Nations 2000)

Perhaps more important, the Brahimi report states unequivocally that "(d) The Secretariat must tell the Security Council what it needs to know, not what it wants to hear, when formulating or changing mission mandates."

The planning of operations is complex. While various factors might appear to be similar to foreign-policy decision-making in national governments, they differ in that most of the elements of decision-making are outside the control of the secretariat.

- The parties to the conflict are often unpredictable, particularly when they are competing internal movements or factions.
- The main resources for peace operations—troops—have to be supplied by states who may not be willing to provide them in the number and time required.
- The financing of operations is in the hands of other actors, whose priorities may differ.
- The operations may be linked to other regional issues, as was the case of the various operations in West Africa or in the Rwanda-Congo area.

The secretariat has a number of assets, however. First, the United Nations is usually considered to be neutral by the other parties in the conflict. Neutrality is difficult to maintain. As Urquhart says: "The Secretary General and his representatives, however, have only skill, patience, determination, and their reputation for integrity and fairness" (Urquhart 2004, 4).

Yet, it is precisely their skill and reputation that make the secretariats players. The secretary-general can compose his representatives of individuals that can *prima facie* be considered unaffected by the political outcome, other than the greater good. When the representative is particularly skilled, as was Lakhdar Brahimi in both Afghanistan and Iraq, or Sergio Viera de Mello at one point in Iraq, the organization can forge agreements where it seemed impossible for them to be reached. While these representatives are sometimes drawn from national figures, increasingly they are drawn from the ranks of career officials or individuals that have at one point been officials. A case in point is Martti Ahtisaari, who, after many years service with the United Nations Secretariat, was elected president of Finland. After completing two terms, Ahtisaari undertook a number of conflict-resolution missions for the United Nations and other international organizations, including, in late 2005 in Bosnia-Herzegovina.

In 2005, there were eighty-five special and personal representatives of the secretary-general either in office or being appointed. About half of these were former—usually retired—international civil servants. This testifies to the value of those whose careers were shaped by dealing with the complex external environment.

A second asset is the ability to mobilize balanced information. National governments often rely on their intelligence services as well as the reporting of their diplomatic missions in other countries. In some cases the United Nations availed itself of this information. However, this information normally is either not available or not considered credible (at least for public presentation) by the United Nations. While much information used in the planning of operations comes from the mass media, the existence of UN offices in most countries of the world provides the organization with a source of information on developments. Between the UNDP and the other development agencies of the organization, and NGOs that can provide information to the United Nations that they would be loathe to provide to national governments, the secretariats can, if they want, avail themselves of solid information on internal political developments. The strengthening of this capacity was also one of the recommendations of the Brahimi report.

A third asset is an ability to deploy civilian officials that can help provide stability. This is particularly true of provision of civilian police cadres to help maintain public order. Unlike peacekeeping troops, which are organized into national contingents and may not be either appropriate or trained for police functions, civilian police cadres are directly contracted by the secretariat and obey the political mission of the organization (Smith 2003). While a relatively new element of peace and security operations, use of civilian police has grown dramatically. This element can be important when restoration of public order is a key ingredient to the mission.

A fourth asset is the ability to convey legitimacy to the result of the political process. The United Nations can certify that the formation of governments or changes of constitutions have been done properly and thus strengthen those who have been elected. The function of electoral supervision has grown dramatically over the past years. In Iraq and Afghanistan these activities have been the most important UN contributions to the processes. According to the website of the Electoral Assistance Division on October 2005, since 1989 the United Nations had received over 140 requests for electoral assistance from member states. These were increasingly part of complex political missions.

One of the most public instances of UN electoral experts affecting political processes took place in 2005 in Iraq when the interim parliament passed a change to the electoral law that was perceived as guaranteeing a favorable result in a referendum on a new constitution. The UN electoral experts who were supervising the process rejected the change, and the parliament was forced to reverse its decision.

In addition to career staff that have been involved in the planning and execution of increasing numbers of mission, the secretariat maintains a roster of short-term experts. This allows the secretariat to field a large number of observers, as well as being able to draw on the short-term services of regular staff of organizations of the UN system, following the model pioneered with the Namibia operation.

Contracting

For the military part of peace operations the secretariats act essentially as contractors. They must identify countries that are willing and able to provide troop contingents, arrange for transport and basic equipment (blue berets, helmets, flags, and radios), often provide other essential equipment up to and including armored vehicles, and oversee the performance of the units.

Selecting military for peacekeeping has proven to be a complex task, because peacekeeping places exceptional demands on military personnel. As Urquhart describes it:

A peacekeeping force is like a family friend who has moved into a household stricken by disaster. It must conciliate, console, and discreetly run the household without ever appearing to dominate or usurp the natural rights of those it is helping. There have been times when the peacekeeping function was more like that of an attendant in a lunatic asylum, and the soldiers had to accept abuse and harassment without getting into physical conflict or emotional involvement with the inmates. The feelings and reactions of peacekeepers must be kept under rigid control and must always come second to those of the afflicted. Thus they must often turn the other cheek, and never, except in the most extreme circumstances, use their weapons or shoot their way out of a situation. But they must also be firm and assert their authority in violent situations. (Urquhart 1987, 248)

Confronted in the early days of peacekeeping with military contingents that did not perform well under these circumstances, the secretariat worked to identify militaries that would routinely provide troops and train them for peacekeeping. Both Fiji and Norway, for example, routinely provided troops for the United Nations Interim Force in Lebanon, and Austria provided contingents to the United Nations Force in Cyprus. A system developed where officers could be seconded to the United Nations for planning purposes, creating a network of military personnel with peacekeeping experience.

Maintaining coherence in military operations that involve coordinating self-contained national contingents has always been a challenge. Part of the response has been to establish supplies that provide a UN identity to the contingents, such as communications equipment that works on a common frequency. The United Nations has established a supply base at Brindisi in Italy that is used to provide contingents with basic equipment.

Many of the contingents in UN operations are provided by developing countries like India, Pakistan, Bangladesh, and Malaysia. The contingents must be transported from their home bases to the operational theaters, and it falls to the United Nations to provide this transport, either by contracting private sources or by convincing another country to make its resources available. This has been a major issue in the timely dispatch of UN military forces, because it can take up to a month for a contingent to form and be transported by sea. Contracting aircraft has been one of the areas of procurement that has been controversial. Similarly, the United

Nations must occasionally obtain transportation services from the few militaries that have significant airlift capabilities.

The experience acquired over the past twenty years, however, has enabled the United Nations to develop contacts that allow it to respond quickly. Contracting procedures have gotten smoother, but the problem has continued. In 2000 Kofi Annan characterized it in the following terms:

> Our system for launching United Nations peace operations has sometimes been compared to a volunteer fire department, but that description is too generous. Every time there is a fire, we must first find fire engines and the funds to run them before we can start dousing any flames. (Annan 2000, 49)

The issue of funding is a central one, and secretariat officials often have to find ways to field operations while waiting for the resources to become available. An example of this is the operation in Mozambique.

Two factions, one supported by the apartheid government of South Africa, engaged in a decade-long civil war after the Portuguese abruptly granted independence and left in the late 1970s. When, in 1992, a political settlement became possible, the Security Council authorized a peacekeeping mission that was a combination of military forces and observers, humanitarian assistance and electoral supervision. Called ONUMOZ, the operation took place between 1992 and 1994 and oversaw an end to the civil war, provision of humanitarian relief, and a successful election and transfer of power to a government considered legitimate by all parties. The experience also demonstrated the management difficulties of peacekeeping. Dirk Salomons, who was the senior administrator in ONUMOZ, describes the initial situation in these words:

> The first months of ONUMOZ's presence in Maputo combined elements of surrealistic theater with flashes from a ghastly nightmare. The United Nations own rules and regulations nearly strangled its young. To begin with, ONUMOZ needed money. The $332 million approved by the Security Council had no monetary value. The Budget Division of the Bureau of Administration and Finance had to draw up a

detailed budget according to the United Nations' standard format, detailing every post, every vehicle, every trashcan. This had to go for review to the Advisory Committee on Administrative and Budgetary Questions (ACABQ), which would conduct hearings requiring the presence of key officials, before sending its comments to the Fifth Committee of the General Assembly (responsible for finance and administration). The Fifth Committee would allow the speakers' list to exhaust itself before sending a draft resolution to the General Assembly, which then had to adopt this resolution. This finally happened in March 1993. In the mean time, the secretariat had no authority to spend money on ONUMOZ. Small allocations, however, were made from some hidden reserve to allow a few of us to fly into Maputo and set up shop.

The secretariat was facing immense pressure. It had to staff and equip several missions simultaneously: Cambodia alone required 7,000 civilians, and then there were El Salvador, Angola, Western Sahara, Somalia—plus all the ongoing relics such as Cyprus and the various entities in the Middle East. The same countries that in the Security Council scolded the United Nations for its inadequacies spoke movingly in the Fifth Committee about bloated bureaucracies, and refused to provide the resources to empower the Field Operations Division. The procurement officers who went out of their way to deliver were met by medieval and hostile auditors who questioned their every move. The combination of financial rules and regulations designed for a static bureaucracy and an overburdened and often hounded staff proved to be as serious a threat to the mission as any violation by the parties to the conflict. (Salomons and Dijkzeul 2001)

Eventually the management problems were solved, and ONUMOZ, headed by an Italian career UNDP official, Aldo Aiello, achieved its objectives.

One way that the problem has been addressed recently by both the secretariat and member states has been the development of standby forces. These are troop contingents that can be called upon on short notice in the event a crisis occurs where UN forces can be decisive. As a result of the Brahimi report's recommendations a UN standby arrangements system has been set up whereby states agree to have troops available for deployment on relatively short notice. A more specific effort has been the Multinational Standby High Readiness Brigade for UN operations that was established by the Government of Denmark together with twelve other regular troop contributors. These and other possible initiatives described by Langille (2002) are expanding the capacity of the secretariat to organize a response in crisis situations.

Management

Secretariats have generally provided solid management of peace operations. The day-to-day minutiae of payments, accounting, and inventory control, which in headquarters are matters of routine, become more complex in field situations. Depending on the extent of confusion that attends the operation, many of the normal facilities, like banks, are simply not available. While there have always been minor issues in field missions, the most dramatic probably occurred in 1994 when US$3.9 million cash that had been brought into Somalia to meet the payroll of the UN operation was stolen from a locked filing cabinet. There were several other irregularities in the operation. From that time the Office of Internal Oversight Services has provided auditing and inspection services that have minimized the amount of financial mismanagement in peacekeeping operations. (The Oil-for-Food program, which was related to the larger Iraq operation, was an exception.)

Because various organizations of the UN system have had extensive experience in managing programs, projects and operations in countries with different levels of development infrastructure, the secretariat has always been able to deploy competent staff, even in difficult circumstances. Even when staff and troop contingents were shown to have committed violations of human rights (specifically sexual exploitation), as in the Congo, administrative measures were put into place to prevent recurrence of the problems.

Because their tasks are different, one problem has been conflicts between the special representatives, formally in charge of operations but focused on political aspects, and the force commanders. Both Urquhart (1987) in the Congo and Margaret J. Anstee (1996) in the Angola operation reported problems with the force commanders. The Angola case is particularly instructive.

After the withdrawal of Cuban troops supervised by United Nations forces, a civil war broke out, with the official government, dominated by one ethnic group, fighting a rebel group built on another ethnic group. In order to broker a cease fire and oversee elections, using the model followed in neighboring Namibia, a new peacekeeping operation was authorized.

Margaret Anstee was named to head it, the first woman to head a major peacekeeping operation. The problems of managing an operation in which the peacekeepers were between two internal factions were very complex. Anstee herself had had extensive experience in Africa, having been the UNDP resident representative in Ethiopia and Morocco, but she had never headed a peacekeeping operation. There were problems of coordination with political positions in New York, where the secretary-general, Boutros-Ghali, was himself from Africa. Anstee describes the difficulties in her book and suggested that, together with lack of coordination with the commander of the peacekeeping forces, the lack of agreements undercut the mission (Anstee 1996).

In other operations, like Namibia, relations were better. The key to ensuring good coordination is a common understanding of both the mission and its constraints. It is also a function of experience, which is another argument for having both special representatives and force commanders with prior experience in peacekeeping.

COUNTER-TERRORISM

Peace and security operations during the first sixty years of the organization have involved either disputes between states or within states. In both cases the actors were states (or the presumptive governments of states). By the 1990s the issue of terrorism as a threat to peace had become widespread. The attack by a terrorist group on the United States on September 11, 2001, was the culmination of a series of attacks that had been ongoing for over twenty years. Because terrorism involves non-state actors, the normal methods of state power do not work well against it and, in fact, there has been no formal definition of terrorism. The issue, however, has begun to be addressed by various international conventions, as well as by decisions of the Security Council. In 2004 the

High-Level Panel on Threats, Challenges and Change defined it as "any action . . . that is intended to cause death or serious bodily harm to civilians or non-combatants, when the purpose of such an act, by its nature or context, is to intimidate a population, or to compel a Government or an international organization to do or to abstain from doing any act" (United Nations 2004, 46).

Because international terrorists work essentially without borders, the role for international organizations and their secretariats in dealing with it can be expected to grow. At the present time work relates to developing the regime and to administering those elements that are already agreed.

The Emerging Regime

The existing regime to deal with terrorism includes a number of elements. One is implementation of specific international conventions on specific terrorist acts (such as hijacking aircraft) and on mechanisms of finance (money laundering and other means of providing funding to terrorist groups). Another is to include terrorist groups as targets for actions to prevent the spread of weapons of mass destruction. A third is to reach broader agreements on the definition of terrorism and a comprehensive approach that all states can follow to prevent the spread of terrorist groups.

The focus of implementation activities is the United Nations Office of Drugs and Crime located in Vienna, which uses technical assistance as its main instrument. This office has responsibility for overseeing a series of twelve treaties, the oldest from 1963, that were intended to ensure that states would move against specific types of acts. The treaties did not establish any verification mechanism, or even an institution to coordinate. Because terrorism as currently defined in the United Nations is conducted by non-state actors, it is similar in its etiology to crime; therefore, many of the instruments that are used to deal with transnational crime, such as prohibition of money laundering, which began in the context of drug trafficking, can be applied.

Preventing terrorist groups from obtaining weapons of mass destruction is a clear priority. The IAEA addresses this aspect under its mandate to ensure the security of nuclear materials. Under its nuclear safety program it provides advisory services to evaluate the security of protection of nuclear installations and training services to upgrade national capacities to protect supplies and equipment and prevent terrorists from obtaining them. This has not been easy, particularly in the newly independent states of the former Soviet Union, where nuclear material has not been as carefully guarded as would be expected under existing standards.

The issue of possible proliferation has been present throughout the nuclear era, and opposition to nuclear enrichment and the reuse of nuclear fuel has often been based on fears that this will lead to materials falling into the hands of states or non-state groups that would use them for non-peaceful purposes. This aspect is now tied to a larger issue of nuclear security as reprocessing and enrichment become more important in the larger context of obtaining more green energy.

The IAEA staff is a recognized repository of expertise in this area, and its role is likely to increase in the early decades of the century.

Finally, the Security Council has established the Counter-Terrorism Committee to monitor developments. This committee, working with other committees, is supported by secretariat staff. From that, and from work in the General Assembly, a comprehensive convention against terrorism may emerge and guide further work by the secretariats.

Future Anti-terrorist Institutions

Terrorism is an area of peace and security where the secretariats are indispensable, but where their work will intersect directly with those of states. Whether there will be formal international institutions that will do more than policy research, technical assistance and training, and information exchange has yet to be determined. To a degree, this would be an international version of law enforcement. Existing multinational arrangements like Interpol—the International Criminal Police Organization—are largely based on networks rather than being operational themselves. However, the model of the international judicial system that is evolving may be applied to work against terrorism.

NOTES

[1] For a good description of the facts, see Boulden 2001, chap. 3.

[2] Historically, the United Nations has supplied communications equipment. For reasons of security, most militaries have communications equipment that works only on certain frequencies. Thus, the contingent from one country would have problems communicating with that of another. As a result, the United Nations would provide communications equipment to all contingents. Often, the United Nations also would provide radio operators from its own staff.

[3] For details of the process, see UNTAGFT n.d.

8

• • • • • • •

Providing Humanitarian Relief

From Palestine to Darfur

> *I asked her [his wife] if, quite seriously, she thought I'd been*
> *a success. Or a failure.*
>> *She said: "I think you've done all right."*
>> *"But is that good enough?"*
>> *"I don't know," she said. "Is it?"*
>> *"I don't know," I replied. "Is it?"*
>> *We sat and looked at each other. It's so hard to tell.*
>> *—THE COMPLETE YES MINISTER, 281*

When the United Nations Secretariat was assigned responsibility for coordinating the tsunami relief effort in Asia in December 2004, the largest international relief effort in history, this
confirmed that humanitarian assistance was an international function. The United Nations Secretariat (and the associated programs
like UNICEF, UNDP, UNHCR, and WFP) have gradually acquired
experience in dealing with humanitarian relief in places where traditional nongovernmental or bilateral relief would not be possible,

either because of the political context or because the places do not have enough importance to the donor countries.

There has been increasing recognition that the services provided by the experienced, multinational staffs of UN relief operations are superior to those provided by alternative institutions, especially those of individual states. Three broad categories of services fall under the heading of humanitarian relief: refugees, persons who have been internally displaced within their own countries, and people affected by natural disasters. While they share similarities in terms of the services delivered, each has its own role for international secretariats.

REFUGEES

Before World War I refugees were not considered an international issue. Those who had been forced to flee from their countries had no legal protection, and there was no perceived responsibility to assist them. The large number of refugees as a result of the Russian Revolution and the realignment of state boundaries (especially Germans) had been addressed in the context of the peace conference. Two temporary high commissions, for German refugees and Russian refugees, were established under the leadership of the Norwegian explorer and statesman Fridjof Nansen and placed within the purview of the League. These eventually were consolidated into what was called the Nansen Commission, formed by the League after Nansen's death in 1930.

The logic favoring establishment of an international body to deal with refugees was that states often did not want to accept refugees, in part because of their inability to determine whether they were legitimate refugees or merely migrants and in part because they did not want to provide economic support for them. Refugees were international charges, and the Nansen Commission (and the League) undertook the responsibility for certifying refugees' bona fides, including issuing travel documents (called Nansen passports) for persons who were legally stateless. Economic and social support for refugees until they could be settled in third countries became an international responsibility, first undertaken by the ILO (Henri Reymond was one of the early staff members concerned) and then by the League itself.

The 1951 Convention relating to the Status of Refugees defines a refugee as a person who, "owing to a well-founded fear of being persecuted for reasons of race, religion, nationality, membership of a particular social group, or political opinion, is outside the country of his nationality, and is unable to or, owing to such fear, is unwilling to avail himself of the protection of that country" (Article 1A(2)). Early refugees were found in Europe, and much of the work of providing them with assistance was undertaken by the host governments. In this, the role of the United Nations high commissioner for refugees and predecessor secretariats was to determine whether an individual had refugee status and provide a certain amount of coordination of national actions to provide protection.

Who Is a Refugee?

Under international law, which carries over into national law for the 146 states (as of October 2005) that are party to the 1951 Convention relating to the Status of Refugees or its 1967 protocol, states take on significant responsibilities for refugees that are in their territory.[1] Under the provisions, refugees are able to obtain work permits, social security, housing, and other services. The determination of who is a legitimate refugee has significant implications both for the individual refugee and for the country receiving the refugee.

As the location of refugee flows has moved from developed to developing countries, the issue of status has taken on an additional element. While many refugees are clearly motivated by fear—especially when they are fleeing armed conflict—others may be motivated by economic considerations. Refugee status is seen as a way of migrating to countries having higher-paying employment or other services. These purely economic migrants are specifically excluded from refugee status.

The Office of the United Nations High Commissioner for Refugees has a responsibility under the convention and its protocol for helping determine who is a refugee. The initial role was one of oversight, ensuring that the individual states—who would apply the conventions themselves to determine refugee status—were following the international norms. This included reviewing national legislation and undertaking inspections on request. As the focus of refugee status shifted to developing countries, the UNHCR had to take on a more operational role. UNHCR officials would themselves determine refugee status in initial receiving countries, and this determination would be honored by third countries that accepted the refugees. Whenever a large-scale refugee situation occurs, UNHCR dispatches officers to undertake the determination of refugee status. Under its procedures refugees must come to the UNHCR officials. The UNHCR has developed elaborate procedures to ensure the correct application of the norms set out in the convention.

Almost by definition, the procedures are slow. Each individual petition has to be reviewed carefully, since the status accords significant obligations to receiving states. In practice, they cannot be applied in cases of sudden population movements, such as occurred in Kosovo or Darfur. In these cases the UNHCR makes a blanket or group determination.

As the number of requests for refugee status has increased, the number of UNHCR staff concerned has also increased. The operations are largely funded from voluntary sources rather than being dependent on the assessed budget.

The State of the Stateless

To the extent that receiving states do not acknowledge or assist refugees, international secretariats are their de facto governments by virtue of managing the refugee camps and providing basic services. This function first developed in the context of World War II and its aftermath—especially among children—but reached its most long-term form with the United Nations Relief and Works Agency for Palestine Refugees in the Near East (UNRWA), which still exists and still runs schools and hospitals in the West Bank, Gaza, and refugee camps in Lebanon, Syria, and Jordan. The Palestine refugees who had left their homes in the 1948 Arab-Israeli war became a responsibility of the United Nations because the whole Palestinian issue was connected to UN mandates.

The organization had undertaken refugee operations before, when the United Nations Relief and Rehabilitation Administration was created at a forty-four-nation conference at the White

House on November 9, 1943. This agency, predating the UN Charter, undertook relief works through 1947, was absorbed into the United Nations proper when the organization was established, and was replaced by another temporary organization, the International Refugee Organization, which itself was absorbed by the UNHCR. In addition to the United Nations Relief and Rehabilitation Administration, a temporary fund was established in 1946 to provide food, clothing, and health care to European children affected by the aftermath of the war: UNICEF.

As the presentation speech by Mrs. Aase Lionaes, member of the Nobel Committee of the Norwegian parliament at the 1965 Nobel Peace Prize ceremony honoring UNICEF, put it:

> What did Europe look like in 1946? And how were Europe's children living at the conclusion of the World War? The Swedish poet Hjalmar Gullberg provides us with an unforgettable picture in his poem "Europe's Children":
>
> "That we had fixed the padlock on our fate, That hardly mattered; Though finespun dreams had lulled the very soul, Our peace of mind was shattered: Beyond the palings, Europe's children hold aloft Their begging-bowl."
>
> These were the children UNICEF came to help in Europe during that fearful, bitter winter of 1947—undernourished, ill, clad in rags, homeless, and starved after five years of war and occupation. We came across them everywhere—in the ruins of cities, in refugee camps, in bombed villages in Hungary, Yugoslavia, Albania, Poland, Italy, Greece, Rumania, and Austria. UNICEF itself calculated that in Europe in 1947 the number of needy children amounted to twenty million. It was for these children in fourteen different countries that UNICEF provided a lifeline—a stream of food, medicine, clothes, and footwear. Never before had we witnessed an international relief campaign for children on such a scale. During the winter of 1947–1948 UNICEF was able to report that it gave six million children and mothers one meal everyday.
>
> Fortunately the economic reconstruction of Europe after the war proceeded relatively quickly. After four or five years our countries were able to look after their children themselves. (Haberman 1972)

UNICEF was first headed by Maurice Pate, an American who had been involved with refugee assistance from World War I through World War II, with a break in the interwar period. He sensed that the need for longer-term assistance to children would increase, especially as more countries became independent. In 1950 he helped promote the conversion of the fund to permanent status.

UNRWA was established by United Nations General Assembly Resolution 302 (IV) of December 8, 1949, to carry out direct relief and works programs for Palestine refugees. Intended to be a temporary organization, its mandate has been extended to 2008, and it provides most of the educational and health services to persons residing in the Occupied Territories. The first commissioner-general of UNRWA was a Canadian military officer, Major General Howard Kennedy, but subsequent executive heads have been civilians, including, from 1954 to 1958, Henry Labouisse, who later became the second head of UNICEF.

In a parallel development, after its establishment as a permanent part of the secretariat, UNHCR begun to manage a large number of refugee camps in countries adjacent to places where internal conflicts had caused persons to flee from their homes. These were largely in Africa, including Somalia, the Sudan, Liberia, Sierra Leone, Cote d'Ivoire, the Democratic Congo, Rwanda, Burundi, Mozambique, and Angola. UNHCR has also managed, at different times, camps in Afghanistan, Vietnam, and Azerbaijan in Asia, and Colombia in Latin America. The number of persons under the direct care of UNHCR has not been calculated, since the populations of refugee camps fluctuate tremendously. In October 2005, UNHCR estimated that it had 19.2 million people who were "of concern," of whom 9.2 million were under the agency's direct charge.

Management of the state of the stateless requires contracting housing and supplies as well as setting up food distribution, transport, and to the extent possible, economic activities. In practice, local employees or contractors run most of the camps, but international staff members provide supervision. In a number of cases, both in the Middle East and in Africa, international officials have had to deal with political forces that have tried to take over and use the refugee camps as protected bases from which to continue insurgencies. Resolving these problems, including expelling the political forces, has not been easy and sometimes has not been successful, leading to the camps being closed, with consequent suffering for legitimate refugees.

The management of services for almost ten million people inevitably makes demands on administrative systems. Funding for refugee administration is international in origin, but the location of the camps is often far outside the normal purview of administrative control. It is to the credit of the UNHCR and its staff that there have been very few allegations of financial mismanagement in its camps, especially since some larger operations, like Somalia, have been sites of major financial scandals.

The main line of defense against mismanagement has been the professionalism and experience of the international staff. As the international role has continued and grown, UNHCR and its nongovernmental partners have developed a cadre of career staff who are able to navigate the difficult terrain of managing the provision of services in an essentially unstable environment.

Durable Solutions

One international mandate that has proven to be particularly difficult is finding lasting or durable solutions for refugee crises. In theory, when the conditions that caused people to flee their home countries have changed, they can return. International humanitarian law, however, does not permit forced return to home countries (the principle of *non-refoulement*). To the extent that economic conditions in the home countries are bad, even when the political conditions have improved, it has proven difficult to repatriate refugees. In those cases, of which the largest is probably that of Afghan refugees in Pakistan, a carefully planned program of return has to be designed and implemented. This design has to include protections for the returnees as well as start-up resources.

When repatriation is not possible, camps have to be maintained for long periods, as has happened in the Middle East or other areas where a political solution has not been reached (such as Western Sahara) or efforts have to be made to place refugees in third countries.

The international system has evolved through a series of partnerships. An intergovernmental organization, the International

Organization for Migration, was established after World War II to facilitate the settlement of refugees in third countries. It still works in close association with agencies like UNHCR but maintains itself outside the United Nations system. Its secretariat works with recipient governments to place migrants. This is based on an understanding of national laws, procedures and limitations, and the needs of refugee populations.

INTERNALLY DISPLACED

While refugees have legal status under international law, persons who are forced to leave their homes but do not cross international borders constitute a special case that has become an international responsibility. As conflicts have increased in the context of failed states and civil war, internally displaced populations have grown. Their own governments are either nonexistent or nonfunctional.

UNHCR estimates that in 2004 there were twenty-five million internally displaced persons worldwide, more than were estimated to be refugees (UNHCR 2005, 12). Who is responsible for helping them, in the absence of their governments, is one issue; the management of assistance is a second.

One of the developments in the late twentieth century was to charge UNHCR with the responsibility for at least part of the displaced population. In 2004 the agency was responsible for 5.6 million people, a 22 percent increase from the previous year (UNHCR 2005, 12). Requests come either from the secretary-general or from the General Assembly. In some cases assistance to displaced populations is part of a broader political solution to a crisis, but mostly it is because there is no other organization able to provide the services.

In other cases assistance is provided by UNICEF, for children, and a large proportion of assistance comes from the WFP, which estimates that in the 1990s about thirty million displaced persons were in need each year as a result of conflicts, and many were attended by the WFP (WFP 2004, 6). A report to its executive board noted that "in 1975, WFP allocated almost 90 percent of its resources to development projects; only 99,000 mt [metric tons] of food went to support emergency activities. By 2002, food resources for emergencies exceeded 3 million mt, delivered to 60 million people" (WFP 2004, 5). The reasons why an international organization like WFP has become the main food supplier for emergencies in the world are discussed below.

Providing services to internally displaced persons raises complex management issues. The advantage that accrues to international officials is that they can maintain a general position of neutrality in the underlying conflicts, unless the United Nations has to support, for reasons of law or political decision, one side or the other. In those cases, as has been shown in Afghanistan, the Darfur region of Sudan, and elsewhere, international staff can become targets themselves.

NATURAL DISASTERS
AND COMPLEX EMERGENCIES

The international system has largely taken over the organization of relief in cases of natural disaster when national authorities have been unable to cope or when armed conflicts interact with national disasters and there is no national government at all. As the WFP notes:

> The number of people affected by natural disasters increased from 50 million in 1980 to 250 million in 2000. Floods alone affect an average of 140 million people each year; in 2002, more than 600 million people were affected by climatic shocks, more than half of them by droughts across much of Africa and South Asia. (WFP 2004, 6)

The increasing role of international organizations derives directly from their assets as institutions. These include experience, scope, and political position. Their reputation is based on a series of operations in Bangladesh, Cambodia, and then the Sahelian region of Africa in the 1970s and 1980s that demonstrated that, in these conditions, an international response is not only possible but is likely to be successful. Of these, the Sahelian operation was the most complex and successful.

The Sahelian Operation

Drought in Africa has existed throughout history. In the 1980s, however, the drought that began in the 1960s had reached an unprecedented scale of intensity and coverage, affecting most of the arid region of central Africa known as the Sahel. International media dramatized the problem, which was compounded by civil war in Ethiopia as well as war between Ethiopia and Somalia, both of which produced massive numbers of refugees. International public concern was reflected in a series of concerts promoted by rock musicians, most notably the Live Aid Concert that was held both in the United States and the United Kingdom.

The scale of the problem—millions of people dying of starvation—severely strained the capabilities to respond of the United Nations system and the world as a whole. NGOs, governments, and United Nations system agencies all wanted to help, but lack of coordination hindered efficiency. Secretary-General Perez de Cuellar, with advice from the field as well as agencies like UNDP, UNHCR, UNICEF, and WFP, decided to create a single organization to coordinate the effort. The United Nations Office of Emergency Operations in Africa (OEOA) was set up in late 1984. Bradford Morse, the UNDP administrator, was placed in charge, reflecting the role UNDP was supposed to play, and Morse convinced Perez de Cuellar to appoint Maurice Strong, who had run the UN Conference on the Environment, as the executive coordinator.

Maurice Strong recalled the origins of the office in a speech:

> The Office for Emergency Operations in Africa was set up by the Secretary-General in December 1984, when it was quite clear that the African emergency was beyond the normal capacities of the organizations of the UN system to respond, and that it was continent-wide in its scale, embracing 20 countries with a population of about 200 million and actually affecting—to the point that their lives were at risk—some 35 million people. In many respects the African emergency can properly be characterized as the largest known example of ecological breakdown.
>
> It was really a question of putting the United Nations on the peacetime equivalent of a wartime footing. The reason

for this was not that these organizations were not able to do their bit, but it was because they all had to be called upon to do a great deal more than they were accustomed to doing. This required far closer co-operation among the UN organizations, and between them and the African governments and donor countries and the non-governmental community.

Only the UN was in a position to sit down and evaluate and point up what was really needed. There were all kinds of possible needs, but to be specific about the needs of 35 million people in 20 countries in 10 000 or more locations isn't easy. Then, to mobilize the resources and move relief supplies in from a thousand locations around the world, streaming them in to more than 10 000 locations in Africa through a small number of seaports—that takes a degree of orchestration and co-ordination which no one government could provide; and only the UN was able to do that kind of thing. (Canada 2005)

The approach taken was to let each organization provide its normal assistance and raise its own funds but to insist that this be coordinated through the United Nations. This involved ensuring that the supplies were sent where they were needed, that order was provided in delivery, and that political problems were addressed. The UN Relief Operation in Dacca and the UN effort to deal with famine in Cambodia in 1979 were precedents. The Cambodia operation, described by William Shawcross in *The Quality of Mercy* (1984), was particularly germane. In that operation a key role had been played by Kurt Jansson, the career UN official who had become UNICEF's representative for the relief operation.

The procedures developed by OEOA have carried over to subsequent operations. However, despite its importance, there has been little public study of the process. Several elements were key. In each of the affected countries an emergency operations committee was established, under the UN resident coordinator, who was usually the UNDP resident representative. This helped guarantee a modicum of coordination in the field. Representatives who had political backing and an ability to deal with local authorities could solve immediate problems. Kurt Jansson was designated the head of the Ethiopian operation at the assistant secretary-general level.

Jansson was an old hand at the United Nations. He had most recently worked with UNICEF, which had originally suggested him for the post, but he had been a member of the United Nations Secretariat—as director of the Social Development Division—and UNDP (as resident representative in Pakistan and Nigeria). He knew both the multilateral negotiation process and field administration. He quickly established close working relations with the donor community and obtained its agreement to work through the field office in Addis Ababa rather than at headquarters (Jansson, Harris, and Penrose 1987). This allowed Jansson to be more hands on in reaching agreements and to deal with political issues quickly. He was also able to establish a personal relationship with the Ethiopian head of state, Colonel Mengistu, which enabled him to address political issues at the highest level. He reported on his first meeting with Mengistu:

> Turning to the famine he warmly welcomed the establishment of the UN Emergency Office in Addis and my own assignment. He stated with a smile that he had been informed of my assignment in Kampuchea and added, graciously, that he hoped the UN role in Ethiopia would he as successful as it was in Kampuchea.
>
> Chairman Mengistu stressed that he would like to see me at regular intervals to be briefed on the famine situation and that he was willing to see me any time I needed his support to fulfil the task to which I had been assigned. During the year I spent in Ethiopia I was to see him many times, mostly at his request but sometimes at mine. (Jansson, Harris, and Penrose 1987, 28)

A second element was the ability to coordinate. In the famine relief effort OEOA worked with WFP to set up a system of tracking when grain ships would arrive in port. Prior to this, the ships often had to wait in harbor, since the dock space in the main Ethiopian port was limited (and there was competition with ships bringing other types of cargo, like military supplies). This capacity enabled WFP in subsequent years to have a clear idea of what food was where and permitted rerouting to deal with emergencies. In addition, this coordination allowed a certain amount of direction to nongovernmental donors about what types of supplies were most needed. The Band Aid charity, for example, had not wanted to be connected with any governmental operation but was then unable to spend the considerable resources it had raised. The OEOA suggested purchasing trucks that could bring grain from the docks inland.

Jansson was an effective coordinator, based on his previous experience as well as his ability to deal with NGOs. The Ethiopia famine was one of the first that involved a significant NGO input and Jansson, at least, learned some lessons from it. He reported:

> Many NGOs had serious management problems. Some took on too much without having the necessary capacity to distribute what they had received from the donors. At one point in the middle of 1985 there was somewhat of a mess developing among a few of the largest NGOs responsible for huge quantities of food. Other NGOs adopted the policy of taking on only as much as they thought that they could handle and insisted on being self-sufficient in transport. This was the policy of CARE and ICRC from the beginning. The other major NGOs gradually developed their own transport and repair capacity but these arrangements came very late and long after the peak of the rescue operation had been reached. Poor leadership plagued some of the NGOs and there were too many changes in personnel, too many absences on leave and business abroad. Competition and jealousy was not uncommon. The home offices needed material for their fundraising and pressured their field staff to show results. (Jansson, Harris, and Penrose 1987, 24)

These lessons would recur in subsequent emergencies, and it would fall to the special representative to deal with them.

A third element was the use of a donors' conference to raise funds. In March 1985 OEOA convened a meeting in Geneva at which, according to Maurice Strong, "we were able to dramatize the needs and really push the donor governments to produce more money and more supplies to meet those needs" (Canada 2005).

First Response

When a natural disaster strikes, such as the tsunami of 2004 or the earthquake in Pakistan in 2005, immediate response has to be provided by institutions already in place. In developing countries where UN system offices exist, there are officials designated to deal with disasters. WFP, for example, has field staff in those countries that have utilized a large amount of food aid. UNDP has country offices in all countries and has a standing charge to assist in disasters.

For large-scale disasters the need for external assistance is usually obvious. However, one function of the international staff is to certify the scale of the emergency. The existence of staff on the ground provides for this.

Historically, organizations like the Red Cross—consisting of both national Red Cross or Red Crescent Societies or the International Red Cross—have provided first response. Some countries use their militaries for immediate assistance.

For some types of relief supplies, like food, the main external providers are international organizations. WFP has developed a system for quickly diverting stocks that are either in transit or are stored near the site of the natural disaster. By maintaining a careful track of where food stocks can be found, WFP can respond quickly. The value of WFP consists in the fact that it is nearly ubiquitous in the developing world, where natural disasters are likely to require an international response. If necessary, the WFP can buy food stocks locally, using its monetary resources. In contrast, other potential donors, like the United States, are restricted in the extent to which they can buy food that is not produced in their own country.

Coordination

History has shown that the main need for external humanitarian relief is in the recovery period. There is a need for emergency housing, medical personnel, supplies and equipment, and repair of physical infrastructure. The amounts needed are often very large. At the same time, particularly when an emergency situation has received considerable media attention, as in the 2004 tsunami disaster, there can be a rush on the part of governments and NGOs to provide relief. To ensure that the resources are both needed and used properly, coordination is required.

There are a number of dangers that humanitarian relief seeks to avoid. The supplies and equipment that are sent should be appropriate. There are many anecdotal stories of inappropriate supplies being sent: sweaters for disasters in the tropics, for example. Meanwhile, needed equipment, like tents, may be in short supply.

The financial resources needed to purchase supplies locally or pay personnel may be inadequate and lead to stoppage of operations, as has occurred frequently. On the other hand, more resources may be provided than can be used effectively, depleting the pool of public and private finances available for subsequent disasters in other areas. The resources provided for relief from the 2004 tsunami reduced the amounts available for the 2005 Pakistan earthquake and drought emergencies in central Africa.

A main international role has been to provide the necessary coordination, and this has expanded the scope of international action. Unlike peace and security operations, where there has to be a close relationship between intergovernmental bodies and secretariats, natural disaster relief depends almost entirely on the secretariats, with intergovernmental responsibility limited to establishing mandates and providing post-operation oversight. The effectiveness of the international effort is determined by the success of the secretariats in mobilizing resources and coordinating operations in the field, both essentially coordination functions.

Coordination of Resource Mobilization
In earlier years resource mobilization in the context of a disaster was done by individual organizations, regardless of whether they were international organizations or NGOs. In effect, the organizations competed with each other for the same funds. The governmental contributors to international organizations for emergencies worked to eliminate this problem by establishing an office in the United Nations secretariat whose responsibilities would include coordination of fund-raising. Now called the Office for the Coordination of Humanitarian Affairs (OCHA), the staff of this office, headed by an under-secretary-general, are responsible for organizing donor meetings that will raise the funds necessary for all of the international organizations to provide necessary relief.

There are two elements to this function. The first is an accurate estimate of needs. Needs assessment in a humanitarian emergency is difficult. If it is a natural disaster, access to the area may be limited. If it is an emergency related to armed conflict, access may be possible but dangerous. Yet without an accurate assessment of needs, almost from the outset, fund-raising can be difficult. If the resources needed are overestimated too often, credibility will be damaged. If needs are underestimated, requiring successive fund-raising efforts, credibility is again affected.

OCHA and its companion organizations have an advantage in this. There are, in most developing countries, UN staff resident in the country who can provide information. Many of these develop a familiarity with areas outside the capital city, because their projects take place there. They also have contacts with local NGOs and local government. One of the assets of the international organizations is their long-term involvement with development in specific countries. This means that, in addition to staff on the ground, there are many staff in headquarters locations who are familiar with the countries in which the emergencies take place.

Moreover, as the number of emergencies coordinated by the United Nations increases, so does the accumulated experience in doing needs assessments. These assessments have to draw on input from other organizations, especially the WFP. Fortunately, these organizations have formal arrangements for this purpose and share staff in emergencies. On the whole, the needs assessments prepared in recent emergencies have been accurate. When donations have exceeded these needs, OCHA has been willing to say so.

While the needs assessments are largely binding on international organizations, they are not on NGOs, who often have a vested interest in raising their own funds in emergency situations. Unlike international organizations NGOs do not have to account to their donors in detail for the results from the funds they spend. There is therefore an incentive to raise as many funds as possible in a given emergency. This is clearly what occurred in the 2004 tsunami disaster. Over a longer period it may happen that information about fund-raising by nonofficial sources will also be tabulated, but at present this does not happen.

The second element of fund-raising is finding a way to convince member states to contribute in an emergency. Many donor states set aside funds for emergency relief, while others can draw funds from contingency lines. The issue is how to get these funds allocated. The global fund-raising appeal is one of the instruments used. In this, a donors' meeting is called, with appropriate press coverage, and the contours of the emergency situation are outlined.

The ability of secretariat officials in encouraging states to contribute to appeals has been demonstrated. Following the tsunami disaster the criticism of the under-secretary-general for Humanitarian Affairs, Jan Egelund, was widely quoted: "We were more generous when we were less rich, many of the rich countries, and it is beyond me, why are we so stingy, really. . . . Even Christmas time should remind many Western countries, at least, how rich we have become." Egeland, who came to the United Nations Secretariat from the Norwegian Red Cross, has become an outspoken champion of funds for relief and reconstruction. The result of his statement, which provoked some criticism, was a significant increase in pledging for the tsunami operation. He continued this policy in other emergency situations in 2005.

Coordination at the Field Level
Humanitarian emergencies in the twenty-first century often provoke a large-scale response from a large variety of organizations, mostly nongovernmental. While in some cases, such as India after the tsunami, the government of the affected country can coordinate the assistance, often the scale is so large or the national capacity so small that the responsibility for coordination has to be assumed by the United Nations.

With an experience that extends back to the Bangladesh operation and before, but particularly to the Ethiopia famine, the United Nations has evolved procedures that provide effective coordination. For organizations of the United Nations system, this has been easy: the General Assembly has mandated that all organizations work together under a single coordinator. For development assistance this is the resident coordinator, who is usually also the resident representative of the UNDP. The resident coordinator can also take responsibility for coordination of humanitarian assistance, or a special coordinator can be appointed. The field coordinator reports in first instance to the under-secretary-general for Humanitarian Affairs, whose second title is emergency relief coordinator. This allows field coordination to mesh with resource mobilization.

The more essential coordination is of the plethora of NGOs that are usually engaged in a relief operation. Often, because of their fund-raising ability, these organizations can mobilize significant resources. As nongovernmental entities they prize their neutrality in political situations that are often complex, and they have specific missions to guide them. Some are concerned with a particular population group (children, women), while others focus on specific types of assistance. Placing disparate groups under a common umbrella is often a challenging task, somewhat akin to herding cats.

International officials have several assets in this type of coordination. First, the international organizations are themselves not hierarchical in structure; they work largely on the basis of consensus that recognizes the need for all parties concerned with the emergency to agree on overall direction, priorities, and relative responsibilities. This style works well with NGOs, which are themselves not hierarchical. Second, because international organizations are themselves politically neutral, they can coordinate without threatening the neutrality of the NGOs. Third, many of the UN staff and other humanitarian relief staff either started or spent part of their careers in NGOs, giving them a demonstrable understanding of the concerns of NGOs. Finally, the resource mobilization organized by the United Nations provides its field staff with an ability to help the NGO community whenever there are shortfalls.

From Disaster to Reconstruction

According to the accepted wisdom at the international level, emergencies should move from relief to reconstruction, and international action should move from relief to development assistance. This transition is expected to be guided by international organizations that can help plan and fund development projects that can provide livelihoods for those affected by the disasters.

This transition moves the process from humanitarian assistance to international economic and social management.

NOTE

[1] The 1967 protocol merely updated the 1951 convention with regard to the definition of refugees and allowed some countries, like the United States, that were not party to the convention to accept its substantive provisions.

9

• • • • • • •

Managing the International Economy and Social Relations

"I think the Minister means, what function do you perform in this Department."

"I'm a professional economist," Dr Cartwright explained. "Director of Local Administrative Statistics."

"So you were in charge of the Local Government Directorate until we took it over?"

He smiled at my question. "Dear me, no." He shook his head sadly, although apparently without bitterness. "No, I'm just Under-Secretary rank. . . . I fear that I shall rise no higher."

I asked why not.

He smiled. "Alas! I'm an expert."

—THE COMPLETE YES MINISTER, 381

While the ideology of the free market has seemingly been pervasive, the international public sector has increasingly begun to play a role in managing the global economy and, to an extent, social development. This growth was foreshadowed in the creation of the Bretton Woods institutions, the World Bank and the IMF. They initially functioned as state-centric organizations with limited mandates, but they have become, at least partly because of the competence of their secretariats, economic players in their own right. The addition of the WTO has completed a trio of international entities that direct much of international economic growth and play a significant role in maintaining stability.

Over time, the importance of the research done by both the World Bank and the IMF has increased and has become a significant ingredient in national policymaking. The role of their staff in stabilization operations has similarly grown. The WTO dispute-resolution process and the staff that runs it are similarly becoming a critical ingredient in international economic management.

Like the World Bank, the development funds of the United Nations have also evolved into entities whose main role is to promote public investment for globally agreed purposes. UNDP, UNICEF, WFP, and UNFPA all function, through their secretariats, to leverage their development-assistance resources to encourage countries to follow international investment and policy priorities.

While management of international social issues has largely been indirect, by way of policy agreements or human rights norms, there is a growing area where non-economic factors have to be guided by international secretariats. This is particularly true in health, where international organizations have been called upon to coordinate and manage national public and nongovernmental responses to real and potential pandemics like HIV/AIDS and avian flu.

ORIGINS OF INTERNATIONAL FINANCIAL AND DEVELOPMENT INSTITUTIONS

The Allied Powers during World War II had assumed that international institutions would be needed for managing the global economy. Their diagnosis showed that many of the causes of the war derived from ruinous international economic policies. At the Bretton Woods Conference in 1944 the Allies agreed to establish two institutions: the IMF, to ensure order in foreign exchange markets as a precondition to effective trade; and the World Bank, with a mandate to provide foreign exchange for public investment and to encourage private investment.

Unlike the United Nations, the Bretton Woods institutions were not to be universal organizations. Instead, they would include those states that were part of the international financial system. Some viewed them as another set of international banking institutions like the Bank for International Settlements in Basel, which had been established initially to manage the collection, administration, and distribution of the annuities payable as reparations by Germany following World War I as well as servicing the external loans contracted to finance them. The bank, however, had been established as a limited company with an issued share capital and had a limited membership.

The first meeting of the World Bank's board of governors, in March 1946, resolved the issue. One group of countries, led by Lord John Maynard Keynes, argued that the World Bank should be located in New York City (where the United Nations was to be established), while the United States argued that it should be located in Washington, D.C., because placing the two institutions in New York would closely link them with the United Nations. US Secretary of the Treasury Fred Vinson stated:

> The Fund and Bank are not business institutions in the ordinary sense. While they must be operated so as to conserve their assets and allow the most fruitful use of their facilities, they are not profit-making institutions. The business of the Fund and Bank involves matters of high economic policy. They should not become just two more financial institutions. (Vinson 1946, 626)

Starting the two institutions was not a simple process. The IMF had a relatively quick start and absorbed many of the staff who had worked on the Bretton Woods Conference. Its first managing director was the head of the Belgian delegation, and by June 30, 1947, the IMF had a staff of 355 from twenty-seven countries.

The World Bank started more slowly. It began its formal operations on June 25, 1946, with a staff of twenty-six, with twelve executive directors and thirty-eight member countries (less than one person to a country) (World Bank 2004). There was confusion about the relative roles of the management staff and of the board of directors, and there were difficulties in appointing the first president, Eugene Meyer, who resigned within the year. The new president, John J. McCloy, insisted, as a condition of accepting the post, that the management (the secretariat) would run the World Bank. His vice-president, who came from the private sector, worked for staffing levels and salary to be related to job descriptions rather than bureaucratic rules. Like other United Nations secretariats, the World Bank drew on persons who had worked with the UN Relief and Rehabilitation Administration. The first head of personnel, William F. Howell, who served in that capacity until his death in 1964, had been director of personnel for UNRRA.

Unlike the United Nations, which drew on the experience of the League, the Bretton Woods institutions were established along an American model (Knorr 1948), because the United States negotiators and the bank managers were reluctant to model them too closely on the United Nations. The staff regulations included some elements of the principles on which the secretariats of the United Nations system had been based (the criterion of independence, for example), but salary levels and grading structures were different. More important, while all of the other specialized organizations of the United Nations system negotiated relationship agreements that clearly indicated that they were obligated to report to the Economic and Social Council and coordinate with the UN Secretariat as well as one another, the Bretton Woods institutions negotiated much looser arrangements.

Both the World Bank and the IMF underwent start-up controversies. The IMF had to set the basis for determining how to regulate currency exchange rates. It established the key role of the staff in setting the basis for policies and decisions on specific countries. As its official history of the period states:

> Now as the Fund's policies are gradually worked out, an almost continuous interchange of ideas, both formally and informally, takes place between the members, the Governors, the Executive Directors, the Managing Director, and the staff. . . .
>
> Preparatory work is done by the staff, whose appraisal and recommendations are approved by the Managing Director; and the agreed staff position is then reviewed and decided upon by the Executive Directors. (Horsefield 1969, 12)

The World Bank underwent a similar, if somewhat more tortu-
ous process. It had to work out problems of capital acquisition
(including how to market its bonds) and project appraisal. It began to move from a role in reconstruction (implying loans to Europe: its first loan was to France) to development, where the main
focus of lending would be developing countries (its first loans of
this type went to Chile).

While the World Bank was focusing on reconstruction, the General Assembly was beginning to consider how to deal with "under-
development." From the beginning, a question before all of the
international organizations was how poorer countries would benefit from membership. Security was the main interest of the industrialized countries of Europe and North America, followed by stable
financial and trade relations. Developing countries claimed their
share in the form of what is now called development assistance.

At its first session the General Assembly adopted Resolution
52, calling for assistance to interested members "who may need
expert advice in the various fields of economic, social and cultural
development." The resolution stated that the United Nations had
the responsibility under the UN Charter to assist in that development, that development was important for world peace and pros-
perity, and that responsibility was shared with the specialized
agencies.

The beginnings of these expert services could be found in
UNRRA, which had been undertaking advisory functions in the
field of social welfare, especially regarding children. The Economic
and Social Council had recommended that these functions be transferred to the United Nations, and in another resolution of the first
session (Resolution 58), the General Assembly authorized the secretary-general to make the transfer, engage experts, and provide
advice to countries on request. It gave a special emphasis to dealing with problems of the physically handicapped. While the initial focus was on rehabilitation in Europe, it set a precedent that
these services would be funded from the regular assessed budget
of the organization. The secretary-general would prepare a program based on the requests received, have them reviewed by the
Social Commission of the Economic and Social Council, and then
build them into the budget.

By the third session of the General Assembly in 1948, the focus of
the expert advisory program had shifted to the underdeveloped

countries. In Resolution 200 (III), the General Assembly authorized the secretary-general to expand the advisory-assistance program to cover economic development. The resolution authorized the organization of expert teams from the secretariat and the specialized agencies, provision of fellowships for overseas training of developing-country experts, provision of in-country technical training, and supplying equipment that might be needed for these tasks. The assistance should be provided on request, be geographically distributed, and "(iii) be designed to meet the needs of the country concerned; (iv) be provided, as far as possible, in the form which that country desires; (v) be of high quality and technical competence." These parameters defined UN technical assistance for much of the next fifty years.

The regular program eventually developed into a system under which different specialized agencies, and the United Nations itself, would receive allotments that could be used to finance technical-assistance activities. These were even approved as predetermined shares in order to ensure continuity in staffing. Each agency was able to hire specialists who could provide advisory services and could do a modicum of planning.

The original idea was to fund assistance from the assessed budget of the organization, but it quickly became apparent to the countries that had the highest assessments, especially the United States, that this was a budget line that would expand infinitely. The UN budget could be adopted by majority vote of the General Assembly, and it was obvious that developing countries would soon be a majority, so the regular program of technical assistance could be seen as a means for an increasing transfer of resources from North to South that could not be formally stopped by the countries that paid the organization's bills.

In the intervening year the dispute was placed before the Economic and Social Council. The developing countries were unwilling to give up the technical-assistance program established under Resolution 200 (III), while the developed countries were unwilling to allow any growth under the assessed budget. The compromise was to establish the Expanded Program of Technical Assistance (EPTA), which would be funded from voluntary contributions. This was motivated by President Truman's Four Point Plan and a commitment by the United States to fund a multilateral effort. The EPTA would have its own administrative machinery, and after a time, its own oversight mechanism, the Technical Assistance Board. While the regular program of technical assistance could not grow, the EPTA could and did.

The EPTA developed a network of field offices and pioneered raising development funds through voluntary sources. When its advisory projects were seen as too small, the UN Special Fund was created in 1958 for larger-scale pre-investment projects.

The field offices were initially staffed by fairly low-level officials whose main responsibilities were administrative (looking after experts assigned to the country, processing payments, and negotiating project agreements).

The funds raised were allotted on the basis of agency shares, which were negotiated through an interagency committee. The structure was obviously wrong, both politically and administratively, and in 1965 the General Assembly, under some pressure from both donor countries and some of the bureaucracies (especially the Special Fund) decided to merge the EPTA into the UNDP.

With the creation of the UNDP (with the exception of the WFP and the UN Population Fund) the major funds, programs, and institutions for economic and social management were in place. Over time, these institutions evolved from a minor supporting role to a major role.

MANAGEMENT OF
INTERNATIONAL FINANCIAL STABILITY

The IMF had one of the most dramatic evolutions. After World War II, currency trading was assumed to be based on fixed exchange rates and the IMF was set up to provide bridge financing while countries facing balance of payments difficulties made the necessary adjustments to make their currencies exchangeable for trade. This system is long gone, but the need for stability in the foreign-exchange markets—to ensure smooth trade and agile payments—continues. The early experience of the IMF helped in dealing with a larger issue: structural adjustment.

Structural Adjustment

Stable currency exchange rates were expected to avoid some of the problems in the international trading system that had been blamed for the economic problems leading to World War II. For the first twenty-five years of its existence, the IMF was a technical organization that used short-term lending to provide stabilization bridges while countries adjusted their exchange rates. The IMF staff role was to monitor global economic trends and, when a specific country encountered difficulties, to determine what types of loans, coupled with national policies, would be necessary to stabilize exchange rates (Horsefield 1969).

Starting in the mid-1970s the exchange-rate system became separated from the gold standard, there was increasing private sector dominance of financial markets rather than governments, world economic growth slowed, inflation increased, and more countries had problems that affected their abilities to function in the global monetary system. As James Boughton puts it:

> As recounted in earlier histories of the IMF, world economic and financial imbalances multiplied in the 1960s and 1970s. The Bretton Woods system of fixed but adjustable exchange rates came under strain and collapsed, and a more flexible system was negotiated. Because the new system imposed few constraints on national economic policies, the IMF was drawn into a more active "surveillance" role in overseeing its implementation. Moreover, as the landscape of the world economy became more precarious, the IMF was drawn into a more active lending role that required a deeper and more sustained involvement in the formulation of macroeconomic policies in countries facing economic crises. During the 11 years covered in this work, 1979 through 1989, a confluence of upheavals propelled the institution into a more central and pervasive role than ever before. (Boughton 2001)

The IMF became an advocate of adjustment policies to address structural imbalances in national economies that were caused by production structure, government macroeconomic policies, trade relations, and consumption patterns. The application of economic policies by developing country governments to remove structural impediments to growth often had profound effects on their populations. They usually consisted of initial shock therapy, called stabilization policies, as currencies were devalued, subsidies removed and consumption costs raised. These steps were then followed by longer-term policies based on privatization of state-run enterprises, encouragement of external investment, and strict controls of imports.

The IMF used its foreign-exchange loans, without which countries could not import goods, as the incentive to induce governments to adopt the recommended policies. The policies would have been worked out as recommendations from the IMF staff economists and then negotiated with government financial officials. The World Bank supported the IMF secretariat through non-project lending, the intention being to provide a longer-term source of foreign exchange (called structural adjustment lending).

The Bretton Woods institutions, using a combination of economic analysis and promotion of market-friendly policies that were agreed by their members (the so-called Washington Consensus, adopted at the end of the 1980s), became global economic managers on a scale unprecedented in history.

Successful management requires a number of different actions. There has to be a sound diagnosis of economic conditions, both global and in individual countries. There has to be an agreement on policies necessary for stability. And, finally, there has to be an external source to verify that states comply with their obligations under these policies.

The basis for enforcement is built into the international financial system. If a state is unable to pay for traded goods in convertible currency, neither other states nor private corporations will sell to that state, and international banks will not lend further. The dependence of almost all economies on traded goods for survival— whether in the form of food, other supplies, or equipment—means that the value of foreign exchange is automatically high. Ensuring that foreign exchange is available is essential in all states.

Problem Diagnosis

Determining the factual basis for the global financial situation requires two things: good information and solid theory. International institutions have a comparative advantage in collecting and publishing statistics because they are considered neutral, impartial, and competent. The IMF, whose national counterparts are central banks that collect most of the financial statistics produced at the national level, has this advantage. The IMF has been able to set a standard for the criteria on which collection is based, including the types of statistics and the format for presentation. The World Bank maintains statistics on national liquidity positions as well as the position of the IMF itself, all of which are available online.

The role of the IMF in developing economic theories that explain international finance is even more important. From the very beginning IMF staff sought explanations for the phenomena with which they were expected to deal. As Barnett and Finnemore note in their study of the IMF, "The intellectual connections created by Fund staff constructed balance-of-payments difficulties as a different type of problem requiring new types of solution" (2004, 56). The development of these connections, done both within the IMF and in the context of professional associations, structured both the policies of the IMF and the cognitive categories that would be used by outside academics to judge them.

The IMF is able to draw on its field missions and the experience of its staff, most of whom have academic training in economics, to produce analytical studies. The IMF maintains its own professional journal, *IMF Staff Papers*, now in its fifty-second volume, to provide an outlet, as well as four series, *Policy Discussion Papers*, *Country Reports*, *Economic Issues*, and *Working Papers*. All of these feed into the IMF's policymaking, as well as into the approaches taken by its staff. The semi-annual *World Economic Outlook*, like the World Bank's *World Development Report*, is used to explore major policy initiatives. The September 2005 edition, for example, explored the types of financial institutions that need to be built. As its preface states:

> The analysis and projections contained in the *World Economic Outlook* are integral elements of the IMF's surveillance of economic developments and policies in its member countries, of developments in international financial markets, and of the global economic system. The survey of prospects and policies is the product of a comprehensive interdepartmental review of world economic developments, which draws primarily on information the IMF staff gathers through its consultations with member countries. (IMF 2005b, x)

Policy Agreement

The next element in successful management is a formal agreement among member states to the policies to be adopted. Unlike the one-state, one-vote system in the United Nations, the IMF, like the World Bank, uses a weighted voting system, in which a state's vote is proportional to its contribution to the IMF's paid-in capital. This means that major contributors have much greater weight in the Bretton Woods institutions than in other international organizations. The board of governors formally makes decisions at the annual meetings of the IMF, while operational decisions are made by the elected board of directors. Most specialized international organizations draw their national counterparts from the respective specialized ministry. In the case of the IMF this is either the Ministry of Finance or the Central Bank (or both). This means that the delegates tend to be likeminded in their approach. There has been enough back-and-forth movement between the IMF and national governments, especially at the highest levels, that many of the delegates are former IMF officials and understand the organization from that perspective.

IMF policies, such as the use of structural adjustment in debtor countries, reflect a combination of policy analysis and common perspective. While criticized outside the IMF (in the General Assembly, for example), they tend to be accepted within it.

Armed with agreed policies, IMF staff who work at the national level to arrange assistance are in a strong position to deal with opposition. If a state does not wish to accept the staff's proposal, the IMF is under no obligation to lend funds. The details of the loan are subject to detailed negotiation, with the IMF staff position guided and circumscribed by the policies that have been adopted.

External Verification

To ensure compliance the IMF staff maintains a constant pattern of surveillance. This function is set out in the Articles of Agreement of the IMF but has expanded over time. The process was set out in a draft of an evaluation of the function being prepared by the Independent Evaluation Office of the IMF (IMF 2005a, 10). As noted, the surveillance function draws on a variety of sources. After periodic country visits the staff of the IMF report to the executive directors, who can, if necessary, make policy decisions on how to influence national governments (see Figure 9–1).

Figure 9-1. Flow Diagram of Multilateral Surveillance

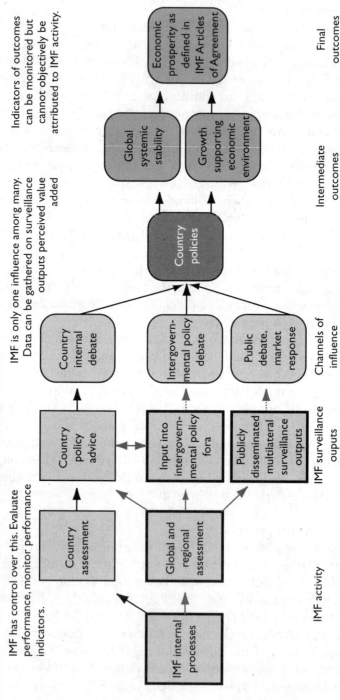

Source: *The IMF's Multilateral Surveillance: Issues Paper for an Evaluation by the Independent Evaluation Office (IEO)* (Washington, DC: IMF, 2005), 10.

Like the intergovernmental bodies in most international organizations, the IMF board of governors makes decisions on policy by consensus rather than vote. Consensus is made easier in the IMF by the extensive networking that exists between staff members and their national counterparts. For 2006, the IMF had 2,802 positions, a fairly sizable number, a large percentage of which were economists. While no study has been done of this, many of the national counterparts, especially in developing countries and at the senior level, seem to have worked with the IMF at some point in their career. This is the kind of networking noted by Slaughter (2004), but with the difference that the glue holding the network together is an international secretariat and the experience of national officials with it.

INTERNATIONAL PUBLIC INVESTMENT

Development assistance has been a major element of the United Nations from the beginning. It was at least partially a response to the smaller states that asked of all UN system organizations, What's in it for me? Provision of technical and financial assistance from developed to developing countries was the answer.

The initial assumption was that the main issue in development was lack of technical skills in developing countries. Even if true at the outset, some fifty years of technical assistance (plus extensive educational mobility of persons from those countries) has made that assumption moot. Instead, there has been an evolution toward the idea of an international function to enable public investment rather than what used to be called development assistance.

The fundamentals for the system were set up when the UNDP was created, largely stimulated by a remarkable document, *A Study of the Capacity of the United Nations Development System* (Jackson report). The new administrator of the UNDP (established at the executive head level) was Paul Hoffman, who had previously headed the Marshall Plan and then the Special Fund. Hoffman wanted an outside view of the best way to respond to the needs of development. He commissioned Sir Robert Jackson, a war hero and former senior deputy director-general of the UNRRA and UN under-secretary-general, to undertake a study of the capacity of the UN system to use the resources generated or to be generated by the UNDP. The study was mandated by the Inter-Agency Consultative Board and was undertaken by a team of persons seconded from the UNDP, led by Margaret Joan Anstee, who had been a field representative.

The study was expected to be narrow and technical, but under Jackson's and Anstee's leadership, it became very critical of the status quo. In terms of the bureaucratic structure, the study was blunt:

> Governments created this machine—which over the years has grown into what is probably the most complex organization in the world. . . . This "Machine" now has a marked identity of its own and its power is so great that the question must be asked "Who controls this 'Machine?'" So far, the evidence suggests that governments do not, and also that the machine is incapable of intelligently controlling itself. (Jackson 1969)

The study recommended that rationality should be built into the system by taking a country—rather than a project—approach, having a unified country presence, and building certainty into programming by establishing agreed figures for allotting funds among countries. It called for the end of the agency shares system. It also included other, more far-reaching recommendations, such as the creation of a United Nations Staff College to train UN system officials in international management. (This was only achieved in 2001.)

When the capacity study was issued, it was widely read in the secretariat and among delegates, if not in the academic community. In 1970 the governing council reached a consensus adopting many of the recommendations. The UNDP was made the central funding organization for UN technical assistance, there would be country programming, there would be regional programs, the UNDP resident representative would be first among equals at the country level, and instead of agency shares, organizations of the system would collaborate (and compete) for projects from which they would draw overhead to finance their technical-assistance support. This structure, with some major modifications, would guide UN development assistance into the twenty-first century.

The World Bank went through a similar process at roughly the same time. The World Bank was not part of the consensus forming the UNDP. George Wood, who had replaced Eugene Black as the World Bank's president, was concerned that at the end of the first development decade progress was faltering. He made a speech at the Swedish Bankers' Association in 1967 in which he said:

"We are ready at the World Bank, together with interested governments, to help to select and finance . . . a group of experts. I am ready to put at their disposal all the information and statistical material the World Bank has accumulated and, if requested, to second staff to their service. Such a Grand Assize—judging the world's record and prospects of growth—should in any case precede any attempt to round off our faltering Decade of Development with a genuine reformation of policy." (World Bank 2005)

Woods was replaced as president in 1968 by Robert McNamara, who moved quickly to establish a nine-member commission "to review the previous 20 years of development assistance, assess the results, and make recommendations for the future." He requested Lester Pearson of Canada to head the group, which has been known since as the Pearson Commission. The World Bank provided thirty staff members to work with the commission, which undertook missions to four continents to discuss issues with government representatives. The combined report, entitled *Partners for Development,* was presented to McNamara in 1969 and led to a change in the policies of the World Bank. The report said that the World Bank must look more broadly at investments for development, that a longer-term perspective must be taken, and that there was a linkage between development finance and other issues, especially trade (Ayres 1983).

As a result, the World Bank made a major change in its lending policies, with an emphasis on use of International Development Association credits and project appraisal involving social cost-benefit analysis. In 1972 there was a major reorganization to decentralize bank operations and turn them over to regions. In 1973, at an address to the World Bank's board of governors, McNamara proposed a strategy for rural development with an emphasis on productivity of smallholder agriculture. This reflected a growing position within the World Bank staff that unless rural development problems were solved, other development problems could not be.

The fundamentals for all the UN system development agencies have remained the same over the past forty years and are similar to those in international financial management, of which they can become a part. Foreign exchange provided to states for which this is a scarce good is still the basis for the assistance. The World Bank (and the regional development banks) provide loans, UNICEF provides equipment and supplies, UNFPA provides condoms and funding for censuses, and the WFP provides food rations for development projects. What has changed is that the elements are now intended to promote international policy objectives through facilitating national public investment, including enabling policy changes.

There has, however, been a struggle about who is really in charge at the country level. The 1970 consensus meant that the UNDP, through its field offices, using a recipient-driven programming structure, should provide leadership to the UN development system. Each developing country was given an indicative planning figure for a five-year period, and projects were to be planned within that limit. The resulting country program would guarantee coordination and linkage with national development plans. So ran the theory.

In 1973 a problem emerged. Expenditures on the projects included in the country programs were being made later than planned, and the UNDP had a large unexpended surplus. Major donors were reluctant to provide additional funds on the grounds that the funds already given were not being spent. The UNDP central administration decided to deal with the problem by authorizing field offices to "over-program." On the assumption that delays were inevitable in projects (and presumably could not be planned for), field offices were allowed to enter into commitments in excess of their planning figures, sometimes by as much as an additional 50 percent. These figures were based on the experience of expenditure in the first years of the cycle. Unfortunately, reality intruded on this policy.

Both field offices and the specialized agencies that provided technical assistance (and much of whose staffing was based on overhead charges calculated against expenditure) accelerated their expenditure. Equipment was pre-ordered; experts were selected promptly and posted quickly. By early 1975 it was obvious that expenditure was likely to be nearly 100 percent against programming. Unfortunately, programming was now at over 100 percent of targets, and the UNDP had an acute financial crisis. There were not enough funds to pay for the experts and the equipment that had been ordered.

Field offices were forced to save funds by delaying delivery of equipment, occasionally reducing the size of contracts or even sending experts home. With considerable effort the financial crisis was addressed. The consequences, however, changed how the development system functioned.

First of all, the credibility of the UNDP as a central source of funding for development activities was damaged and never recovered. Recipients had discovered that UNDP country programming and indicative planning figures could not be trusted. Donors had discovered that UNDP financial management was uncertain. Specialized agencies, many of whom had to lay off staff when promised overheads were not obtained, began to find ways of funding their own technical-assistance programs.

At the same time, formally in order to reduce costs and also to recognize that in many areas, developing countries no longer needed expatriate expertise, the UNDP authorized "national execution" of projects. In this system the government could contract with a national institution to manage a project. Paid at local rates, which were lower than those paid to internationally recruited experts, the projects would cost less and there would be fewer overhead costs. For some critics this implied that the UNDP would become a check-writing agency and its extensive system of field offices would become redundant.

On the basis of a conclusion that the specialized agencies were unable to deliver technical assistance quickly, the UNDP also set up its own in-house executing agency, the Office of Project Execution, which began to grow, to the further dismay of the specialized agencies. It has since become the Office of Project Services, is independent of the UNDP, and reports to the secretary-general.

The notion that the UNDP resident representative would coordinate UN system development assistance was also replaced. The resident representatives reported to the administrator of the UNDP, but the other organizations argued that the administrator did not have the credibility to provide coordination. The organizations of the system convinced the governments, as part of the re-structuring exercise of 1975, to create the position of UN resident coordinator, who would be appointed by the secretary-general. In most cases the UNDP resident representative would perform that role, mostly for financial reasons, but the option existed to appoint someone else (and this happened in Ethiopia during the famine).

Additionally, at least part of the UNDP's purpose was to pro-vide "pre-investment" technical assistance whose end result was supposed to be World Bank projects. After the financial crisis the World Bank increasingly financed its own pre-investment techni-cal assistance and, since it did not formally participate in the resi-dent coordinator system, this meant that the largest component of UN-supported development assistance was outside that system.

Finally, the complex system of country offices and the notion of a career development service went into a long process of self-ex-amination and search for purpose. Even though the UNDP was officially a temporary organization (since it was funded completely from voluntary funds), it had issued career appointments to staff who had an expectation of advancement. UNDP staff were usu-ally graded somewhat higher than regular secretariat staff and were less likely to be picked up by other organizations. They had originally been administrators, but as the administrative respon-sibilities decreased, they increasingly depended on a representa-tion and policy-advice function.

Determining Global Priorities

The history of development assistance has been a dialectic between the priorities felt by national governments, usually having to do with developing their economic capacity to compete in world trade, and the priorities felt by the major donors to development-assistance organizations, usually having to do with social aspects of development, including reduction in poverty. In the end, with appropriate bows to national sovereignty, the donors' priorities have tended to prevail. The focus on market-based systems, international trade, and investment, rather than capital resource transfers through public institutions, has muted the UN–centric debate about how to spur national economic development.

Financing of UN secretariats (the main expenditure in budgets) through mandatory assessments based on ability to pay means that, in real terms, developing countries pay as much of their gross domestic product in foreign exchange to the organizations as the developed countries. Since the contribution of the United States has been capped at 22 percent, they pay more than some. Part of the bargain has been to ensure that there are development activities by the organizations. At the same time, many of the donors to development organizations—especially from Europe—have found it more economical to exert policy influence through multilateral institutions than through maintaining overhead-expensive bilateral programs.

From the time of the first UN development decade, a debate between the donor countries and the developing countries about whether internal (national policies and conditions) or external (structural elements like trade and debt) factors should be emphasized has dominated the determination of global development policies. The debate has never been resolved. The donors like to focus on internal matters like tax policies, meeting basic needs, democratization, and elimination of public corruption. In contrast, developing countries emphasize the need for access to markets for their products, improved public resource transfers from North to South, and increased private investment.

The difficulties of reaching consensus were reflected in the fact that the Agenda for Development proposed by Boutros-Ghali was never adopted. Instead, Kofi Annan took advantage of the celebration of the millennium in 2000 to use that summit to adopt the millennium development goals. These were largely social goals but included a commitment by developing countries to address internal issues and by developed countries to provide financing for development. Subsequently, at the UN Conference on Financing for Development held in Monterrey, Mexico, in March 2002, the agreement was made more solid through the Monterrey consensus. The main sections of the consensus, under the heading "Leading Actions," indicate the compromises made:

- Mobilizing domestic financial resources for development
- Mobilizing international resources for development: foreign direct investment and other private flows
- International trade as an engine for development

- Increasing international financial and technical cooperation for development
- External debt
- Addressing systemic issues: enhancing the coherence and
  consistency of the international monetary, financial and
  trading systems in support of development

The secretariats of the main development organizations were
involved in defining the consensus. The World Bank's 1999/2000
World Development Report was entitled *Entering the Twenty-first
Century: The Changing Development Landscape* and sought to codify
the issues involved. The abstract for the report states:

> [The report] focuses on two forces of change: the integration
> of the world economy and the increasing demand for self
> government, which will affect responses to key issues such
> as poverty reduction, climate change, and water scarcity. The
> forces of globalization and localization will require nation
> states to sustain a dynamic equilibrium with international
> and subnational partners. The nature of this equilibrium will
> have far reaching implications for the gains from trade and
> capital flows, the fruitfulness of global environmental agree-
> ments, the pace of regional growth, and the scope of urban
> development. (World Bank 2000)

The UNDP's *Human Development Report* for 1999 was entitled
Globalization with a Human Face. Other publications of international
organizations focused on the broader debate.
  International secretariats influence the selection of development
policies for the same reason that they affect regime creation: they
provide the factual basis for discussion, formulate and guide agen-
das, articulate middle-ground solutions, pass on information from
the nongovernmental and academic communities, and provide
institutional memory. In the case of development policies, international secretariats can be intellectual leaders because they are
far more likely to do the underlying research than academics, who
depend on the data that the secretariats generate. Moreover, like
the IMF, the development organizations have a fairly high degree
of networking with national officials in developing countries.

A major factor in influencing policy, however, is the extensive use of evaluation by operational organizations, which permits an empirical assessment of the effects of different policies by observing them in specific projects over a wide spectrum of situations. These evaluation results are often summarized in comprehensive reports like UNDP's periodic *Development Effectiveness Report.* These evaluations draw on the network of field offices to provide information that can be analyzed and disseminated to national delegations.

A classic case of policy formulation derived from the work of international secretariats is microcredit. Microcredit programs provide very small loans to poor people to enable them to undertake new economic initiatives. It is now a mainstream concept, but it was initially opposed because it was assumed that poor people would not repay the loans and that the costs of administering a large number of small loans would be prohibitive. The first major experience was the Grameen Bank in Bangladesh, started—as is often the case—as an experiment by an NGO. The project would have lapsed had it not received financial support from the IFAD. IFAD staff undertook an evaluation of results and discovered that, when the borrowers were women, repayment rates were high and the loans were used effectively. IFAD's professionals reported the results, and microcredit, particularly for women, became a standard development practice.

Leveraging to Influence National Priorities

Given a consensus on global priorities, development organizations use their resources to encourage national governments to adopt policies that will implement the global policies. In all cases the resources are based on provision of foreign exchange, either directly, in the form of loans and grants, or indirectly, in the form of equipment, international travel funds, or supplies. In effect, these provide goods and services that a country would not be able to obtain using domestic resources (in the case of countries that are extremely strapped for funds) or which would not have as high a priority.

While foreign exchange was usually a factor in technical assistance, with foreign-exchange resources used to acquire the services of expatriate experts, this was not always the case for the World Bank. In its early years the World Bank insisted on the use of its foreign-exchange components only for direct use to cover imports. As the poverty-alleviation policies in the World Bank evolved, a new policy was developed that allowed the government to exchange World Bank foreign exchange for local currency to use in projects dealing with social development. This substitution meant that the foreign exchange could be used for other purposes.

The process of leveraging was built into the development system. In the early 1970s the UNDP country program was expected to provide the opportunity for a dialogue about how development assistance would match global and national priorities. While this fell into disuse after a time, it has reemerged as the United Nations Development Assistance Framework (UNDAF):

> Through the common country assessment and the United Nations Development Assistance Framework (UNDAF), the United Nations has for the first time the tools needed to provide strategic and coordinated support for the development goals of national Governments. The common country assessment provides a common analysis for use by the United Nations, donors and other institutions, so that all have a shared understanding of the challenges and potential risks they face. The United Nations Development Assistance Framework is the planning and programming mechanism that coordinates the United Nations response to meeting these challenges. (United Nations 1999c, para. 128)

While this was not the first time that tools like this had been used—despite the secretary-general's statement—it implied a revival of the earlier practice of permitting the secretariats of international organizations to negotiate with national governments about how international development resources were to be used.

In effect, the UNDAFs were a form of public investment plan, specifying those types of social and economic infrastructure into which international organizations would invest and, by so doing, enable developing countries to implement global priorities.

The key staff in this process include the country-based representatives of the organizations of the UN system, one of whose key functions has traditionally been to conduct the discussions. In many countries UNDP staff prepares the government's submission to the executive board of the UNDP.

Within the framework there is considerable scope for individual organizations to elaborate projects that can implement their specific priorities. UNICEF, whose main asset is its ability to provide supplies and equipment, has developed a noted skill in trading supplies and equipment for child-friendly policies consistent with those adopted at the global level. Similarly, the WFP, in its development mode, creates projects in which food rations can substitute for cash (food for work) as an incentive to create public infrastructure or support initiative. The WFP's programs in school feeding serve as an incentive to families to send children to school who might not otherwise be sent, for example. Governments create school-feeding programs because they are low cost, given that the main materials are supplied by the WFP.

Creating an International Management Infrastructure

Over time, the UNDP and the UN system organizations involved in development work have created a network of national offices. These can be found in most countries in the world and constitute the most extensive network of offices of any public organization. Originally established to provide field-level management of development-assistance projects, their main current function is to provide the infrastructure of international management. Each developing country now has a resident coordinator, usually the UNDP resident representative, who acts as the representative of the secretary-general at the country level. Not an ambassador, since the United Nations is not sovereign, the resident coordinator nonetheless functions in some respects as though the office were representational.

The UN office has become an administrative center, issuing tickets and travel documents for national officials traveling to UN system meetings. It also performs administrative liaison with national governments in such mundane matters as visas and customs clearance. For many organizations the office oversees national banking, disbursement, and accounting for development projects.

There has been a long-term effort, especially on the parts of donor countries but also by the UNDP and the United Nations itself, to consolidate all UN system organizations within a single office area and, to the extent possible, place officials under the guidance of the resident coordinator. While this has not been attained for all organizations—the Bretton Woods institutions have resisted—there has been progress.

THE TRADE REGIME AND ITS MANAGEMENT

International economic management has been strengthened by the creation of the WTO. Clearly the dispute resolution mechanism (described in Chapter 6) is designed to help manage international trade flows by providing an institutional means to ensure that states live up to their obligations under the GATT. The regime, however, goes beyond that in terms of management.

As one of its major activities, the WTO undertakes periodic surveillance of national trading policies (trade policy reviews). States report on their policy compliance with the GATT and these reports are reviewed by an expert body and an analysis prepared by the WTO secretariat. The four largest trading states (the European communities, the United States, Japan, and Canada) are reviewed every two years, the next sixteen largest every four years, and the rest every six years. Between 1995 and November 2005 there were 153 reviews, including four each of the largest trading states.

When the WTO was formed, UNCTAD became more important. Its focus, however, shifted to helping developing countries enter and cope with the WTO. WTO did not develop a research arm (other than the division dealing with trade policy), while UNCTAD strengthened its capacity to do research.

UNCTAD also has taken on the role of consultant to developing countries to deal both with the WTO and the private sector. In 1993 the United Nations Centre on Transnational Corporations was incorporated into UNCTAD and morphed into the Investment, Technology and Enterprise Development Division. That division analyzes investment trends, provides advice on investment agreements, and undertakes studies to identify possible sources of investment. The International Trade and Commodities

Division provides, among other things, support for the participation of developing countries in international trade negotiations. Staffed largely by economists, UNCTAD has a close relationship with the WTO; they jointly sponsor a technical-assistance program, the International Trade Centre. The closeness of the relationship is shown by the fact that the secretary-general of UNCTAD in 2005, Supachai Panitchpakdi, had previously been the director-general of the WTO.

HIV/AIDS AND AVIAN FLU

In the social area WHO has begun to expand its regulatory role, managing an increasing number of global health problems beyond its international campaigns to deal with infectious diseases like malaria, polio, and smallpox.

WHO was established as a specialized agency in 1948. There had been a small program in the League, but WHO was a major step forward. In determining its tasks, eradication of the infectious diseases that afflicted much of the developing world became an early priority. WHO decided to focus on two diseases that were believed to be both important and curable: yaws and malaria. Yaws is a disfiguring, debilitating, highly infectious non-venereal disease transmitted by direct (person-to-person) contact. Malaria is a highly infectious disease transmitted by insects. As Donald Henderson, who later led the successful smallpox-eradication program, points out:

> The launch of each [programs to combat yaws and malaria] was triggered by the introduction of a new technology—an injectable single-dose long-acting penicillin, for the treatment of yaws, and the availability of large quantities of the inexpensive insecticide DDT, for use in the malaria programme. Surprisingly, prior to the launch, neither campaign could draw on the experience of large-scale pilot programmes in critical areas which would have served to demonstrate the feasibility of eradication, given the tools and resources available. If they had, neither programme would have been initiated. (Henderson 1999, 2)

While there were no international programs to serve as a model, the United States, where malaria was not too common, had undertaken a successful eradication program between 1947 and 1950. After WHO launched its program in 1955, it came to take up one-third of the budget and had five hundred staff, mostly in different developing countries. The campaign was set up on the basis of three principles:

> First was the relationship of the programme itself to the health services. It was a tenet of the malaria eradication directorate that the programme could not be successful unless it had full support from the highest level of government. This translated into a demand that the director of the programme in each country report directly to the head of government and that the malaria service function as an independent, autonomous entity with its own personnel and its own pay scales. Involvement of the community at large or of persons at the community level was not part of the overall strategy.
>
> Second, all malaria programmes were obliged to adhere rigidly to a highly detailed, standard manual of operations. It mandated, for example, identical job descriptions in every country and even prescribed specific charts to be displayed on each office wall at each administrative level. The programme was conceived and executed as a military operation to be conducted in an identical manner whatever the battlefield.
>
> Third, the premise of the programme was that the needed technology was available and that success depended solely on meticulous attention to administrative detail in implementing the effort. Accordingly, research was considered unnecessary and was effectively suspended from the launch of the programme. (Henderson 1999, 2)

WHO was visible in most of the developing world, as a result of the program, which clearly helped ensure its prestige for future campaigns. By 1975 this first campaign was considered a failure. As the United States Center for Disease Control indicates:

> Successes included eradication in nations with temperate climates and seasonal malaria transmission. Some countries

such as India and Sri Lanka had sharp reductions in the number of cases, followed by increases to substantial levels after efforts ceased. Other nations had negligible progress (such as Indonesia, Afghanistan, Haiti, and Nicaragua). Some nations were excluded completely from the eradication campaign (most of sub-Saharan Africa). The emergence of drug resistance, widespread resistance to available insecticides, wars and massive population movements, difficulties in obtaining sustained funding from donor countries, and lack of community participation made the long-term maintenance of the effort untenable. Completion of the eradication campaign was eventually abandoned to one of control. (CDC 2004)

WHO, in the face of difficulties with malaria eradication, decided to focus on eradicating smallpox. This was, in one sense, simpler. In most countries, thanks to inoculation programs and health controls in travel that had been in place for many years, smallpox had already been eradicated, and there was an easy technological fix in the form of a very heat-resistant vaccine. Still, Henderson concluded:

Despite this, eradication was achieved by only the narrowest of margins. Its progress in many parts of the world and at different times wavered between success and disaster, often only to be decided by quixotic circumstance or extraordinary performances by field staff. Nor was support for the programme generous, whatever the favourable cost-benefit ratios may have been. A number of endemic countries were themselves persuaded only with difficulty to participate in the programme; the industrialized countries were reluctant contributors; and, UNICEF, so helpful to the prior malaria programme, decided that it wanted nothing to do with another eradication programme and stated that it would make no contributions. Several countries did make donations of vaccine and the West African programme, directed by the US Communicable Disease Center was a critical addition. However, cash donations to WHO during the first 7 years of the smallpox programme, 1967–73, amounted to exactly US$79,500. That is not per year but the total for that entire period. (Henderson 1999)

The key to the program was that, unlike malaria, it was not conceived as a separate program but was built into existing health programs. The international input was to facilitate delivery of vaccines and to assist in organizational arrangements at country level. A second element was research. As Henderson puts it:

> Research initiatives included the development of new vaccination devices to replace traditional lancets; field studies, which revealed the epidemiology of the disease to be different from that described in the textbooks and, in consequence, the need for modification of basic operations; the discovery that the duration of vaccine efficacy was far longer than that normally stated, making revaccination much less important; operational research, which facilitated more efficient vaccine delivery and case detection; and studies which demonstrated conclusively that there was no animal reservoir. The principle was to ask again and again, how could this programme be made to operate more efficiently, more effectively. (Henderson 1999)

Henderson notes that senior WHO executives resisted this element, but it is consistent with what is now called results-based management, where feedback from the field is used to improve program delivery.

The third element of success was the use of intensive surveillance to detect new cases, so that they could be isolated and dealt with.

The last two cases of smallpox were found in Bangladesh in October 1975 and in Somalia in October 1977.

In 2005 international secretariats were directing campaigns to prevent or control the outbreak of avian flu as well as seeking to control HIV/AIDS. HIV/AIDS has had international management almost since the outset, first through WHO and subsequently through the Joint United Nations Programme on HIV/AIDS (UNAIDS), which is a joint program with WHO and others (located at WHO headquarters).

In June 1986, after several global AIDS conferences dramatized the increasing problem, WHO held an international conference on HIV/AIDS. As a result, WHO established the Global AIDS

Programme and appointed Jonathan Mann as its executive director. Mann took a broad view of the nature of the problem, arguing that while it had medical dimensions, its transmission was favored by social and economic factors that had to be addressed. He assembled an enthusiastic and competent staff that began to reach out to other secretariats on issues of concern. The issue was also debated in the UN General Assembly.

WHO began to receive information about HIV infections among women. It also determined that prostitution was a major vector in the virus's transmission. WHO contacted Jacques du Guerny in the UN Division for the Advancement of Women. Du Guerny was a demographer by profession and saw immediately that once the virus entered the heterosexual population, its spread would be rapid. He saw that its main vectors were behavioral in nature, and therefore its spread would be determined by those behaviors. Women's subordinate status in society—their inability to say no or to enforce the use of condoms by infected partners—would place them at particular risk. The infection would also affect the middle part of the age distribution, persons from twenty to forty-five, and if mortality rates increased would create a distorted distribution in the population, with the predominant parts very young or very old. Moreover, an increasing burden of caretaking would fall on women, who perform that role in most societies.

The division began to cooperate with the Global AIDS Programme; sent a report to the UN Commission on the Status of Women, alerting it to the nature of the problem; and organized a seminar on women and HIV/AIDS that brought together policymakers, AIDS activists, and scholars. Mann was very supportive of further work on the subject.

WHO had also reached out to other UN programs working in the area, such as UNICEF and the UNFPA. Within WHO there were disputes about how to deal with the problem. One school based its approach on detection, medical treatment, and quarantine. Mann rejected this, arguing that the context for HIV/AIDS infection was more important. By 1990 Mann came into conflict with the director-general of WHO, who felt threatened by Mann's approach, which was taking up an increasing proportion of the organization's budget. As a result of the conflict Mann was either fired or resigned, depending on which source is believed. He was replaced by Dr. Michael H. Merson, a career staff member who had headed both the Diarrheal Diseases Control Program and the Acute Respiratory Infections Control Program. Merson was more attuned to the medical approach to dealing with infectious diseases and was less supportive of many of Mann's initiatives.

One immediate consequence of Mann's departure was that many of the initiatives that he had been supporting found that their financing was not secure. This included the work being done by the UN's Division for the Advancement of Women. The division, however, continued its work with its own resources, and a strong section on HIV/AIDS and women was written into the Beijing platform for action.

The HIV/AIDS pandemic increased in size and severity, and because the vectors by which the disease spread were behavioral rather than medical, a number of different UN organizations became involved. The management solution was to create, in 1994, UNAIDS. Peter Piot of Belgium, an early collaborator of Jonathan Mann, was picked to head it. The program has become the main coordinator for diverse activities to address the pandemic and its consequences.

UNAIDS serves as a main channel to assemble statistics on the incidence of HIV/AIDS, but it also has become a significant coordinator of aid flows directed against the disease. UNAIDS has sought to coordinate national responses by following the "three ones":

- **One** agreed HIV/AIDS Action Framework that provides the basis for coordinating the work of all partners.
- **One** National AIDS Coordinating Authority, with a broad based multi-sector mandate.
- **One** agreed country level Monitoring and Evaluation System. (UNAIDS 2004)

WHO, which is closely involved with the UNAIDS program, also has worked with NGOs like Rotary International to eradicate polio. Like smallpox before it, polio is now found only in some countries, largely due to the use of immunization in most countries (aided by UNICEF vaccination campaigns in many developing countries). The issues related to polio have to do with resistance to vaccination among some parts of the populations where the polio virus can still be found. For that reason WHO focuses on providing information as well as mobilizing political pressure on local authorities to permit vaccination campaigns.

A newer development has been WHO's role in identifying new infectious diseases and acting vigorously to prevent their spread. In 2003 the identification of the SARS virus in China and Canada led to WHO requiring those countries to take measures, including quarantine and cancellation of conferences and meetings. WHO also took the lead in planning for a potential outbreak of avian flu among humans in 2005. These types of measures, now that they have been accepted, will continue to be important.

WHO's role in dealing with avian flu has been dramatic. Scientists in WHO, and those working with it, estimated that a cyclical major pandemic of influenza was likely. The main issue was when and starting where. Based on previous immunological studies the scientists concluded that an influenza virus that was endemic to poultry was likely to mutate and spread in the human population. With almost no resistance from states, WHO became the leader in determining how to control the pandemic. This included overseeing national monitoring, especially in China and other parts of Asia; maintaining a tally of available vaccine supplies; and, with the help of the World Bank, estimating the likely cost of the pandemic.

Besides the technical competence at WHO headquarters, the value of the secretariat included the credibility of its field staff in Asia, which could observe developments firsthand and be considered neutral. The one difficulty faced by WHO—the same one it had initially in terms of HIV/AIDS—is that the problem is not exclusively medical. As long as the problem is seen as mostly about health, WHO can lead with little difficulty, but when it involves other elements (such as its economic cost), other organizations become involved and do not necessarily accept WHO's leadership.

In the case of avian flu the solution has been for the secretary-general, as the first among equals with other executive heads, to appoint a special representative to coordinate responses. The first coordinator, named in 2005, is David Nabarro, who was a senior official of WHO.

10

· · · · · · ·

How the International Public Sector Manages Itself

I stared at him, and enquired if he was being sarcastic. He denied it. I accepted his denial (though doubtfully) and continued to explore my theory of what's wrong with Brussels.

"The reason that Brussels bureaucrats are so hopeless is not just because of the difficulty of running an international organisation—it's because it's a gravy train."

"A what?" asked Bernard.

"A gravy train," I repeated, warming to my theme. "They all live off claret and caviar. Crates of booze in every office. Air-conditioned Mercedes and private planes. Every one of those bureaucrats has got his snout in the trough and most of them have got their front trotters in as well."

Humphrey, as always, sprang to the defence of the bureaucrats. "I beg to differ, Minister," he said reproachfully. "Brussels is full of hard-working public servants who must endure a lot of exhausting travel and tedious entertainment."

—THE COMPLETE YES MINISTER, 275

To a large extent the international public sector has to manage itself, and how well it does so will help determine the future of secretariats. The main administrative issues for national public administrations are finance, recruitment of staff, and procurement, and the same is true for international secretariats. However, how the issues are addressed is qualitatively different in international organizations.

These administrative issues are central to the growth of international organizations, and determine whether the secretariat is seen as competent, honest, and neutral. Critics of international organizations usually focus on them rather than on substantive issues. In the period 2004–5 the focus of criticism was the Iraq Oil-for-Food scandal—fraud in what was the largest UN-administered program up to that point. The Oil-for-Food scandal is, in many ways, the exception that proves the rule about managing the international public sector. The secretariats' only protection is to ensure that management is as close to perfect as possible.

FINANCE AND BUDGET

Determining how to finance the international public sector is a significant issue. The organizations of the United Nations system use two methods: a system of mandatory assessments on the membership, and voluntary contributions to fund activities. In addition, the Bretton Woods institutions fund personnel and other administrative costs from the interest earned on loans.

Since assessed contributions are mandatory once the budget is approved, determining the size and composition of the budget has been a major political activity. The assessment, after considerable debate, was set on the basis of ability to pay, using a complex formula based on gross domestic product per capita and population size. The largest economies were expected to pay the most, while a minimum assessment was set for states with small economies. Despite the fact that the system was designed to ensure that all states paid the same in relative terms, the major contributors realized at an early stage that the majority of states that paid only small amounts in absolute terms could vote to increase budgets. This was one reason that the United Nations regular program of technical cooperation was capped almost at the outset and development assistance moved to financing from voluntary funds. As a result, a series of reform efforts were undertaken to control the budget process while permitting changes in orientation, such as the so-called restructuring exercise in 1974 and the Group-of-18 reform in 1986.

The Group-of-18 reform addressed weighted voting on the budget. Since weighted voting would have required an amendment of the UN Charter, the compromise chosen was that the budget had to be adopted by consensus. In effect, this provided a veto to any government that believed that the amounts were too large or wrongly allocated. In addition, the role of the General Assembly Committee for Programme and Coordination (CPP) was strengthened to include determining the overall size of the budget through review of what was called the budget outline. The idea was that the year before the biennial budget was to be approved, the CPP would agree on the total amount that the secretary-general could request, based, in theory, on his medium-term plan. This would be agreed by consensus as well (Mathiason 1987).

The budgetary process set up by the Group of 18, with the exception of the introduction of "results-based budgeting" in the late 1990s, continued until 2003. Results-based budgeting had been developed in a number of governments, like Canada, Australia, the United Kingdom, and under the Clinton administration, the United States. It was part of the "reinventing government" movement and sought to make governments more responsive and cost effective. Each government department would specify in its budget the results that it expected from its activities and use this to justify requests for funding. As has often been the case, these types of national reforms are often carried over to the international system, in part because they help make the payment of assessed and voluntary contributions more palatable to national legislatures. In 1997 Annan proposed the adoption of results-based budgeting in the United Nations. A number of specialized agencies were already using variations on this. However, there was resistance from many developing-country governments that saw this as an effort to cut programs that they might favor. The process required a change in the management culture of the organization, both at the level of the secretariat staff and the governments (Mathiason 2004).

Over the period 2000–2004 results-based programming was instituted. Secretariat managers must specify what is expected to happen as a result of the outputs that they produce. For example, statistical offices are expected to indicate what use will be made of their statistics; policy research divisions are expected to indicate what will be done with their research studies; and standards-setting offices are expected to indicate who will adopt the standards. In some respects, promising results is more difficult for international secretariats because most of their services are delivered indirectly. At the same time, the discipline of thinking through what is supposed to happen as a result of work is a way of sharpening focus and defining programs that are likely to work.

The purpose of the move from a line-item budget to a program budget and then to a results-based program budget is to give states control over the content of the programs by making expected results clear and linked to resources. If the system works, it should permit flexibility in the management of resources, which could be redeployed from ineffective to effective programs. Administrative systems, however, are designed to restrict the ability of the secretariats to change expenditure patterns. The budgets are divided into sections that correspond to "major programs," but in practice they correspond to secretariat departments. The secretariat is not allowed to transfer funds from one section to another without specific authorization from member states. The secretariat is also not permitted to transfer funds from certain lines (for example, established posts) to others (such as equipment or travel). Kofi Annan's reform proposals in 2006 sought to address this by having the General Assembly authorize the secretary-general to make resource transfers between sections but within major departments (United Nations 2006).

Each biennial budget is built on the previous budget, so that any changes in the size of major programs, or component programs, are immediately noticeable. Since each program has its governmental supporters, change has been resisted. Moreover, the major contributors, who meet regularly in an informal caucus called the Geneva Group to determine maximum contribution levels that they are willing to sustain, have resisted increases in the overall budget. Over most of the history of the United Nations, its budgets have formally involved zero real growth, that is, no growth in constant terms, although inflation and currency fluctuations have been absorbed. In some recent periods the major contributors have insisted on zero nominal growth, that is, no change in the dollar amounts in the budget, irrespective of inflation or currency fluctuations.

The difficulty for the secretariats has been that the total size of the assessed budget has usually not increased and the relative shares of different program components have been difficult to change. As a result, the organizations have been far less flexible than might be desired.

In practice, several devices have been employed to build a certain amount of flexibility into the system, usually with the tacit consent of the major contributors. Several are technical, and one involves using structural change as a means of readjusting the budgets.

As a matter of practice, each budget proposal is only compared with the previous biennium. The budget documents do not attempt to show historical series (say four or five budget periods). The amounts used to calculate the previous biennium's budget (the base for the next budget) are not the amounts that were originally budgeted but rather the estimated final approved sums. Since these are often adjusted to reflect inflation and currency fluctuations, as well as increases that might be added in the off-budget year, they always lead to a slight real increase in the next budget base.

Another technical device is to change the composition of established posts in given programs without changing the total number. This has historically involved reducing the number of general service posts (secretarial and clerical) while increasing the number of professional posts or upgrading the professional posts. On this basis it appears that staffing levels will remain constant. More recently this has also involved outsourcing some of the clerical functions, which can be included in a different budget line from established posts.

Even these technical solutions are difficult, since budget-review bodies sometimes object to them. The organizations usually solve the problem of relative allocation of resources among programs by reorganization. As part of a large-scale reorganization, departments can be created or divided and posts reallocated. There are periodic reorganizations in most of the organizations, resulting in redeploying resources. In a few cases, although not in recent years, the reorganization process has led to an overall increase in assessed resources.

The increased focus on the cost of the organization involves two ideas: The first is that the organization has become top heavy, with too many posts at the assistant- and under-secretary-general levels. The second is that the organization has become sclerotic because too many staff have been in office too long and have become "dead wood."

Upon his election in 1991 Boutros-Ghali moved on the first issue by unilaterally abolishing the post of director-general for development and international economic cooperation and consolidating several departments, including merging the Department of International Economic and Social Affairs and the Department of Technical Cooperation for Development into a single Department of Economic and Social Affairs. This merger did not work well, largely because the top manager was not able to control the new entity. In 1993 Boutros-Ghali made a second reform, which in effect broke the new department into three: Policy Coordination and Development, Policy Analysis, and Technical Cooperation, each with an under-secretary-general. However, in the process he eliminated the Centre for Social Development and Humanitarian Affairs in Vienna and moved most of its parts back to New York. It was replaced in Vienna by the Division of Outer Space Affairs. He also merged the Centre on Transnational Corporations with UNCTAD and moved it to Geneva. The net effect of these moves was to reduce the number of assistant secretaries-general.

Most of these changes were cosmetic. They did not affect the underlying programs, although the reorganizations made it difficult for the staff to carry on their work smoothly. The units being moved from Vienna to New York, for example, were in the process of preparing world conferences in their fields. The changes did not appease the United States, which was under pressure from its Congress (now under the control of conservatives who were hostile to the United Nations) and which began to withhold significant parts of its assessed contributions.

Despite his efforts, Boutros-Ghali was unable to satisfy the United States and, faced with its veto in the Security Council, did not stand for reelection. He was replaced by Kofi Annan, the first secretary-general to come from within the secretariat. Annan proposed a series of reform measures. These included some management improvements, such as establishing a cabinet style of governance (organizing department heads into committees), changing the name of the interagency coordination body from the Administrative Committee on Coordination to the Chief Executives Board, and creating a new post of deputy-secretary-general. These did not change the management structure.

Under the Annan secretary-generalship, there was steady growth in higher-level posts, as well as an effort to give the secretary-general more flexibility in managing resources by permitting shifts between budget sections and swaps of posts.

The secretariats have an additional difficulty in that the budgets all assume that the funding levels agreed by the member states will be available for use. This has never been the case. In every budget period some states, usually smaller ones, do not pay any of their assessment because they have a foreign-exchange shortage. However, larger contributors, for different reasons, sometimes refuse to pay all of their contribution. In early days the Soviet Union objected to certain peacekeeping operations and refused to pay for them; more recently, the United States, forced by its legislative branch, which simply does not appropriate enough funds to cover the assessment, has withheld certain amounts. Additionally, most states do not pay their assessment on time. The United States, whose fiscal year does not begin until October, is responsible for paying for most of the final quarter of each budget. Most organizations either live in a constant cash-flow crisis or in the shadow of an imminent one.

Almost no international organizations have the authority to borrow money externally in order to cover cash flows (member states do not want the organizations to accrue interest charges and therefore be forced to increase their budgets).[1] A number of the organizations are not allowed to make adjustments when assumptions about inflation and currency fluctuation turn out to be incorrect. WHO and the International Telecommunication Union, in recent years, did not make correct estimates about probable inflation and foreign-currency exchange rates—their budgets are in US dollars but their expenses are largely in Swiss Francs and Euros—and had to undertake budget reductions and other cash-flow correctives. Most organizations are also not permitted to carry over assessed budget amounts from biennium to biennium. Unexpended amounts are to be returned to the member states as credits on their next contributions.

Given these facts, the managers in the controllers' offices have to dole out budget funds carefully. This tends to mean that programs cannot spend as scheduled during the first quarter, perhaps during the first year, and sometimes during the entire budget cycle.

Since the reorganizations have not addressed the basic inflexibility in the assessed budget, and the chronic cash-flow problems make realistic planning difficult, an increasing number of programs depend on voluntary funding to complete their work. The development funds (UNDP, UNICEF, UNFPA, WFP) have always been completely dependent on voluntary contributions, mostly from major contributors. Other programs, like refugees and humanitarian coordination, have a small core from assessed resources but most of their funds are also raised from voluntary sources.

For the secretariats this means that programs have to be planned to attract donor funding and that over time certain donor countries become the basic support of specific programs. The secretariats have to be sure that the domestic political interests of these countries are kept in mind when programs are planned. Most donors build their contributions to specific funds and programs into their domestic budgets, with little available for contingencies. To the extent that domestic budgets are inflexible, donors themselves have restrictions on what they can support at the international level, and for some, like the United States, this can be affected by a change in government.

For example, under the administration of Ronald Reagan, the United States stopped providing funds for UNFPA on the grounds that abortion was supported by projects in some countries. Although this was denied by the UNFPA (and inspections by the US government showed that it was not true), the United States did not contribute to UNFPA until the administration of Bill Clinton. The next administration, under George W. Bush, again stopped funding the UNFPA, even though the United States Congress appropriated the funds.

This is not exclusively a problem of the United States. The United Nations Institute for Training and Research for the Advancement of Women is an autonomous institute headquartered in the Dominican Republic. The largest funders for much of its history were Norway and the Netherlands. In 1992 these countries commissioned an evaluation of the institute that was highly critical of its performance and suggested that it be merged with the United Nations Development Fund for Women (UNIFEM). When this did not happen, largely because of political factors (the Dominican Republic mobilized other developing countries to oppose the merger), Norway and the Netherlands withdrew their funding. The institute has been in crisis ever since; it currently subsists on subventions (grants of financial aid) from the UN assessed budget while it seeks to replace the withdrawn funding.

Where a given country is willing to contribute is determined by that country's political interests as well as historical factors. The Nordic countries, for example, have been particularly interested in contributing for human rights activities. Italy has provided funds for drug control and crime prevention. Japan has provided funds for management reform and disability. Often the donor has a wider purpose. Japan, for example, endowed a fund dealing with violence against women to be implemented by UNIFEM as a response to criticism about its treatment of "comfort women" during World War II.

Because of the dependence on voluntary funding, most senior managers of international organizations have to be entrepreneurial rather than bureaucratic about their program planning. Ironically, even though the international secretariats are bureaucracies, they have to function somewhat like private-sector entities (or NGOs) to obtain sufficient resources to carry out their programs. Some consciously model themselves on large NGOs and call their strategic planning documents business plans.

The difficulty with reliance on extra-budgetary funds is that doing so can distort the organization's overall priorities. For example, many argued that endowing UNIFEM with funds for dealing with violence against women changed its priorities from its development focus to a human rights focus. Relying on extra-budgetary funds can also involve difficult political tradeoffs. Because of Italy's large voluntary contribution to UN drug-control and crime-prevention programs, the heads of both programs have been, for the past fifteen years, Italian. Similarly, in 1999, when a Danish candidate for head of UNDP was not selected, the Danish government reduced its contribution. (The United States, which had provided the administrator to UNDP since the beginning, did not field a candidate, preferring to maintain UNICEF with a US executive head, but it reduced its contribution to UNDP by half.)

Alternative methods of obtaining funds have been considered to address the problem of resource flows. One obvious method is for international organizations to charge a fee for services provided. Most of the services provided by international organizations are expected to be free; in fact, making them free is one reason for using assessments as the basis for financing. Only a few organizations, other than the Bretton Woods institutions, who can use interest paid on their loans for administrative expenses, have developed fees for services (other than charging for some publications). The World Intellectual Property Organization charges for international registration of copyrights and patents covered by its treaties, and the International Telecommunication Union charges fees for its 620 sector members—mostly from telecommunications companies—and its 100 associates—mostly from other types of corporations concerned with communications. These arrangements have been criticized as restricting open access to the organizations, especially by NGOs that cannot afford the fees.

An alternative to user fees is to charge overhead on funds administered by international organizations for others. Early development assistance was built on the idea that specialized agencies would be paid for their overhead in delivering technical assistance. This would be the equivalent of interest rates, but since the development assistance was grant based, it was a budgeted charge. Some of this still occurs when an organization of the United Nations system agrees to do field administration of funds from other donors, although the overhead rates are kept low.

A few organizations, notably UNICEF, but now including UNIFEM and UNFPA, obtain funds by commercial transactions (such as selling greeting cards). The funds raised by such means, which are similar to a private corporation in terms of management, amounted to almost US$56 million in 2004 (UNICEF 2005).

Another possible method for financing the development organizations, suggested by the American economist James Tobin, would be to levy a fee or tax on an international transaction that benefits from the international order. Transactions might include international air traffic and international banking transactions. This so-called Tobin Tax has been promoted by academics and some governments, as well as the UNDP Office of Development Studies (Ul-Haq, Kaul, and Grunberg 1996). Countries like the United States resist this because they assert that providing international organizations with a taxing mechanism would undercut national sovereignty.

Taken as a whole, secretariats have learned to function in a financing system that is not optimal, largely by knowing how to use the rules in place and by acting as entrepreneurs to obtain voluntary funding. Little by little the alternatives to assessed budget funding are becoming more common.

HUMAN RESOURCES: CAREER VS. ROTATION

The cost of the secretariat staffs is the largest budget item of most international organizations. The creation of these staffs and their maintenance as politically neutral has been a long process. There have been essentially two management issues: achieving geographic balance in the secretariats, and ensuring competence. While the two are not contradictory, they are often thought to be.

Recruitment is in part a technical issue: posts are classified using standard methods, they are advertised, candidates apply, are screened on the basis of fit with job criteria, and then a selection process takes place using a system of committees and boards, leading to an offer. The differences between this and normal practice in national administrations is that the reach of the process has to be international and the internal screening has to be seen to be neutral.

How to recruit staff on the basis of highest standards of competence, integrity, and efficiency with due regard to geographical representation was resolved early in UN history and has applied as well to the other organizations of the UN system. Recruitment involves advertising posts, considering candidates against job descriptions, having those who meet standards reviewed by managers, whose recommendations are considered by appointment-and-promotion bodies that include staff representation. When all of those steps are accomplished, the person will be hired. Geographical factors are taken into account in the review process along with certification of professional qualifications.

Among the defects in the system initially was the fact that job openings were not widely known except to insiders. They were sent to "national recruitment services" who would suggest candidates. This was important for those countries that only provided their nationals on secondment (the Soviet Union and its allies). The process was sufficiently cumbersome that there was an incentive for program managers to identify their own candidates. These were usually persons who were known to the programs, either because they had been interns or field experts, had worked with other related programs, or attended meetings. Being a "known quantity" was often determinative. Program managers knew that a good geographical balance was necessary to obtain political support, so they sought to achieve balance in their staffing.

This system was shown to be problematic, particularly at the entry level. The international civil service was conceived as a career service, and careers should start with entrance at the lowest professional levels. The "known quantity" criterion worked against this. Candidates from under-represented or unrepresented nationalities would not be "known" and therefore had little chance to be hired. For others, the main factor was being in the right place at the right time.

In 1975 the system became untenable. The Joint Inspection Unit, through Inspector Bertrand, looked at the composition of the secretariat and analyzed personnel data. Bertrand found that the average age of staff in each grade was greater at each higher level, as would be expected, with one exception. The exception was the entry-level professional (P-2), which had the highest average age. This was because entry-level posts were being used to reward senior general-service staff who were nearing retirement. This permitted them to retire with international benefits. Many of these general-service staff were, in fact, performing professional duties and, many having been in service since the beginning of the organization, were part of the institutional memory. But a consequence of the situation was that few entry-level posts were available to recruit younger staff, which would ensure constant renewal of the civil service.

Bertrand's recommendation was to establish a system of examinations for appointment to the entry-level positions. In order to deal with the issue of qualified general service, some of the places in the examination were to be reserved for internal candidates, but the examinations should be the same. In order to ensure geographical representation, the examinations should be given in countries that were under-represented or unrepresented in the secretariat and should also be given by occupational groups. These recommendations were implemented over a period of years and proved to be very successful in bringing qualified young staff into the organization.

To achieve an effective process, all posts now must be advertised. Most are advertised on the website of the organizations concerned. Many national governments steer their nationals to these posts by linking to them from their websites. Many organizations also advertise senior posts in the international press, such as *The Economist* or the *International Herald Tribune.*

For most organizations there is no formal quota requiring preference for under-represented nationalities, but there is an informal effort to do so. The United Nations Secretariat, the most visible international civil service, follows a fairly strict system of near-quotas for non-language (and non-mission) posts. Each country has a "desirable range" based on its size and contribution to the budget. Each country's range includes a minimum, a maximum, and a midpoint. Candidates from countries that are below the midpoint (or are completely unrepresented) are expected to receive preference, while a candidate from a country that is at or near its maximum should be successful only if no other candidate with equivalent qualifications is available. The net effect of this policy is that geographical balance can be maintained.

The use of competitive examinations at the entry level is now standard in the UN Secretariat. The examinations are given in countries that are under-represented in the secretariat, below the midpoint (or expected to be, based on anticipated retirements or other staff changes). A certain percentage of slots is reserved for nonprofessional staff who have passed the examination. The examinations are administered by the secretariat, and the examiners are almost always serving staff. As a result, the exams should provide, for career-line staff, the best candidates, reflecting geographic balance, who have the characteristics of existing staff members.

In the UN Secretariat those selected through the examination process are expected to be career employees and are given career appointments after a probationary period. Over the course of the postwar history of international organizations, a large percentage of staff holds permanent contracts. This reflected the early debates about what an international civil service would be. At the time, the global norm for public administrations was the career service, epitomized by those found in the United Kingdom, France, and the United States. Within national civil services, especially in the United States, career civil services began to fall into disrepute, replaced by a "business model" approach to staffing, in which management-level jobs were largely political appointments.

A critique by opponents of international organizations, again especially in the United States, was that the career system led to bureaucratic inefficiency. Staff members protected by permanent contracts were believed to become lazy, set in their ways, and resistant to innovation. Unlike the private sector, which uses cost-benefit calculations to measure efficiency, international secretariats lacked a "bottom line" to measure productivity, so there was no empirical evidence available either way.

An example of anecdotal evidence appears in Shirley Hazzard's novel about the early secretariat, *People in Glass Houses*, which begins:

> "The aim of the Organization," Mr. Bekkus dictated, leaning back in his chair and casting up his eyes to the perforations of the sound-proof ceiling; "The aim of the Organization," he repeated with emphasis, as though he were directing a firing-squad—and then, "the long-range aim," narrowing his eyes to this more distant target, "is to fully utilize the resources of the staff and hopefully by the end of the fiscal year to have laid stress"—Mr. Bekkus frequently misused the word "hopefully"— . . . to have laid greater stress upon the capacities of certain members of the staff at present in junior positions." (Hazzard 1967, 9)

Based on such images the secretariat begins to look less competent and more like any other bureaucracy, only more so.

Reality is different. Within the limits of what can be achieved by an international secretariat, staff members of the organization have proven remarkably adaptable and resilient. They have shown a strong ability to learn, both from mistakes and failures and from successes. In the face of almost constantly constrained budgets, and increasing tasks, they have demonstrated an ability to absorb additional work. Even though an organization is run through the use of carefully defined administrative rules, staff members have proven able to adjust to the rules and still deliver programs in an agile way in most services.

One consequence of zero-growth budgets has been an aging of the secretariats. Reduced intake at the entry level has meant that in many organizations the generations of civil servants who entered at a time of expansion have stayed on and are now reaching retirement. This means that a large number of vacancies is expected in a short time.

Concerns with effectiveness also affect personnel policy. Personnel policy always involves a tradeoff between the need to obtain good staff quickly and the need to ensure that fairness and transparency are maintained. The procedures for recruitment and promotion have become increasingly complex and time consuming. One of the consequences has been a very long delay in filling posts, with, at one point, an average of thirty months being required. In addition, although the organization presupposed a career service, there was no working career-development system. In practice, staff members created their own patterns, moving from one office to another, but this was not always rewarded. As the needs of the organization for staff to serve in less pleasant duty stations (for example, some of the regional commission offices or field missions), increased mobility of staff was considered essential. In the late 1980s a system of internal applications for vacant posts, which in the past would have been filled in a nontransparent way, was set up.

The United Nations had been established on the principle of permanent contracts for staff who were to form the central core of personnel, to ensure their employment, to protect them from political influence, and to ensure an institutional memory. However, by the 1990s almost 80 percent of the staff of the UN Secretariat had permanent contracts, and many governments (and some internal managers) believed that this made it difficult to remove less competent staff. In the absence of good career planning and a sound performance-appraisal system, ineffective staff would be kept and would make the organization inefficient.

A major part of the internal reforms that could be enacted by the secretary-general without recourse to the General Assembly had to do with personnel policies. After five years staff members had to move to new posts. Proof of mobility (defined as having been in more than one duty station) was a requirement for promotion to management grades. A system of program performance reviews based on annual work plans and reviews of the extent to which the plans had been completed was put in place instead of the previous rating system. Program managers were given more authority over hiring.

One approach to dealing with personnel is to adapt a business model, somewhat similar to the situation when the League of Nations was being formed (see Chapter 2) and when states thought that the League could be staffed by personnel seconded directly from governments. This was also argued by the Soviet Union during the first forty-five years of the United Nations, when nationals of the countries of Eastern Europe were only made available by secondment. The most modern case consists of the IAEA and other organizations concerned with verification of the elimination of weapons of mass destruction. These were set up with the idea that the staff would rotate and that there would be no permanent contracts. The experience of the IAEA shows that this does not work in practice; in some key services the proportion of long-term contracts is high (Andemicael and Mathiason 2005). Sound performance of some functions requires experience with international organizations.

Most organizations have compromised and have set up a system where some posts are filled by short-term personnel and others by career staff. The distinction in terms of posts is whether the main criterion for selection is the technical skill needed or an understanding of the organization and how it works in its complex environment. In this sense most management personnel would be expected to come from the career staff, many of whom, having started as fixed-term personnel, showed a particular aptitude for international service.

Still, part of the issue of career versus rotation turns on whether staff appointed on a career basis can be eliminated if they become "dead wood." One element in the reform proposals presented by the UN secretary-general was a large-scale buy-out of one thousand career employees intended to eliminate "dead wood." Critics have argued that this does not work in most organizations because the persons most likely to take the buy-outs are the productive staff members who perceive opportunities outside the organization rather than the "bad" staff who are the real targets of the program. Moreover, as a Heritage Foundation researcher notes, "Few details were provided on these 1,000 staff employees, their current employment status, how close they are to retirement, and why a buy-out of $100,000 was deemed appropriate" (Schaefer 2006, 8). It is not at all clear how the number was reached.

In practice, international secretariats increasingly use mobility in assignments to address the problem of "dead wood." Staff members are encouraged to undertake mission assignments, movement between international organizations has been made easier, and, in the United Nations, rules have been instituted to limit staff to a maximum of five years in a given post. If successful, these policies will decrease "dead wood."

The larger issue, which has not been addressed, is how international service, which is qualitatively different from national or private-sector service, can provide a good and recognized training ground for these other types of services. The effect of prior service experience (national or private sector) on effectiveness in international service has not been studied empirically. Nor has the effect of international experience on subsequent national or private-sector experience been analyzed. As issues at the national level become more internationally interdependent, and as movement among national, private, and international levels becomes more common, such analysis will be important.

PROCUREMENT

Procurement of equipment, supplies, and personnel is a major administrative function of any government. The function is driven by rules in any public sector in order to ensure transparency, fairness, and efficiency. At the international level this is particularly important because the sources of finance are external. The major contributors to the various budgets want to be sure that at least some of the procurement is from their national suppliers.

All of the organizations of the system have adopted rules that are based on competitive bidding for contracts, advertising of openings and tenders, and the use of committees to screen and select suppliers. On the whole, this has worked well. Procurement statistics are routinely provided to member states.

As the size of orders has increased, the organizations have had to adapt. During periods of emergency the systems have been tested and, with few exceptions, have worked well. Since equipment and supplies are tools that are used in operational activities, the ability to provide the tools quickly and fairly has been a major asset of the secretariats concerned.

OIL FOR FOOD: WHAT CAN POSSIBLY GO WRONG?

The Oil-for-Food program that was set up in the context of sanctions against Iraq is arguably the largest administrative scandal suffered by the United Nations. The negative publicity surrounding the program clearly provided ammunition for opponents to the secretariats. The scandal grew out of allegations that individuals, states, corporations, and the secretariat all engaged in improper activities relating to the sale of Iraqi oil in order to provide for the import of food and other essential supplies during the period in which Iraq was under sanctions from the Security Council. The independent inquiry (the Volcker Committee) found evidence that the Iraqi government had used oil contracts to bribe officials, received kickbacks from contractors, and that some secretariat officials were suborned in the process (United Nations 2005).

The Oil-for-Food program, in monetary terms, was the largest program administered up to that point by the United Nations, amounting to US$69.5 billion in proceeds (United Nations 2005, 5). The program showed the problems of international administration in a particular light and could be considered a test bed for whatever could possibly go wrong in managing a program. The lessons learned from the scandal will likely strengthen the ability of the international secretariats to undertake programs in the future, but the scandal itself had at least the short-term effect of discrediting the administration of the United Nations.

A dispassionate analysis of the scandal shows that, on the whole, the United Nations administration functioned well, although several of its secretariat officials made bad choices, and at least one was evidently corrupt.

As a result of the Gulf War in 1991, Iraq was placed under economic sanctions by the Security Council as a means of ensuring that it eliminated its programs for weapons of mass destruction, as an incentive to pay reparations to Kuwait, and to deter any further actions by the government against its own population. As a consequence, Iraq was unable to sell oil on the international markets. At the same time, its inability to sell oil meant that it could not import food and other basic supplies that were not produced in sufficient quantity domestically. Iraq, like many oil-producing countries, was a net food importer. Over the first years of the sanctions regime, some efforts were made by humanitarian agencies to provide food, but these were insufficient. International organizations, both public (like UNICEF) and nongovernmental (like CARE and Medicins sans Frontieres) documented an increase in malnutrition and child mortality. These organizations, as well as the humanitarian relief coordinators appointed by the United Nations, like Dennis Halliday and Hans Sponeck, argued that something had to be done to reduce the effects of the sanctions on the civilian population.

The compromise reached in the Security Council was to set up a carefully monitored program to sell oil and use the proceeds to purchase food and other supplies. The idea was that the supervision would ensure that the funds would be used properly and would not undermine the sanctions regime. In the negotiations, however, the Iraqi government argued, on the basis of the principle of state sovereignty, that it should issue the contracts and select the contractors, although the funds received would be administered by the United Nations. If this condition was not acceptable, it would not participate in the program. The choice, in effect, was to accept this condition or let the civilian population of Iraq starve. This choice would arise throughout the program.

The decision to accept the Iraqi terms was made by the members of the Security Council without the strong support of the secretariat. In this case, the secretariat—headed at the time by Boutros-Ghali—may have raised concerns but, as the matter was intergovernmental, saw its task as one of implementing whatever the states agreed. The secretariat proceeded to establish an office to administer the program.

Two structural flaws were thus created in the program at the outset. The process of selecting contractors was completely outside UN purview, and the review of the process was in the hands of an intergovernmental committee (the Sanctions Committee), which was also outside the purview of the secretariat. As a result, the bulk of the activities that constituted the scandal took place outside normal UN Secretariat administrative controls.

The Oil-for-Food program had both political and administrative dimensions. The political dimensions involved the relationships with the government of Iraq, while the administrative dimensions had to do with the mechanics of selling oil, purchasing supplies, and overseeing them. The United Nations had experience from previous operations, although not on the scale of Oil-for-Food. Senior career official Benon Sevan was selected to head the program. Politically, his previous experience made him a good choice. During his UN career he had been primarily involved in supporting intergovernmental negotiations, and later he had undertaken several good offices assignments, including ones in Afghanistan and Iraq. As a Cypriot of Armenian origin he was as close to a political neutral as could be found in the Middle East. His administrative experience, however, was more limited; he had headed only relatively small secretariat units that were concerned with support to negotiations rather than managing large-scale financial and administrative transactions. The skills at negotiating in the context of the Middle East, where personal relationships are important, made him vulnerable in the end to influence when, as the Volcker Committee showed, he had a personal financial problem that "friends" helped solve.

Because at least part of the program was at an intergovernmental level, the usual internal auditing controls would not be as effective. Internal audit focused on the procedures and application of rules by the secretariat but did not extend to activities of intergovernmental bodies. Thus, on the critical issues of contracting and their oversight, the Office of Internal Oversight Services was in a weak position. The Volcker Committee noted that that office suspected problems in the program but could not prove them and, although it—and program administrative staff—brought many to the attention of the secretary-general's office, they were not addressed.

The contracting process also had flaws. A major outsourced function of the program was the monitoring of contract implementation. This was to be provided by private contractors and was sent out to bid. The first successful bidder was a Swiss company, COTECNA, which had employed the son of the secretary-general. This gave the appearance of favoritism and constituted one of the most visible public questions in the scandal. As it happened, confirmed by the Volcker Committee, COTECNA was a qualified contractor and was also the low bidder in a process in which there was no evidence of interference by the secretary-general. Still, the *appearance* of a conflict was in some ways as bad as a real one.

Additionally, two other secretariat officials, one involved with the support to the Security Council and the other a middle level officer in the procurement division, were found to have sought to influence the process of selecting contractors. Both were dismissed, although the former was reinstated on the basis of an appeal; the latter was prosecuted by national authorities in the United States in 2006.

Clearly, at certain points while evidence of problems in the program was accumulating (and which only came to public attention after the 2003 war when internal Iraqi documents were released), the secretariat felt that its choice was (1) to pursue investigations that would have required slowing or halting the program, with consequent suffering of the Iraqi civilian population, or (2) to continue the program despite the probable corruption. It was decided at the time that the first alternative was less desirable. It will be for historians to determine whether this was the proper choice.

A number of key lessons were learned. One was that programs of this type need to be set up within the United Nations own system of administrative controls. The administrative-control structure had worked to prevent corruption on those elements that fell under its control. Second, the personal financial integrity of senior officials cannot be guaranteed, so it is necessary to set up more rigorous financial-disclosure regulations. Finally, the internal oversight and accountability mechanisms of the organizations needed to be strengthened. This final point recognized that the secretariats were now actors in their own right in international politics and that, as for other actors, they needed control mechanisms.

NOTE

[1] The United Nations Secretariat routinely borrows from peacekeeping accounts, which have a separate assessment and can defer payments to troop-contributing countries, to cover cash shortages in the regular budget accounts.

11

. . . .

The Accountability
Problem

Quis Custodiet Ipsos Custodes?

> But more shocking still, Humphrey just didn't seem to care.
> I asked him how that was possible.
>
> Again he had a simple answer. "It is not my job to care.
> That's what politicians are for. It's my job to carry out gov-
> ernment policy."
>
> "Even if you think it's wrong?"
>
> "Almost all government policy is wrong," he remarked
> obligingly, "but frightfully well carried out."
>
> —THE COMPLETE YES MINISTER, 454

International secretariats are gaining power and influence, using their ability to use legitimacy, information, and their structural position to provide a form of international governance. They
primarily regulate themselves, given the complexity of the system and its rules. The question has to be asked, How are they to
be held accountable? Who will watch the watchers?

In national governments the political process—through elections and the workings of parliaments—serves as a check on the

civil service. No similar check exists at the international level. Other than the oversight provided by the intergovernmental machinery, which is partial and fragmented, there is no central means to ensure that the international public sector responds both effectively and efficiently to demands for its services.

The Oil-for-Food scandal was framed in terms of financial accountability, and, as noted in Chapter 10, the real problem was in those aspects of the program that fell outside the purview of the normal UN financial control systems. The investigation of Oil-for-Food did not ask whether the program succeeded in achieving its objective of ensuring that the effects of sanctions on the civilian population were not inhumane. That question would have been the most important one to ask.

A real threat, unless checks are built in, is that the career international civil service could become beholden only to itself and not accountable for results, like the mandarinate of imperial China. The old Roman query *Quis custodiet ipsos custodes?* (who will guard the guardians) clearly applies. Over a fifteen-year period I have explored this issue in a series of articles in *Public Administration and Development* (Mathiason 1987, 1997, and 2004). Despite all of the reforms, the answer is still unclear.

There has been progress, but it has been slow. However, as the international public sector becomes more prominent and its functions continue to expand, the issue of accountability will take on increased importance. There is little precedent for a public service that is removed from the public for which it provides services, and as new models emerge, they will define how the machine will be controlled.

FORMAL ACCOUNTABILITY: AUDIT

When the United Nations and the specialized agencies were established, oversight was to be provided with the help of external auditors and an internal audit function. All of the organizations designated external auditors, usually from one or more of the member states. Every year they would look at specific programs and determine whether financial rules were being followed. They were, by definition, independent, although it could be argued that they reflected the views and cultures of the countries from which they came. Internal audits were prepared for the executive head and were intended to help the head maintain administrative control over the organization.

The Joint Inspection Unit was a later creation, intended to serve as an independent body to review management performance and make recommendations. The recommendations, however, were not mandatory. Most governments had internal inspection services, which reported either to a minister or to a head of government, while others had inspection services that reported directly to the legislature.

In the mid-1990s governments became concerned with the possibility of misspent funds and corruption. A few widely publicized cases, such as the theft of a UN payroll in the Somalia Operation (mentioned in Chapter 7), helped create a fear that an organization as large as the United Nations, with a far-flung set of operations, is vulnerable to abuse.[1] Critics believed that locating these functions within the Department of Administration (later called the Department of Management) would not make them sufficiently independent to be credible. One of the reforms forced on Boutros-Ghali by the member states was the creation of an Office of Internal Oversight Services (OIOS) in 1995. In a typical compromise the under-secretary-general for OIOS would be named by the secretary-general but confirmed by the General Assembly. The under-secretary-general would serve for one five-year term that would not correspond to the term of the secretary-general. All public reports would go directly to the General Assembly. The new office encompassed previous units dealing with internal audit, program performance monitoring, evaluation, and management consulting, as well as new units dealing with inspections and investigations.

There have been three under-secretaries-general of OIOS: a German diplomat, an auditor from the private sector in Singapore, and most recently, the former auditor-general of Sweden. The office has undertaken a large number of investigations as well as normally programmed evaluations. Most of the other organizations of the UN system have developed similar mechanisms. In the most recent set of proposals by the secretary-general, provisions have been made increasing the resources of the office and making it more independent, partly as a consequence of its perceived inability to affect the Oil-for-Food scandal.

All international organizations have internal audit mechanisms, and all have had external auditors, appointed from national audit services. The internal audits report to the executive heads, and the external auditors reports are made to both the executive heads and the member states. In that sense the financial affairs of the international organizations are an open book. In addition to the organization-specific arrangements, for over thirty years the Joint Inspection Unit, whose members are elected and are independent, has provided oversight over the organizations of the UN system.

As the organizations have evolved, the standard audit function has been supplemented by investigation and monitoring services. In the 1990s, based on national models of inspectors-general, most organizations established comprehensive offices of internal oversight. Most of the operational organizations, from the World Bank to UNICEF to the UNDP, have set up evaluation units—in the case of the World Bank the Operational Evaluation Department— to do more in-depth analyses of program and project results.

The UN model, based on the OIOS, has begun to be applied throughout the system. Evidence in all of the organizations to date has been that financial controls work. In the few cases where there have been irregularities, they have been quickly detected, dealt with and, if necessary, procedures tightened. The funds provided by member-state legislatures to the international system have not been pilfered.

REAL ACCOUNTABILITY: RESULTS

While the funds have not been pilfered, have they been successfully used for the purposes for which they were appropriated? Finding a way to answer this question has been an issue from the beginning.

The current means for providing accountability is to require international secretariats to undertake results-based program planning and budgeting. The central idea is that secretariats define what they expect to see happen as a direct consequence of what they produce. They then manage programs to maximize those outcomes. They monitor and evaluate whether the results are obtained, and they use that information to improve both planning and management of programs. The approach comes from the "reinventing government" movement developed at the national level by a number of major contributors to the United Nations (see Osborne and Gaebler 1993). The difference is that for national governments, the results of service provision are typically direct (roads built, health care provided), while for international secretariats the results are typically indirect (governments influenced to build roads in a particular way, governments influenced to provide particular types of health care).

Results-based management is both an accountability and a management tool. By reviewing secretariats' promises in terms of what they actually achieve, functional accountability can be obtained. Member states can decide whether the secretariats' proposals are realistic given past performance and if they correspond to stated priorities. Results-based management provides a check against allocating resources to programs that sound good rhetorically but are not within the ability capacity of the secretariats to achieve. If implemented properly, it should increasingly ensure that resources are directed to important programs for which the secretariat has a demonstrated ability to effect change.

Organizations of the UN system now routinely present their program budgets in terms of expected results. Some, such as the IAEA, have used results-based programming for several biennia. The United Nations Secretariat has been incorporating results-based budgeting since the late 1990s. As noted in a review by the Joint Inspection Unit, results-based management has been largely adopted in the UN system, although the extent to which the organizations are able to comply with the Joint Inspection Unit's benchmarks is variable:

> The changeover to a results-based culture has been lengthy and difficult, with organizations struggling to establish environments that promote high performance and accountability, empower managers and staff alike and include them in the setting and accomplishing of programmatic goals. (United Nations Joint Inspection Unit 2004, 3)

The results-based management systems used by international secretariats draw from earlier approaches, such as the logical framework matrix that was originally developed for bilateral development-assistance programs. The essence of the system is that planning is a deductive process of working from larger goals to more specific objectives that can be achieved in a fixed time. Then, the outcomes that must occur in a budgetary period to achieve the objectives are specified. Finally, the outputs and activities that the organization should undertake and the inputs necessary are detailed. Because the starting point is a view of what the future should look like, the exercise is somewhat counter-intuitive. Most managers would take the present and project it into the future. However, since most of the problems addressed by international secretariats are long term, and the organizations have a sufficient funding base and political stability to think in the longer term, results-based management can be a very powerful tool.

While the planning for results-based management has advanced, and an increasing number of organizations have been able to specify what is expected to happen as a result of their work, the second element, ensuring that the promises implied in the program budgets have been kept, has proven more difficult. The intended outcomes are only partly under the control of the secretariats, whose work usually only influences others to make the outcomes happen. Measuring whether the outcomes have occurred requires secretariats to obtain information that they did not traditionally collect.

Both the United Nations and the IAEA have developed databases in which program managers can enter evidence of the existence of outcomes. This implies that programs include self-evaluations of their work. UNIDO has begun the process with the 2006–7 program budget. Like other organizations, UNIDO undertook to identify the changes that the program's outputs, mostly advisory services and training, were expected to produce and then set up a system for capturing information on each expected outcome.

To the extent that the secretariats can prove that their programs provoke changes in the beneficiary population, they will demonstrate their accountability and should mobilize support.

ACCOUNTABLE TO THE PUBLIC:
INFORMATION

Results-based management, for accountability purposes, is a matter for discussion between secretariats and member states, who are represented on program-review and budget-review committees. When international secretariats were minor actors in international affairs, this level of oversight was probably sufficient. Since services were delivered indirectly, public concern with issues were focused on governments rather than on the international public sector.

This clearly suits the international secretariats, who correctly perceive that if their role is too visible, the notion of state sovereignty on which the international system is formally structured will be challenged. In fact, like the English bureaucrats in *Yes, Minister*, the international civil service prefers to work in the shadows.

Within the last decade the independent and noticeable role of the secretariats in dramatic circumstances like natural disasters, the Iraq War, the issue of weapons of mass destruction, pandemics, and international financial crises raises the question of whether or not visibility will increase accountability.

Public opinion is a major means of controlling governments. Its use with international secretariats has not been explored. Would a more public international civil service be more accountable? Or would it become less effective?

Public information and international organizations was debated from the outset of the United Nations. Discussion, in the first budget of the organization in 1946, centered on allocations for public information. Trygve Lie proposed a model budget to allow the secretariat to explain policies. Member states, however, did not want to give the secretariat the ability to conduct propaganda. As a result, they restricted the public information program to the preparation of "information products" (books, pamphlets, press releases, radio clips), rather than information campaigns. This model continued for most of the first fifty years of the organization and was reproduced in most of the organizations of the UN system.

The system served to insulate the secretariats from public opinion, since, like the official documents of the intergovernmental bodies, public information material was distributed indirectly. Official documents were distributed to a network of depository libraries, at least one in each country, but individuals who wished to access these documents had to go to the foreign ministry or the library to which the documents had been sent. Public information documents were likewise available at these places, or through UN information service offices, which were usually set up in conjunction with UNDP offices.

Organizations like the World Bank, the IMF, and the UNDP had arrangements with commercial publishers like Oxford University Press to publish and distribute flagship publications, although the prices made the publications somewhat inaccessible.

Press coverage of the United Nations was largely provided by local correspondents of the major international press, although a few had resident correspondents specifically assigned to international organizations. These tended to cover only major intergovernmental meetings rather than less visible but perhaps equally important activities.

With the election of Kofi Annan as secretary-general, the approach changed. In part, this was because the United Nations had become more important, but it was also in large measure due to the influence and expansion of the Internet.

The Internet is essentially borderless. It allows anyone to make information available to anyone who wants it. It permits a direct connection between an organization and the public, as long as the organization makes its information available and people know where to look for it. The UN system, led by the UNDP, quickly perceived the utility of the Internet as a means for distributing information. Without violating the norm of "information product," the secretariats could make information about their programs, including all official documents, available. The organizations quickly developed complex websites that were open to anyone with access to the Internet.

One immediate consequence of the Internet has been to permit NGOs to participate more actively in the discussions being undertaken by member states in intergovernmental forums. In the past these organizations and their members had to physically attend the various meetings to see what was happening. With the

Internet, civil society organizations can communicate with one another and, through representatives physically present at negotiations, have input. This means that the secretariats can enlist the support of civil society for their work by making their own work available and consulting with NGOs in preparing papers on the basis of which government discussions begin. This process, called gatekeeping, involves secretariats acting as filters for the ideas that are presented, taking those that are likely to be acceptable to intergovernmental negotiators and making them available (Mathiason 1998a). Additionally, to the extent that civil society organizations support secretariat initiatives, they develop greater legitimacy.

The availability of public information makes the work of the international press in dealing with secretariats easier. Beyond that, the secretariats have become more open to providing information to reporters. Staff members are still restricted in the interviews that they can give, but middle and senior management are allowed to provide interpretive information. Some organizations have been particularly effective in providing context to the press in dealing with otherwise contentious issues. The IAEA, in the period preceding the Iraq War and in nuclear issues in North Korea and Iran, has been able to project its image as a politically neutral and technically proficient organization.

The press does not usually distinguish among the governments that formally make up the intergovernmental organizations and the secretariats that run them on behalf of the governments, as was the case in its coverage of the Oil-for-Food scandal. Increasingly, however, it is making the necessary distinction between what the governments decide and what the secretariats do with those decisions.

As this distinction is made, public scrutiny of their work will help the international secretariats maintain their credibility by demonstrating their competence and transparency.

NOTE

[1] Many nongovernmental or non–United Nations operations have argued that in some field situations managers have arranged for kickbacks on contracts or have committed other forms of abuse. A few of these, such as a case of contracts in the establishment of the war-crimes tribunal in Arusha, have been investigated and found to be true.

12

. . . .

International Secretariats in Future World Politics

She then explained the reason for her move. "Quite hon-
estly, Minister, I want a job where I don't spend endless
hours circulating information that isn't relevant about sub-
jects that don't matter to people who aren't interested. I
want a job where there is achievement rather than merely
activity. I am tired of pushing paper. I would like to be able
to point at something and say 'I did that.'"

—THE COMPLETE YES MINISTER, 371

Where does the evolution of international secretariats go from here? Critics of the United Nations have essentially said that the organization must reform or it will become irrelevant. An increasing number of public functions are being assigned to international organizations because individual nation-states or states grouped in "coalitions of the willing" are unable to solve public problems. As globalization of both the economy and society proceeds, with an attendant priority to maintaining stability in trans-border flows of goods, people, and resources, the role of international public administrations set up to oversee stability will increase. Rather than becoming irrelevant, international organizations and their secretariats will become even more relevant.

What can we expect to see? More regimes will be created to regulate transactions. Some of these can be predicted: governance of the Internet will have to be decided, international migration will be placed in a comprehensive framework, a global system for resource allocation for energy production and distribution will be developed, and arrangements for international monitoring and control of infectious diseases will be completed. Other regimes will develop as new global problems emerge.

More important, existing regimes will be modified and expanded as their utility becomes obvious. Climate change, verification of elimination of weapons of mass destruction and nuclear proliferation, coverage of global trade agreements, and international criminal legislation are all areas where existing developments suggest expansion. In these the secretariat role will be much the same as it is today. However, the dramatic increase in the number of regimes and their overlap will require secretariats to monitor state action in different regimes, where change in one will affect others. This, in turn, will require greater exchange of information and personnel as organizations acquire expertise in more areas in order to avoid duplication and inconsistency.

As international regimes proliferate and expand, finding ways to hold states accountable for compliance will be a major task for secretariats. This will involve finding a balance between information provided by NGOs and by other states. The analytical neutrality of secretariats will be consistently tested. How successful they will be at promoting enforcement of norms will depend on the quality of information generated and analyzed by the international public sector. As more information becomes available more quickly, thanks to technological progress in information collection and distribution, the secretariats will need more skills to extract that information essential for making and enforcing policy.

The size and complexity of operations managed by international organization are also likely to grow. Strains on systems of personnel management, finance, and procurement have already become evident. There are few models for dealing with this scale in the private sector, where multinational corporations are able to avoid accountability. At the same time, the international public sector has to operate in the same places as the private sector, while resisting temptations to corruption and inefficiency. New models of operations will be necessary, including rules that provide for both probity and effectiveness in managing peace and security as well as humanitarian operations.

While debates will no doubt continue about who will determine global development, secretariats of international organizations will increasingly be asked to find ways of channeling public investments on a global scale. To an extent this will be done through revision and expansion of existing regimes, but it will also, and perhaps increasingly, be accomplished by international institutions providing funds for investment directly, particularly for investments for which there is no short-term monetary return. This will increasingly include the energy sector. The existence of global environmental constraints will increasingly require international certification that transnational public investments do not have negative environmental effects. These, in turn, will require new types of economists, administrators, and policy analysts.

Whether the existing international secretariats can meet these challenges is a fair question that needs to be answered now. In 2006, in the wake of events like the Oil-for-Food scandal and the difficulties in implementing UN reform, critics of the international organizations were questioning whether the international public sector can function properly and are seeking different organizational methods to address problems, including avoiding the structured secretariats entirely by replacing them with interstate "networking" or by letting the "magic of the marketplace" provide the services.

A better alternative would be to restructure the international secretariats in ways that will allow them to perform their increasing tasks with growing success. This implies changes in both the theoretical perspective applied to international organizations and to the way their operations are managed.

RECOGNIZING THE ROLE
OF INTERNATIONAL SECRETARIATS

The theoretical perspective, applied to studying international politics, shapes what can be observed. The dominant theories exclude international administrations as actors. But we have shown that the secretariats are, in fact, actors, and a first step is to recognize that. To do so, we will have to resuscitate the functionalist perspectives that were applied to planning the United Nations at the outset and use functional analysis to specify the role of international secretariats clearly. We must see them as public administrations, subject to theories of public management and control, but in a new context. That way, the secretariats can be visible, can be measured and analyzed, and can be judged by scholars. This will contribute both to their growth and to their control.

International-relations theory will give a proper place to international administration, and an effort must be made to answer some of the questions raised in this book that are as yet unanswered.

GIVING SECRETARIATS THE TOOLS TO SUCCEED

The owners of these international administrations—their member states, their governments, their publics, and civil society organizations—will have to act so as to permit the organizations to carry out their tasks. This implies several things.

First, governance of the organizations should be provided on the basis of capacity to deliver results rather than rhetoric. Results-based management must become pervasive in planning, implementation, and evaluation. Whenever a new international problem occurs, the question needs to be asked: Can the market or national governments address this successfully, or is it a problem for which collective solutions, managed by international administrations, are more likely to provide the desired results? There will have to be a dual system, a classical Westphalian model for some issues, a new model for others.

Second, international secretariats need to be given management tools, including secure financing and professional staff. Secure financing implies an ability to raise revenue directly. The Tobin Tax or similar methods of collecting fees for transactions that are made possible by international management should be considered on their merits, rather than being dismissed by arguing that they infringe on national sovereignty. A core of international secretariat staff should be, as at present, career officials. However, the process of selecting career staff also needs to be structured to ensure that those who are given these appointments merit them. Training the staff in the meaning and history of international service, to ensure continuity, is important.

Third, as international secretariats increasingly deliver direct services, or services that affect the general public directly, they need to become accountable to those publics. The model of indirect oversight through member states, which means, in practice, oversight by foreign ministries, will be increasingly inadequate. Procedures must be developed to allow a more direct relationship between publics and international administrations. New approaches to the role of civil society organizations, which in some areas already interact with international secretariats, can be foreseen.

Increasingly, international administrations are in the news, but unless the media professionals understand the systems on which they are reporting, the coverage will be flawed. This will be an increasing challenge for media, public communication schools, and scholars.

Newer methods, such as the use of the Internet to permit direct public input into international decision-making, can be developed and applied. International regimes are inevitably specialized, and decision-making in them involves specialized knowledge. The issue will be how to involve the publics of these specialties (epistemic communities) in those processes.

The job of building the expanding international public sector will fall to a new generation of international civil servants. Many of them are being trained in universities today, and many are already working in international organizations. At the end of the day, I hope that they will conclude, as did Henri Reymond: "I never regretted having, at an early age, been drawn into it. In that, as in much else, I have been very fortunate" (Reymond 1994).

References

Andemicael, Berhanykun, and John Mathiason. 2005. *Eliminating Weapons of Mass Destruction: Prospects for Effective International Verification.* London: Palgrave.

Annan, Kofi. 2000. *We the Peoples: The Role of the United Nations in the Twenty-first Century.* New York: United Nations. Available online.

Anstee, Margaret J. 1996. *Orphan of the Cold War: The Inside Story of the Collapse of the Angolan Peace Process, 1992–1993.* New York: St. Martin's Press.

Ayres, Robert L. 1983. *Banking on the Poor: The World Bank and World Poverty.* Cambridge: M.I.T. Press.

Barnett, Michael, and Martha Finnemore. 2004. *Rules for the World: International Organizations in Global Politics.* Ithaca, NY: Cornell Univ. Press.

Beigbeder, Yves. 1988. *Threats to the International Civil Service.* London: Pinter Pub., Ltd.

Benning, Joseph F. 2001. "That's Where the Money Is": An Exploration of the International Effort to Contain Transnational Organized Crime through the Formation of an Anti-Money Laundering Regime." Ph.D. diss., Wagner Graduate School of Public Service, New York Univ.

Boughton, James M. 2001. *The Silent Revolution: International Monetary Fund, 1979–1989.* Washington, DC: IMF.

Boulden, Jane. 2001. *Peace Enforcement: The United Nations Experience in Congo, Somalia, and Bosnia.* New York: Praeger.

Bunn, George. 2003. "The Nuclear Nonproliferation Treaty: History and Current Problems." *Arms Control Today.* December.

Canada. 2005. "Maurice Strong: African Operation on the Scale of the Invasion of Normandy." Department of Foreign Affairs and International Trade. Available on the DFAIT website.

CDC (Center for Disease Control). 2004. "Eradication Efforts Worldwide: Success and Failure (1955–1978)." *The History of Malaria, an Ancient Disease.* National Center for Infectious Diseases. April 23. Available on the cdc.gov website.

263

Chisholm, Donald. 1985. *Coordination without Hierarchy: Informal Structures in Multiorganizational Systems.* Berkeley and Los Angeles: Univ. of California Press.

Clinton, Hillary Rodham. 1995. Remarks to the United Nations Fourth World Conference on Women Plenary Session. Beijing. September 5. Available online.

Cox, Robert W., and Harold K. Jacobson. 1973. *The Anatomy of Influence: Decision Making in International Organizations.* New Haven, CT: Yale Univ. Press.

Donnelly, Jack. 1986. "International Human Rights: A Regime Analysis." *International Organization* 40, no. 3 (Summer): 599–642.

Emmerij, Louis, Richard Jolly, and Thomas G. Weiss. 2005. "Economic and Social Thinking at the UN in Historical Perspective." *Development and Change* 36, no. 2: 211–35.

Goldhammer, Herbert, and Edward Shils. 1939. "Types of Power and Status." *The American Journal of Sociology* 45, no. 2 (September 1939): 171–82.

Grotius, Hugo. 1916. *The Freedom of the Seas.* Translated by Ralph Van Dammen Magoffin. New York: Oxford Univ. Press.

Gruson, Sydney. 1954. "U.S. Bows on Pay to Ex-UN Aides." *New York Times.* December 4.

Haas, Ernst B. 1958. *The Uniting of Europe: Political, Social, and Economic Forces, 1950–1957.* Stanford, CA: Stanford Univ. Press.

———. 1964. *Beyond the Nation-State: Functionalism and International Organization.* Stanford, CA: Stanford Univ. Press.

Haberman, Frederick W., ed. 1972. *Nobel Lectures, Peace 1926–1950.* Amsterdam: Elsevier Publishing Company.

Hacker, The Right Honourable James. 1984. *The Complete Yes Minister: Diaries of a Cabinet Minister,* edited by Jonathan Lynn and Antony Jay. New York: Harper and Row.

Haggard, Stephan, and Beth Simmons. 1987. "Theories of International Regimes." *International Organization* 41, no. 3 (Summer): 491–517.

Hammarskjöld, Dag. 1953a. "Statement to the Press on Arrival at Idlewild Airport, New York, 9 April 1953." UN Press Release, SG/287. April 9.

———. 1953b. "The United Nations and the Political Scientist." *American Political Science Review* 47, no. 4: 975–79.

———. 1961. *The International Civil Servant in Law and in Fact.* Lecture delivered May 30, 1961, at Oxford University. Oxford: Clarendon Press.

Hasenclever, Andreas, Peter Mayer, and Volker Rittberger. 1997. *Theories of International Regimes.* Cambridge: Cambridge Univ. Press.

Hazzard, Shirley. 1967. *People in Glass Houses: A Novel.* New York: Random House.

Henderson, Donald. 1999. "Eradication: Lessons from the Past." *Morbidity and Mortality Weekly Report* (December 31):16–22.

Horsefield, J. Keith. 1969. *The International Monetary Fund. 1945–1965: Twenty Years of International Monetary Cooperation.* Vol. 1, *Chronicles.* Washington, DC: IMF.

Howson, Susan. 2004. "Review of International Organizations and the Analysis of Economic Policy, 1919–1950: By Anthony M. Endres and Grant A. Fleming." *History of Political Economy* 34, no. 2: 405–8.

Hurd, Ian. 1999. "Legitimacy and Authority in International Politics." *International Organization* 53, no. 2 (Spring): 379–408.

IMF (International Monetary Fund). 2005a. *The IMF's Multilateral Surveillance: Issues Paper for an Evaluation by the Independent Evaluation Office (IEO).* Washington, DC: IMF. September 25.

———. 2005b. *World Economic Outlook.* (September). Washington, DC: IMF.

Jackson, Sir Robert. 1969. *A Study of the Capacity of the United Nations Development System.* 2 vols. Sales no.: E.70.I.10. Geneva: UN.

Jansson, Kurt, Michael Harris, and Angela Penrose. 1987. *The Ethiopian Famine.* Atlantic Highlands, NJ: Zed Books.

Johnson, David M. 1952. Seventh Session of the General Assembly. Vol. 18, record 284. "Letter no. 724" (June 11). Documents on Canada External Relations. Available online.

King, Jeff, and A. J. Hobbins. 2003. "Hammarskjöld and Human Rights: The Deflation of the UN Human Rights Programme 1953–1961." *Journal of the History of International Law* 5: 337–86.

Knorr, Klaus. 1948. "The Bretton Woods Institutions in Transition." *International Organization* 2, no. 1 (February): 19–38.

Krasner, Stephen D. 1982. "Regimes and the Limits of Realism: Regimes as Autonomous Variables." *International Organization* 32, no. 2: 497–510.

Langille, H. Peter. 2002. *Bridging the Commitment—Capacity Gap: Existing Arrangements and Options for Enhancing UN Rapid Deployment.* New York: The Center for United Nations' Reform Education.

Langrod, Georges. 1963. *The International Civil Service: Its Origins, Its Nature, Its Evolution.* Dobbs Ferry, NY: Oceana Publications.

Luck, Edward W. 2003. "Reforming the United Nations: Lessons from a History in Progress." *International Relations Studies and United Nations Occasional Papers,* no. 1.

Mathiason, John R. 1972. "Old Boys, Alumni, and Consensus in ECLA Meetings." In *Communication in International Politics,* edited by Richard L. Merritt, 387–404. Urbana: Univ. of Illinois Press.

———. 1987. "Who Controls the Machine? The Programme Planning Process in the Reform Effort," *Public Administration and Development* 7, no. 2.

———. 1997. "Who Controls the Machine, Revisited: Command and Control in the United Nations Reform Effort." *Public Administration and Development* 17, no. 4.

———. 1998a. "UN Secretariat: The Gatekeepers of Ideas." In *Beijing! UN Fourth World Conference on Women*, edited by Anita Anand and Gouri Salvi, 195–201. New Delhi: Women's Feature Service.

———. 1998b. "World Citizenship: The Individual and International Governance." Paper presented at the third Pan-European Conference on International Studies, Vienna, Austria, September 16–19.

———. 2001. *The Long March to Beijing: The United Nations and the Women's Revolution*. Vol. 1, *The Vienna Years*. Mt. Tremper, NY: Associates for International Management Services.

———. 2004. "Who Controls the Machine, III: Accountability in the Results-based Revolution." *Public Administration and Development* 24, no. 1: 61–73.

———. 2005. "What Went Wrong with the Women's Revolution." Paper prepared for the Ray Smith Symposium on Gender Justice beyond Beijing, Syracuse, NY, September 16–18.

Mathiason, John R., and Dennis Smith. 1987. "The Diagnostics of Reform: The Evolving Tasks and Functions of the United Nations." *Public Administration and Development* 7, no. 2: 143–63.

McDiarmid, John. 2003. "Recollections of a Most Worldly Neighbor." The New Canaan Historical Annual [New Canaan, CT] 12, no. 2.

McLean, Donald, ed. 2004. *Internet Governance: A Grand Collaboration*. New York: United Nations ICT Task Force.

Meron, Theodor. 1998. "War Crimes Law Comes of Age." *The American Journal of International Law* 92, no. 3 (July): 462–68.

Mitrany, David. 1946. *A Working Peace System: An Argument for the Functional Development of International Organizations*. 4th ed. London: National Peace Council.

Moynihan, Daniel P. 1978. *A Dangerous Place*. Boston: Little, Brown and Co.

Mueller, Milton, John Mathiason, and Lee McKnight. 2004. "Making Sense of Internet Governance: Defining Principles and Norms in a Policy Context." In *Internet Governance: A Grand Collaboration*, edited by Donald McLean. New York: United Nations ICT Task Force.

Ness, Gayl D., and Steven R. Brechin. 1988. "Bridging the Gap: International Organizations as Organizations." *International Organization* 42, no. 2: 245–73.

Nye, Joseph S., Jr. 2004. *Soft Power: The Means to Success in World Politics*. New York: Public Affairs.

Osborne, David, and Ted Gaebler. 1993. *Reinventing Government: How the Entrepreneurial Spirit Is Transforming the Public Sector*. New York: Plume.

Paterson, Matthew. 1996. *Global Warming and Global Politics (Environmental Politics)*. London: Brunner-Routledge.

Phillpot, Dan. 2003. "Sovereignty." *The Stanford Encyclopedia of Philosophy*. Summer ed. Edited by Edward N. Zalta. Stanford, CA: Online.

Pollock, David, Daniel Kerner, and Joseph L. Love. 2001. "Raúl Prebisch on ECLAC's Achievements and Deficiencies: An Unpublished Interview." *Cepal Review* 75 (December): 9–22.

Ranshofen-Wertheimer, Egon F. 1945. *The International Secretariat: A Great Experiment in International Administration*. Washington, DC: Carnegie Endowment for International Peace.

Reymond, Henri E. 1994. *The International Service: Experiences and Recollections*. December. Available in the UNESCO archives on the unesco.org website.

Reymond, Henri, and Sidney Mailick. 1985. *International Personnel Policies and Practices*. Westport, CT: Praeger.

Rosenthal, A. M. 1952. "Morale of U.N. Staff Is Shaken by Attacks." *New York Times*. December 7.

Royal Institute of International Affairs. 1944. *The International Secretariat of the Future: Lessons from Experience by a Group of Former Officials of the League of Nations*. London: Royal Institute of International Affairs.

Ruggie, John Gerard, Peter J. Katzenstein, Robert O. Keohane, and Philippe C. Schmitter. 2005. "Transformation in World Politics: The Intellectual Contributions of Ernst B. Haas." *Annual Review of Political Science* (2005): 271–96.

Salomons, Dirk, and Dennis Dijkzeul. 2001. "The Conjurer's Hat: Financing United Nations Peace-building in Operations Directed by Special Representatives of the Secretary General." Fafo report 359. Oslo: Fafo.

Schaefer, Brett D. 2006. "A Progress Report on U.N. Reform." Heritage Foundation Backgrounder #1937. Washington, DC: The Heritage Foundation. May 19. Available on the heritage.org website.

Schultz, Lillie. 1952. "Spies or Sappers? Who Is Undermining the UN?" *The Nation* (December 20, 1952), 576–79.

Shawcross, William. 1984. *The Quality of Mercy: Cambodia, Holocaust, and Modern Conscience*. New York: Simon and Schuster.

Slaughter, Anne-Marie. 1995. "International Law in a World of Liberal States." *European Journal of International Law* 6, no. 4: 503–38.

———. 2004. *A New World Order: Government Networks and the Disaggregated State*. Princeton, NJ: Princeton Univ. Press.

Smith, Dennis. 2003. "Managing CIVPOL: The Potential of Performance Management in International Public Services." In *Rethinking International Organizations: Pathology and Promise*, edited by Dennis Dijkzeul and Yves Beigbeder. New York: Berghahn Books.

Thornberry, Cedric. 1997. "The Changing Management Structure of UN Peacekeeping and Peace Support Operations." *In Brassey's Defence Yearbook, 1997,* 376–87. London: Brassey's.

Ul-Haq, Mahboob, Inge Kaul, and Isabelle Grunberg. 1996. *The Tobin Tax: Coping with Financial Volatility.* New York: Oxford Univ. Press.

UNAIDS (Joint United Nations Programme on HIV/AIDS). 2004. "Three Ones: Key Principles: Coordination of National Responses to HIV/AIDS." Conference Paper 1. Washington Consultation. April 25. Available on the data.usaids.org website.

UNHCR (United Nations High Commissioner for Refugees). 2005. *Refugees by Numbers, 2005.* Geneva: UNHCR.

UNICEF (United Nations Children's Fund). 2005. "Financial Report and Statements for the Year Ended 31 December 2004." Private Sector Division. E/ICEF/2005/AB/L.5. July 25.

United Nations. 1975. Group of Experts on the Structure of the United Nations System. *A New United Nations Structure for Global Economic Co-operation.* E.75.II.A.7. New York: United Nations.

———. 1986. *Report of the Group of High-level Intergovernmental Experts to Review the Efficiency of the Administrative and Financial Functioning of the United Nations.* A/41/49. January 1.

———. 1999a. *Report of the Secretary-General pursuant to General Assembly Resolution 53/35: The Fall of Srebrenica.* A/54/549. November 15.

———. 1999b. "Letter dated 15 December 1999 from the Secretary-General addressed to the President of the Security Council enclosing the report of the Independent Inquiry into the actions of the United Nations during the genocide in Rwanda." S/1999/1257. December 16.

———. 1999c. "The Independent Inquiry into the Action of the United Nations during the 1994 Genocide in Rwanda." S/1999/1257. December 16.

———. 1999d. *Report of the Secretary-General on the Work of the Organization.* A/54/1.

———. 2000. "Report of the Panel on United Nations Peace Operations" (Brahimi Report). A/55/305–S/2000/809. August 21.

———. 2004. *A More Secure World: Our Shared Responsibility: Report of the High-Level Panel on Threats, Challenges and Change.* A/59/565. December 2.

———. 2005. Independent Inquiry Committee into the Oil for Food Programme (Volcker Committee). "First Interim Report." New York: United Nations. February 3.

———. 2006. "Investing in the United Nations for a Stronger Organization Worldwide." Report of the Secretary-General. A/60/692.

United Nations Joint Inspection Unit. 2004. *Overview of the Series of Reports on Managing for Results in the United Nations System.* Geneva: Joint Inspection Unit.

UNTAGFT. N.d. "Namibia–UNTAG Background." Available on the un.org website.

Urquhart, Brian. 1984a. *United Nations Oral History Collection.* Leon Gordenker, interviewer. Interview no. 5. October 19. Available on the un.org website.

———. 1984b. *United Nations Oral History Collection.* Leon Gordenker, interviewer. Interview no. 6. October 22. Available on the un.org website.

———. 1987. *A Life in Peace and War.* New York: Harper and Row.

———. 2004. "The United Nations Rediscovered?" *World Policy Journal* 21, no. 2 (Summer): 1–5.

Urquhart, Brian, and Erskine Childers. 1994. *Renewing the United Nations System.* New York: Ford Foundation.

US Environmental Protection Agency. 2006. "Ozone Science: The Facts behind the Phaseout." Available on the epa.gov website.

Vinson, Fred. 1946. "After the Savannah Conference." *Foreign Affairs* 24 (July): 622–32.

Waldheim, Kurt. 1986. *In the Eye of the Storm: A Memoir.* Bethesda, MD: Adler and Adler.

Westby, David L. 1966. "A Typology of Authority in Complex Organizations." *Social Forces* 44, no. 4 (June): 484–91.

World Bank. 2000. *Entering the 21st Century: World Development Report 1999/2000.* New York: Oxford University Press. Abstract (source of quotation) available on the worldbank.org website.

———. 2004. *World Bank Group Historical Chronology.* Available on the worldbank.org website.

———. 2005. *Pages from World Bank History: The Pearson Commission.* Available on the worldbank.org website.

WFP (World Food Programme). 2004. *Nutrition in Emergencies: WFP Experiences and Challenges.* WFP/EB.A/2004/5–A/3. April 6.

Young, A. Sylvester. 2003. "Statistics in the ILO: Roles and Responsibilities." *Bulletin of Labour Statistics,* no. 1.

Zacher, Mark. 1992. "The Decaying Pillars of the Westphalian Temple: Implications for International Order and Governance." In *Governance without Government,* edited by James Rosenau, 58–101. Cambridge: Cambridge Univ. Press.

Index

• • • • • •

About the Author

John R. Mathiason is an adjunct professor of international relations at Syracuse University. For thirty years he was a career staff member of the United Nations Secretariat, working in different parts of the secretariat and completing his career as a principal officer and deputy director of the Division for the Advancement of Women, responsible for management of substantive support to the UN women's program. Since taking early retirement he has been consultant to a number of other UN organizations, including the International Atomic Energy Agency, the Comprehensive Test Ban Treaty Organization, and the United Nations Development Program, as well as several NGOs. He has published in the areas of management of the international verification regime for the elimination of weapons of mass destruction, United Nations accountability, Internet governance, and other fields in which the role of international secretariats is growing.

Also from Kumarian Press...

Governance and United Nations Reform:

Piecing a Democratic Quilt: Regional Organizations and Universal Norms
Edward McMahon and Scott Baker

Peace Operations Seen from Below: UN Missions and Local People
Beatrice Pouligny

Culture, Development and Public Administration in Africa
Ogwo J. Umeh and Greg Andranovich

Building Democratic Institutions: Governance Reform in Developing Countries
G. Shabbir Cheema

New and Forthcoming:

NGOs in International Politics
Shamima Ahmed and David M. Potter

Humanitarian Alert: NGO Information and Its Impact on US Foreign Policy
Abby Stoddard

A World Turned Upside Down: Social Ecological Approaches to Children in War Zones
Edited by Neil Boothby, Alison Strang, and Michael Wessells

Complex Political Victims
Erica Bouris

Visit Kumarian Press at **www.kpbooks.com** or
call **toll-free 800.289.2664** for a complete catalog.

*Kumarian Press, located in Bloomfield, Connecticut, is a
forward-looking, scholarly press that promotes active international
engagement and an awareness of global connectedness.*